"Drawing on the all-too-familiar reality of our inaction on climate change, Frédéric Samama offers a deeply innovative, interdisciplinary perspective that leads to a powerful idea: our past successes have created societal 'bubbles' that now hold us back from the exploration and adaptation we urgently need. This book is a timely and creative call to rethink how societies learn, evolve, and build resilience. A brilliant and essential contribution from someone who deeply understands both the financial and institutional landscapes."

Philippe Aghion, Professor at Collège de France, and 2025 Nobel Laureate in Economics

"What our failure owes to our past successes. Questioning a collective sleep walk to an assured disaster of our own making, Frederic Samama does not tell the over-rehearsed tale of conflicting interest. Addressing the issue at a more fundamental level, he blends together insights spanning from anthropology to cognitive science and economics to describe a society shaped by and trapped in past successes. Something we can escape by re-discovering that what we have in common and what we share is more important than what we compete for."

Jean Boissinot, Former Secretary General of the Network for Greening the Financial System

"Claude Lévi-Strauss observed that 'the world began without man and it will complete itself without him.' In *The Enigma of Climate Inaction*, Frédéric Samama shows us how to postpone that ending—if our species can grasp the opportunity in time. Drawing on neuroscience and evolutionary biology, he reveals why our greatest survival mechanisms have become obstacles to addressing existential threats. 'Societal bubbles' of overconfidence—from agriculture to neoliberalism to our faith in modeling the world—now paralyze us in pure exploitation mode when exploration is desperately needed. But Samama offers hope! His vision of humans acting within nature, not above it, provides both diagnosis and cure for breaking free from our bubbles and rediscovering the exploratory mindset essential for survival."

François Candelon, Partner at private equity firm Seven2 and the former global director of the BCG Henderson Institute

"Why is humanity not taking action in the face of the impending disaster that is climate change? For anyone like me who is committed to the fight against climate change, this is the key question. Going beyond the usual explanations about geopolitical conflicts or economic interests, Frédéric Samama draws on neuroscience and applies it to collective action. A fascinating and thought-provoking book to read and reread."

Pascal Canfin, Member of the EU Parliament, Former Chair of the European Parliament's Environment, Public Health and Food Safety Committee

"I'm betting that you, like many of the rest of us, have wondered why we human beings have done so little to stop the onrushing catastrophe of climate disaster that threatens us. I urge you to take a spin with Fred Samama, an experienced veteran in the worlds of both climate change and finance, and read his new book entitled The Enigma of Climate Inaction. It will take you back through the history of big challenges that humans have had difficulty confronting, and apply some of that analysis to the most enormous global challenge of all that confronts us today. And this will, hopefully, generate understanding that will help us do better."

Peter Goldmark, Former Budget Director, New York State; former President, Rockefeller Foundation; Former Executive Director, Port Authority of NY & NJ; former Publisher and CEO of the International Herald Tribune; former Director, Climate + Air Program, Environmental Defense Fund

"This book addresses one of the most vexed questions of our time—what underwrites our nihilistic response to climate change? The answer on offer rests upon an enlightened move: the same (Bayesian) principles that dictate our individual sense-making and decision-making apply to societal self-organisation. On this view, the inertia, rigidity and inaction—in the face of self-destruction—evinces exactly the pathology of disorders like Parkinson's disease. So, is there a cure? Is there a 'societal dopamine'? If this book's thesis is right, then the answer is yes: we need to reinstall a childlike wonderment and curiosity about our lived—and living—world. Crucially, just reading this book is a step in the right direction."

Karl J. Friston, MBBS, MA, MRCPsych, MAE, FMedSci, FRBS, FRS Professor: Queen Square Institute of Neurology, University College London, UK; Honorary Consultant: The National Hospital for Neurology and Neurosurgery, UK; Chief scientist: VERSES, California, USA

"A fascinating and enlightening book that calls us to confront the defining problem of climate inaction. Samama blends cognitive insight and financial expertise to reveal how adaptive social coordination shapes our responses—and why rethinking our systems is vital to our survival."

Martin Guzman, Professor, Columbia University's School of International and Public Affairs, Member of the Pontifical Academy of Social Sciences, Vatican, Former Minister of Economy of Argentina

"In this powerful book by one of the world's experts in climate finance, Frédéric Samama draws on psychology, anthropology and history to unpack our 'normal' ways of thinking and behaving, showing us why change at the deepest level is not only vitally important but also eminently possible. A passionate and important read."

Rebecca Henderson, John and Natty McArthur University Professor at Harvard University

"Ernest Hemingway once noted that people go bankrupt 'gradually, then suddenly.' Fred Samama similarly looks at the causes and consequences of human inattention, here in the vital arena of climate change. This book is both fascinating and important."

Josh Lerner, Jacob H. Schiff Professor, Harvard Business School

"I had, over the years, the pleasure of working with Frédéric Samama, and I was always impressed by his ability to reconcile the practical mindset of someone deeply involved in business with a strong determination to ground his actions in rigorous intellectual and scientific thinking. For many years, he has worked tirelessly to promote action against climate change and to develop the tools—both financial and conceptual—that are essential to addressing this major challenge of our generation. This book reflects that commitment and the result of years of intellectual investment."

Xavier Musca, Chairman of the Supervisory Board of Tikehau Capital; former Secretary-General to the President of France; former Director of the French Treasury

"A decade ago, Nicholas Stern published an urgent call to climate action entitled *Why Are We Waiting?* We are still waiting as the climate crisis accelerates. In this ground-breaking work, Frederic Samama builds on cognitive science to trace the roots of successful survival strategies at the individual, organizational, and societal levels, as well as the roots of failure. In Samama's telling, the coordination mechanisms humanity has used to solve other problems of resource scarcity have promoted mental habits ill-suited for organizing effective climate action. The antidote is a shared realization of our planet's fragility and beauty—and of our shared responsibility for avoiding its destruction."

Maurice Obstfeld, C. Fred Bergsten Senior Fellow, Peterson Institute for International Economics, Former Chief Economist at the IMF

"In this book, Frédéric Samana, explores the 'urgent, difficult action' of fighting climate change, one of the most important threats that humanity faces today. Drawing from several disciplines, he asks the question of when society succeeds or fails when facing catastrophe, as this is a threat that has so far failed to inspire widespread mobilization. The three imperatives for action that emerge from his analysis are urgency, complexity, and ethics. They require, as he correctly argues, actions by the state, business and society in general —that is, collective social responsibility. It is a significant contribution to the analysis of one of the critical problems that humanity faces today."

José Antonio Ocampo, Professor of Professional Practice at Columbia University, former United Nations Under-Secretary-General for Economic and Social Affairs, and former Minister of Finance of Colombia

"Frederic brings together economics, cognitive science, and culture to explain why humanity is collectively lax at confronting the existential threat of climate change. Understanding the 'why' is critical to resolution. This book is critical. Coming from New Zealand, I am intensely proud that the legal rights recently allocated to natural resource are referenced as part solution: 'Manaaki whenua, Manaaki tangata, Haere whakamua. Care for the land, care for the people, go forward.'"

Adrian Orr – ex-Governor of the Reserve Bank of NZ, CEO of the New Zealand Superannuation Fund, and Chair of the International Forum of Sovereign Wealth Funds

"Why are we not acting to save our world from climate change? Sometimes, the magnitude of a problem demands that we think in radically new ways. This brilliant and original book weaves insights from cognitive science, philosophy and economics to illuminate the roots of our inaction and to push us to respond. Samama's analysis is powerful, surprising and convincing—I daresay his book is a vital read."

Hélène Rey, Lord Raj Bagri Professor of Economics, London Business School and Vice President, Centre for Economic Policy Research

"When Bayesian inference meets anthropology, we uncover a compelling new perspective on the roots of our climate inaction. Frédéric Samama takes us on a fascinating journey to illuminate one of the most critical challenges of our time."

Olivier Rousseau, former co-CEO of FRR, The French Pension Reserve Fund (Fonds de Réserve pour les Retraites)

"The lack of collective mobilization in the face of climate change is worrying and puzzling. In *The Enigma of Climate Inaction*, Frédéric Samama—a long-standing pioneer in aligning finance with climate action—draws on cognitive science, economics, history, and anthropology to introduce the powerful concept of 'societal bubbles': overconfidence born from past success. His innovative, interdisciplinary approach not only exposes the roots of our paralysis but also charts a path toward systemic transformation. A vital, urgent, and inspiring read."

Nicholas Stern, IG Patel Professor of Economics and Government, Chair of the Global School of Sustainability, and Chair of the Grantham Research Institute on Climate Change and the Environment, LSE

"The enigma of climate inaction is important and timely. Frederic has held prominent roles in Finance but his book goes much deeper than any finance analysis. He drills into the core question of why humanity is doing so little about the climate threat."

Thomas Sterner is professor of environmental economics, has been President of the European Association of Environmental and Resource Economics and has a lifelong career of research in climate economics

"People often talk about the climate crisis as if it was just about science. It is not: as Samana depicts so well, social psychology and political science are critical, since we seem powerless today to act in the face of mounting evidence of the climate catastrophe that is looming. This is one of the first books that describes this issue of mass psychology so powerfully and it not only offers a lucid and potent analysis of the problem, but also a very valuable framework for tackling this in the future. A must-read for anyone who cares about the climate and is engaged in efforts to build popular support for the action we all so desperately need."

Gillian Tett, Columnist and Editorial Board, FT, Provost, King's College, Cambridge

"This compelling and original book addresses one of the most urgent questions in climate politics today: why our societies continue to fall short, even as the evidence of crisis becomes overwhelming. By drawing on cognitive science and history, Frédéric Samama offers a powerful framework for understanding the roots of collective inertia—and a hopeful path toward transformation. A must-read for anyone seeking to move beyond incrementalism."

Laurence Tubiana, CEO of the European Climate Foundation, France's Climate Change Ambassador and Special Representative for COP21.

"*The Enigma of Climate Inaction* is a major contribution to the renewal of human and social sciences in the face of ecological and political impasses. This book does not limit itself to diagnosing paralysis. It offers a rich theoretical and interdisciplinary framework. *The Enigma of Climate Inaction* exemplifies the type of critical, ambitious scholarship that must inform both research and education today. It will resonate with scholars, students, and citizens alike who seek to reimagine agency in a world marked by uncertainty, urgency, and the need for transformation."

Luis Vassy, President of Sciences Po.

THE ENIGMA OF CLIMATE INACTION

The Enigma of Climate Inaction explores humanity's perplexing passivity in the face of the looming climate crisis—despite our having known about it for decades, the fact that we brought it into existence, and the existential threat it poses to our species.

Drawing on cutting-edge insights from cognitive science, anthropology, history, economics, finance, and philosophy, Samama argues that our success in accessing resources has bred an overconfidence in the systems that enable it. By uncovering the roots of our inaction, he moves beyond merely identifying the problem and offers a framework for action. He invites readers to experience a jolt in perspective—one that prompts a re-evaluation of our relationship with nature and our sense of responsibility.

This powerful and innovative examination of the cognitive and societal blind spots that obstruct urgent climate action and solutions provided will be especially valuable for professionals in environmental policy, the social sciences and humanities, and finance.

Frédéric Samama, PhD in Economics and MPhil in Philosophy, is a pioneer of green finance. He created the first mainstream low-carbon equity indices and launched what was at that time the world's largest green bond fund to finance green infrastructure in emerging markets. He co-initiated the first coalition of investors committed to climate action, representing the entire financial sector at COP21. He also co-edited *Sovereign Wealth Funds and Long-Term Investing* with Patrick Bolton and Nobel laureate Joseph Stiglitz, and has testified before the US Senate on climate finance. He is an adjunct professor at Columbia University and Sciences Po.

THE ENIGMA OF CLIMATE INACTION

Why Are We Doing Nothing (or Almost Nothing) in the Face of Catastrophe?

Frédéric Samama

Routledge
Taylor & Francis Group

LONDON AND NEW YORK

Designed cover image: Getty Images - ABIDAL

First published in French by Editions Hermann, 2024
Revised and expanded edition in English Routledge, 2026
4 Park Square, Milton Park, Abingdon, Oxon OX14 4RN

and by Routledge
605 Third Avenue, New York, NY 10158

Routledge is an imprint of the Taylor & Francis Group, an informa business

© 2026 Frédéric Samama

For Product Safety Concerns and Information please contact our EU representative GPSR@taylorandfrancis.com. Taylor & Francis Verlag GmbH, Kaufingerstraße 24, 80331 München, Germany.

British Library Cataloguing-in-Publication Data
A catalogue record for this book is available from the British Library

ISBN: 978-1-041-07005-4 (hbk)
ISBN: 978-1-041-03064-5 (pbk)
ISBN: 978-1-003-63838-4 (ebk)

DOI: 10.4324/9781003638384

Typeset in Joanna
by codeMantra

CONTENTS

FOREWORD

by Jean Jouzel

As a paleoclimatologist specializing in the study of past climate variations through the analysis of ice cores extracted from deep within Antarctica and Greenland, I have been deeply interested in climate change since the early 1970s, when the greenhouse effect was steadily intensifying. This increase is linked to human activities, primarily our use of coal, oil, and gas, the combustion of which produces carbon dioxide—better known as CO_2. Deforestation and cement manufacturing also contribute to CO_2 emissions. Other greenhouse gases, including methane and nitrous oxide, are also produced, with agriculture accounting for a significant proportion of these emissions.

This was the era when the first climate models were developed. Suki Manabe, winner of the 2021 Nobel Prize in Physics, was one of the pioneers in this field, focusing on what would happen to our climate if the amount of CO2 in the atmosphere doubled. In 1979, the findings of Manabe and his colleagues at Princeton formed the basis of the Charney report, which concluded that such a doubling—then considered possible for the second half of the 21st century—would result in a temperature increase of around 3°C once equilibrium was reached. While the precise consequences of this level of warming were uncertain, the report emphasized that they could be significant at regional scales.

The alarm was sounded, and numerous scientific meetings throughout the 1980s echoed this concern. In 1987, the warning from climate modelers was reinforced by ice core analysis from the Vostok site in Antarctica, conducted through collaboration between French and Soviet teams—an effort in which I was fortunate enough to be involved. This work revealed the greenhouse effect's crucial role in past climate changes.

Politicians began to take these warnings seriously, driven more by the potential economic impacts—especially in the energy sector—than by concern for the planet itself. In 1988, at the initiative of the G7, the Intergovernmental Panel on Climate Change (IPCC) was established under the auspices of the United Nations to "assess the potential impact of human activities on climate."

In the 1970s, global warming was not yet perceptible. Indeed, a Danish paleoclimatologist even predicted we were entering a cooling period, possibly leading to a new ice age. Personally, I was convinced by the climate models that forecast a markedly warmer 21st century—a conviction that would increasingly guide my research career, particularly through my contributions to the IPCC from 1994 to 2015.

The Climate Convention, launched at the 1992 Rio Earth Summit following the IPCC's first report, led to a series of international agreements—Kyoto in 1997, Copenhagen in 2009, Paris in 2015—intended to limit global warming. However, reality has fallen far short of these ambitions: since 1970, global greenhouse gas emissions have more than doubled, from 27 billion to nearly 60 billion tonnes per year when accounting for all anthropogenic sources. Sadly, the warnings from the scientific community have largely gone unheeded, even though the urgency of reducing emissions is absolute.

For a long time, I attributed this failure to the difficulty of motivating action whose benefits would only become tangible in the second half of this century. I hoped that once global warming became an undeniable reality with clear consequences, decisive action would follow. We are now at that point. Global warming is a reality. The latest IPCC report confirms with certainty that it is due almost entirely to human activity. Moreover, the changes we are witnessing align closely with what the scientific community has been predicting for over 50 years. As forecast in successive IPCC reports, each decade is warmer than the last, and extreme events—heatwaves, droughts, floods—are becoming more intense and/or more frequent.

The same trends apply to forest fires and sea-level rises, which have doubled since the 1990s. The impacts of global warming on both human populations and the natural world have become unmistakable.

And yet, contrary to my ultimate hopes, this evidence has not been enough to set us on a trajectory aligned with the Paris Agreement's ambitions. To be clear, some progress has been made: 20 years ago, global warming of 4–5°C by century's end seemed plausible, whereas now hopes are pinned on staying below 3°C. Yet this remains well above the critical threshold of 1.5°C—beyond which today's youth may face overwhelming challenges by the century's end. While the battle is not yet lost, we are falling short of the objectives laid out in the Paris Agreement.

How did we get here? How can we explain that, despite credible scientific warnings, inaction so often prevailed over action? For me, this remains a troubling mystery—one to which Frédéric Samama's book offers some particularly illuminating answers.

Drawing on his deep involvement in green finance—an area I have followed for more than a decade—and his multidisciplinary background spanning economics and philosophy, Samama examines why societies sometimes respond effectively to challenges and sometimes fail, as on Easter Island. Using examples like the development of agriculture and the information society, he proposes that societies behave like living organisms: They flourish by accessing natural and human resources.

However, these undeniable successes have led to overconfidence in science and capitalism, and, for Frédéric Samama, it is this overconfidence in the models that we use to represent the world that appears to be the cornerstone of our inaction in the face of the climate crisis.

He argues that this may be the first major challenge that requires societies to limit access to resources, in contrast to their traditional path to success.

Nevertheless, Samama—and I—retain hope. A real mobilization is still possible, provided it involves both governments and businesses, and permeates society as a whole. He stresses that the beauty and fragility of our planet must lie at the heart of this effort. His remarkably well-written book is both fascinating and inspiring, inviting each of us to act.

Jean Jouzel
Emeritus Research Director at the CEA
Member of the French Academy of Sciences
and the US National Academy of Sciences

PREFACE

Our inaction in the face of climate change is an enigma.

We have known about the danger for decades. We are the source of that threat—and it is an existential one. And yet, meaningful action remains unrealized.

The enigma deepens when we consider how effectively societies have mobilized in other moments of crisis. During the Covid-19 pandemic, governments acted rapidly to fund vaccines and enforce life-saving public health measures. When the ozone layer was under threat, harmful chemicals were swiftly banned. Ahead of the Y2K bug, entire systems were overhauled: airplanes grounded, hospitals secured, infrastructure updated.

Of course, history also offers examples of failure. On Easter Island, societies built massive stone statues—each weighing dozens of tonnes—as part of a prestige competition driven by gigantism. In doing so, they deforested the land to build the necessary transport systems. Their civilization ultimately collapsed. Some accounts even suggest that the last survivors resorted to cannibalism.[1]

---

1   J. Diamond (2021), *The Last Tree on Easter Island* (London: Penguin). Another thesis (P. McAnany and N. Yoffee, eds. (2010), *Questioning Collapse: Human Resilience, Ecological Vulnerability, and the Aftermath of Empire* (Cambridge: Cambridge University Press) highlights the role of rats and virus importation.

This, in a nutshell, is the central question of this book: why does a society succeed—or fail—when facing catastrophe?

In 2007–2008, I was living in New York and working at the core of the global financial system. From the inside, I witnessed just how close our economic infrastructure came to collapse—and how fragile our societal coordination mechanisms truly are. The crisis struck the most vulnerable the hardest, especially in a country where the safety net was thin. As a European, I knew that crises in history often evolve into catastrophes—and the looming climate crisis was already visible on the horizon. It became clear to me that new thinking was needed, and new actors had to step in. At that time, climate change was not yet on the financial sector's radar. It was seen, like nuclear risk, as the domain of government. Even so, I decided to act. I founded a research center on climate and finance in partnership with Columbia University, developed the first mainstream low-carbon indices, and introduced financial instruments that priced the cost of inaction—echoing a key message from the IPCC. I co-launched an investor coalition that would ultimately represent the financial sector at COP21. Over time, I contributed articles, books, and testimony before the US Senate—all focused on aligning finance with climate action.

Fifteen years later, broad recognition of the threat has emerged, and a range of solutions has been proposed—GDP impact studies, carbon pricing, and more. But none of it has sparked the scale of action we truly need. We can keep waiting for a distant technological breakthrough—but it may never come.

The situation is urgent: our remaining carbon budget will be exhausted within a few years if we want to stay below the dangerous threshold of 1.5°C above pre-industrial levels. It's no surprise that current strategies are falling short—they rely on the very logic that caused the crisis. Attempting to solve a problem with the very tools that created it is a precarious wager—they were designed for a different purpose altogether.

That's why I chose to dig deeper—to investigate the fundamental forces that drive our societies. What if societies functioned like living organisms, always seeking out resources for survival? If this is so, how can we study these dynamics? Could lessons from the human brain—an organ naturally hungry for energy—offer us a model? And could those insights scale to human systems?

This book is the result of a long, multidisciplinary inquiry—often well outside my comfort zone. Yet I believe that by drawing on insights from cognitive science, anthropology, finance, philosophy, and history, we can begin to understand why our societies stall in the face of existential risk— and how we might break through that paralysis. I don't claim to hold any absolute truths. What I offer is the outcome of a patient investigation—an intricate puzzle whose pieces this book seeks to assemble.

ACKNOWLEDGMENTS

This book is the fruit of an investigation that I conducted and then sought to share. It led me to explore new intellectual territory. My only objective was to seek an explanation for a situation that, were it not so serious, might simply be considered unusual.

I have been able to count on the support of Jean Boissinot, Patrick Bolton, François Candelon, Ariane Chebel d'Appollonia, Gilonne d'Origny, Gilles de Margerie, Jean-Christophe de Swann, Thomas Gaucher, Peter Goldmark, Sylvie Goulard, Roger Guesnérie, Haizhou Huang, Eugene Kandel, Yann Le Pallec, Jean Jouzel, Christophe Jurczak, Bruno Levy, Olivier Paquier, Laurinda Pereira, Ghislain Périsse, Hélène Rey, Olivier Rousseau, Félix Schoeller, and David Vaillant. Although they bear no responsibility for the contents of the book, I would like to thank them warmly for their kind yet rigorous feedback throughout the writing process.

Finally, thanks to Arthur Cohen and Noëlle Meimaroglou, for publishing the original French edition of this book, and to Guillaume Dervieux, Rebecca Marsh, and Frances Tye, for their help in preparing this revised and expanded English version.

1

CLIMATE CHANGE[1]:
DANGEROUS INACTION

Understanding the depth of our inaction begins with recognizing the full scope and urgency of the climate crisis. Despite clear scientific warnings and widespread, firsthand observations, climate change still hasn't triggered a collective response proportionate to the threat. The greenhouse effect has been known and scientifically documented since the 19th century,[2] and the impact of human activity on the planet has been known since the 1970s. There is no longer any doubt: climate disruption is an existential threat to

---

1 The term "climate change" (or "climate" or "climate disruption" in this book) refers here to the effects of the greenhouse gas emissions produced by the human species, and more generally to the disruption of conditions for human life on earth (rising temperatures, more extreme climatic events, loss of biodiversity, etc.).

2 S. Arrhenius (1896), "On the Influence of Carbonic Acid in the Air upon the Temperature of the Ground," *Philosophical Magazine and Journal of Science* 5 (41) (April): 237–276.

DOI: 10.4324/9781003638384-1

humanity. In the IPCC's "business-as-usual" scenario,[3] some 4–5 billion people will be in mortal danger by the end of this century.[4] This extreme danger emerges in regions where heat and humidity make it impossible for perspiration to cool the body—putting human lives at considerable risk (see Figure 1.1).

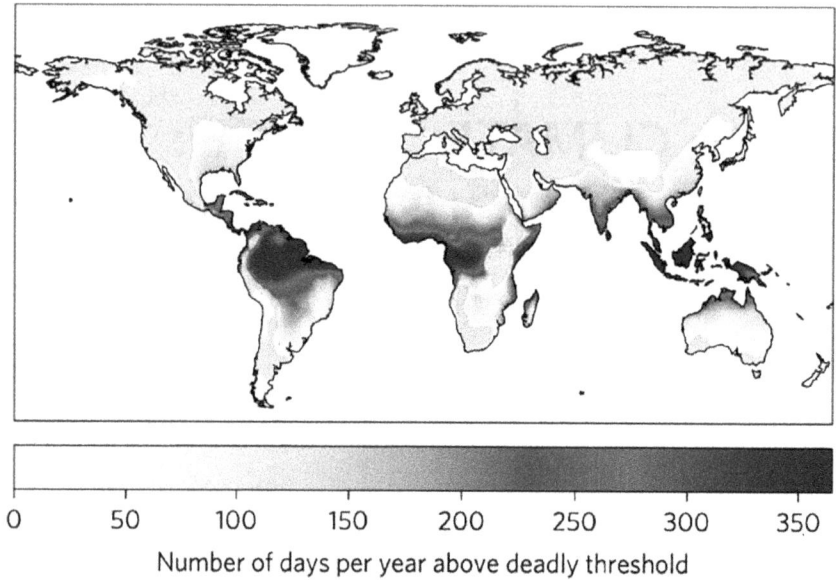

Number of days per year above deadly threshold

Figure 1.1 Graph of populations at risk in the IPCC's "business as usual" scenario author

Source: C. Mora *et al.* (2017).[5]

Note: In the so-called "business as usual" scenario—typically referring to a high-emissions trajectory—nearly 4–5 billion people could be living in conditions that exceed lethal heat and humidity thresholds by the end of the century. Darker areas indicate regions where this is projected to occur year-round.

---

3 The Intergovernmental Panel on Climate Change ("IPCC"), established in 1988 at the request of the G7, synthesizes scientific climate research. The IPCC was co-recipient of the Nobel Peace Prize in 2007.
4 C. Bielecki, I. Caldwell, C. Counsell, B. Dietrich, B. Dousset, E. Johnston, R. Geronimo, T. Giambelluca, E. Hawkings, L. Leon, L. Louis, M. Lucas, M. McKenzie, C. Mora, F. Powell, A. Shea, C. Trauernicht, and H. Tseng (2017), "Global Risk of Deadly Heat," *Nature Climate Change* 7: 501–506.
5 C. Bielecki, I. Caldwell, C. Counsell, B. Dietrich, B. Dousset, E. Johnston, R. Geronimo, T. Giambelluca, E. Hawkings, L. Leon, L. Louis, M. Lucas, M. McKenzie, C. Mora, F. Powell, A. Shea, C. Trauernicht, and H. Tseng (2017), "Global Risk of Deadly Heat," *Nature Climate Change* 7: 501–506.

In the last 20 years, more than 3 billion people have already begun to suffer the impacts of global warming, including almost 1.5 billion people in areas of severe drought.[6] The number of extreme weather events has quadrupled in the last 40 years.[7]

As a result, and based on studies of just six major regions, the World Bank[8] estimates that there will be 216 million climate migrants by 2050: 86 million from sub-Saharan Africa, 49 million from East Asia and the Pacific, 40 million from South Asia, 19 million from North Africa, 17 million from South America, and 5 million from Eastern Europe and Central Asia. Action is therefore imperative.

The challenge is daunting—due to its scale, complexity, and the limited time we have in which to act. It is also daunting in its magnitude, because we must reverse a trend that would otherwise lead to a doubling of greenhouse gas emissions by the end of the century, and drastically reduce them by 2050. All countries, all sectors, and all agents are concerned (see Figure 1.2).

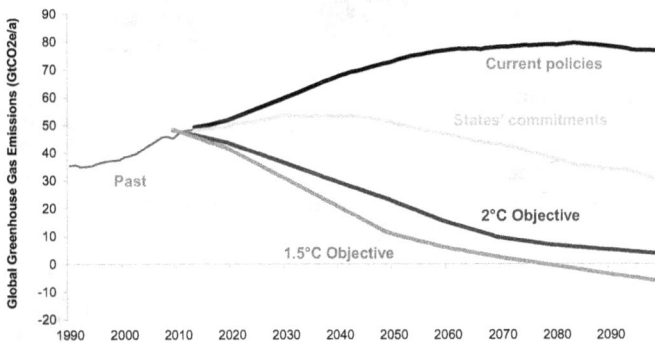

Figure 1.2 Graph of greenhouse gas emissions and the global effort required

Source: Climate Analytics and NewClimate Institute,[9] author.

Note: While the emissions are to double by 2050 in the business as usual trend, the goal of carbon neutrality requires a drastic reversal of the trend to bring emissions close to zero by the same date.

6   R. Below, J. Blatter, D. Delforge, C. Donatti, G. Fedele, P. Moraga, K. Nicholas, N. Speybroeck, and A. Zvoleff (2024), "Global Hotspots of Climate-Related Disasters," *International Journal of Disaster Risk Reduction* 108: Article 104488.

7   E. Rauch (2017), "Climate Stress Seen Through Munich RE's Risk and Opportunity Lens," Munich RE, 2017.

8   S. Adamo, V. Clement, A. de Sherbinin, B. Jones, K.K. Rigaud, N. Sadiq, J. Schewe, and E. Shabahat (2021), "Groundswell Part 2: Acting on Internal Climate Migration," *World Bank*, Washington.

9   https://climateactiontracker.org.

Complexity, because the forces at play are multiple and nonlinear and interact with each other. This complexity renders traditional policymaking—modeling and deliberating before acting—ineffective (see Figure 1.3).

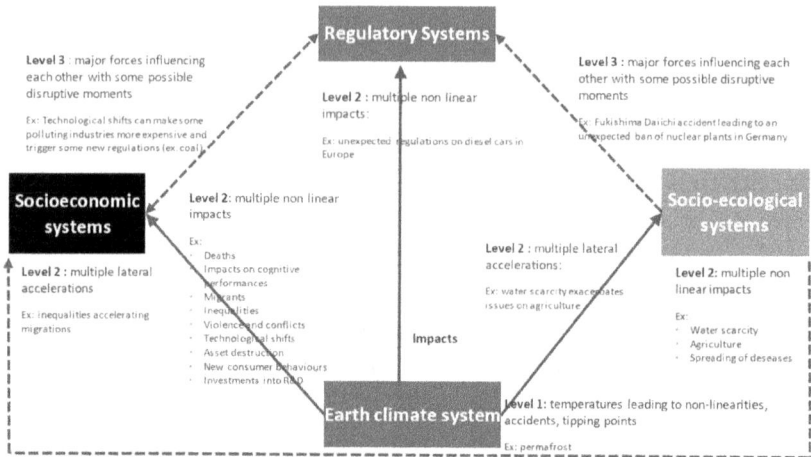

Figure 1.3 Graph of climate entropy

Source: P. Bolton et al. (2020).[10]

Note: The climate is generating high and growing entropy,[11] due to three main forces. First, societal forces—public opinion, changing consumer preferences, etc.—second, physical forces (heat waves, extreme weather events, etc.), leading to inflection points—[12] and third, regulatory forces (introduction of carbon credit markets, taxonomies, industrial constraints, etc.). These three types of forces are nonlinear and interact with each other.

---

10 P. Bolton, M. Després, L. Pereira da Silva, F. Samama, and R. Svartzman (2020), *The Green Swan: Central Banking and Financial Stability in the Age of Climate Change* (Basel: Bank for International Settlements), January.

11 Entropy is understood here as a situation of disorder, caused by nonlinear forces interacting with each other, and as therefore without organization, even statistical organization. Wars and Covid can be seen as similar situations of high entropy. This is the meaning adopted in the remainder of the book.

12 A. Barnosky, S. Cornell, M. Crucifix, J. Donges, I. Fetzer, C. Folke, S. Lade, T. Lenton, D. Liverman, J. Rockström, K. Richardson, M. Scheffer, H. J. Schellnhuber, W. Steffen, C. Summerhayes, and R. Winkelmann (2018), "Trajectories of the Earth System in the Anthropocene," *Proceedings of the National Academy of Sciences of the United States of America* 115 (33): 8252–8259.

If we take nature-related risks as an example, climate disruption increases the risk of drought, which will suddenly disrupt food production, leading to massive population movements and an exponential increase in conflicts. In Syria, drought, amplified by global warming, has forced rural populations to migrate to the cities. It now appears that global warming is partly responsible for the civil war in that country. Regulatory shocks are another major source of disruption. Consider the Dieselgate scandal: in 2015, a small Californian NGO exposed Volkswagen's excessive emissions of nitrogen oxides and CO_2. The fallout was swift—Volkswagen's share price collapsed, and the scandal shifted the balance of power between automakers and regulators, ultimately prompting the European Commission to impose radical new emissions standards. While combustion-powered cars still accounted for 65% of production in 2022, they are now set to be banned from sale in Europe from 2035. The climate crisis is a true turning point in human history—a *green swan*—marked by massive, nonlinear, interlocking forces that threaten human life.[13]

This is all the more threatening given the short time frame. To achieve carbon neutrality—i.e., a rise limited to 1.5°C warmer than the pre-industrial era, with 83% probability— at the start of 2020, the world's remaining carbon budget stood at just 300 $GtCO_2$.[14] However, we spent 34.3 $GtCO_2$ in 2020, then 36.5, 36.8, and 37.4 in the following years, and this has reduced today's carbon budget to 118 $GtCO_2$. Assuming that CO_2 emissions will remain constant in the future, in 2025 humanity will have a carbon budget of only three more years if we are to stay within the limit of 1.5°C.[15] This fact alone underscores the urgency of the crisis (see Figure 1.4).

---

13 P. Bolton, M. Després, L. Pereira da Silva, F. Samama, and R. Svartzman (2020), *The Green Swan: Central Banking and Financial Stability in the Age of Climate Change* (Basel: Bank for International Settlements), January.

14 IPCC (2021), *Climate Change 2021: The Physical Science Basis. Contribution of Working Group I to the Sixth Assessment Report of the Intergovernmental Panel on Climate Change*, Summary for Policymakers, Table SPM.2: Estimates of historical carbon dioxide (CO2) emissions and remaining carbon budgets."

15 P. Bolton, M. Kacperczyk, and F. Samama (2022), "Net-Zero Carbon Portfolio Alignment," *Financial Analysts Journal* 82(2): 19–33. Since the residual budget is now 118 $GtCO_2$ in 2025 and current emissions are 37.4 $GtCO_2$, assuming they remain constant, humanity only has 118/37.4 years of carbon budget left, or just over three years.

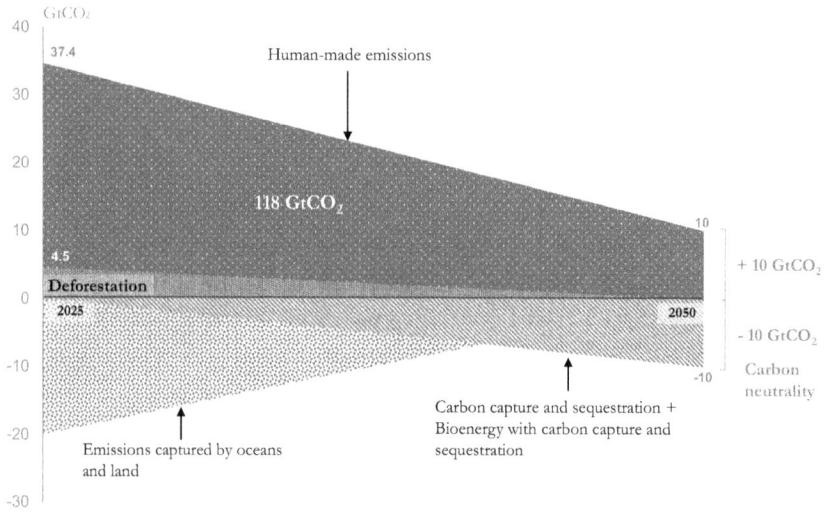

Figure 1.4 Graph of the climate emergency linked to a limited carbon budget (in 2025)

Source: P. Bolton, M. Kacperczyk, and F. Samama (2022),[16] author.

Note: The carbon budget is only 118 $GtCO_2$ in 2025 if we want to limit the rise in temperature to 1.5°C warmer than the pre-industrial era, with 83% probability. The oceans and land, which until now have absorbed the vast majority of emissions, have reached their saturation point. Achieving net zero by 2050 will require both a drastic reduction in CO_2 emissions and the ability to sequester what remains.

As a logical consequence, every year that passes makes our world's adjustment to carbon neutrality more difficult, if not impossible: by 2025, achieving this goal would require cutting emissions by 24% annually. If this effort is postponed, the necessary annual reduction in CO_2 emissions will rise from 24 to 32% in 2026, and will become impossible to achieve before 2030 (see Figure 1.5).

---

16 P. Bolton, M. Kacperczyk, and F. Samama (2022), "Net-Zero Carbon Portfolio Alignment," *Financial Analysts Journal* 82 (2): 19–33.

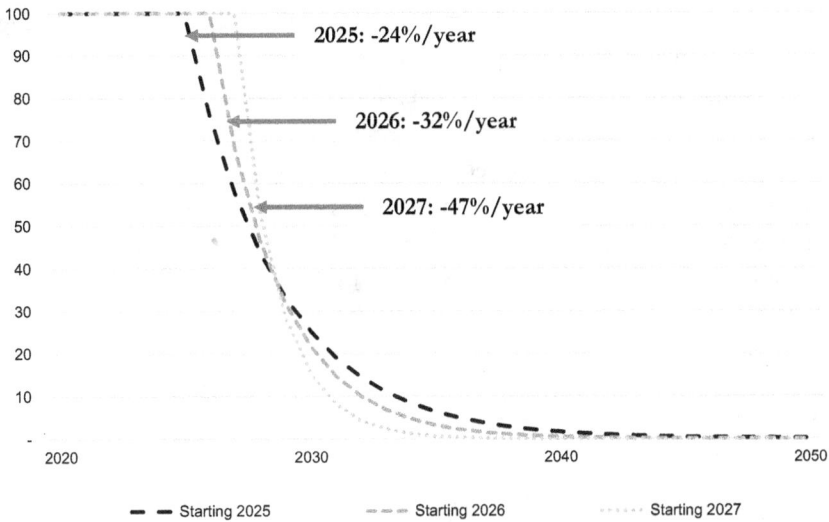

Figure 1.5 Graph showing the impact of time on the annual rate of decarbonization to achieve carbon neutrality

Source: P. Bolton, M. Kacperczyk, and F. Samama (2022),[17] author.

Note: The gradient of annual CO_2 reduction efforts is increasing very rapidly over time. The window of opportunity to avoid exceeding a temperature rise of 1.5°C is therefore very small.

At the same time, mankind is facing another crisis with certain similarities to—and partly correlated with—global warming[18]: the destruction of biodiversity. Even now, "75% of the Earth's surface is significantly altered"[19] by human activity; the Intergovernmental Platform on Biodiversity and Ecosystem Services (IPBES) estimates that around 1 million species are

---

17 P. Bolton, M. Kacperczyk, and F. Samama (2022), "Net-Zero Carbon Portfolio Alignment," *Financial Analysts Journal* 82 (2): 19–33.
18 P. Bolton, M. Després, L. Pereira da Silva, F. Samama, and R. Svartzman (2020), "Penser la Stabilité Financière à l'Ère des Risques Écologiques Globaux: Vers de Nouveaux Arbitrages entre Efficience et Résilience des Systèmes Complexes," *Revue d'Économie Financière* 138: 41–58.
19 IPBES (2019), *The Global Assessment Report on Biodiversity and Ecosystem Services: Summary for Policymakers*, p. 11.

already threatened with extinction.[20] Environmental disruption is leaving species with little time to adapt—where adaptation is even possible.[21]

The climate crisis and the biodiversity crisis are linked and mutually reinforcing—the climate alters biodiversity, while at the same time biodiversity helps to limit the effects of greenhouse gas emissions by creating carbon sinks.[22] Both stem from the excessive exploitation of resources, whether fossil—which has a direct effect on the climate—or natural, such as water—which has direct consequences for biodiversity.

*

In conclusion, the data are unequivocal: global warming poses an existential risk to humanity. If the solution were purely technical, we likely would have implemented it by now. But the urgency of this crisis runs deeper—it forces us to question the very logic that led us here. We must look beyond conventional tools and ask a more fundamental question: how do human societies function? This book explores a hypothesis: that societies may behave like living organisms. If so, perhaps we can learn—starting with the brain—how they operate in order to survive.

This is the subject of the next chapter.

---

20 IPBES (2019), *The Global Assessment Report on Biodiversity and Ecosystem Services: Summary for Policymakers.*

21 A. Arneth, D. Barnes, M. Burrows, S. Diamond, C. Duarte, W. Kiessling, P. Leadley, P. McElwee, S. Managi, H. Ngo, H. Pörtner, G. Midgley, D. Obura, U. Pascual, M. Sankaran, R. Scholes, Y. Shin, and A. Val (2023), "Overcoming the Coupled Climate and Biodiversity Crises and Their Societal Impacts," *Science* 380 (6642) (April 21): eabl4881.

22 A. Arneth, D. Barnes, M. Burrows, S. Diamond, C. Duarte, W. Kiessling, P. Leadley, P. McElwee, S. Managi, H. Ngo, H. Pörtner, G. Midgley, D. Obura, U. Pascual, M. Sankaran, R. Scholes, Y. Shin, and A. Val (2023), "Overcoming the Coupled Climate and Biodiversity Crises and Their Societal Impacts," *Science* 380 (April 21) (6642): p. 1:

Overall, climate change and sea level rise are projected to exacerbate the direct impacts of human activities, causing further losses in biomass, habitats, and species.

Conversely, biodiversity loss contributes to climate change through loss of wild species and biomass. This reduces carbon stocks and sink capacity in natural and managed ecosystems, increasing emissions.

2

HOW OUR BRAINS MODEL
THE WORLD

Like all living organisms, humans are driven by a fundamental imperative: survival. Our brains have evolved to optimize our actions in order to stay alive, to develop mechanisms for accessing resources, and to minimize energy consumption whenever possible. These intertwined drives shape how we perceive the world, anticipate outcomes, and make decisions. Understanding these cognitive processes—especially through the lens of modern neuroscience—can offer crucial insight into how we respond to threats, including the climate crisis.

Examples from everyday life

A baby is looking at a yogurt pot balanced on the edge of the kitchen table. A dog accidentally jostles the table, causing the yogurt pot to fall: untouched, it follows a vertical trajectory, from top to bottom. When the

DOI: 10.4324/9781003638384-2

baby reproduces this movement with their toy, they will observe the same result: when they let go of it, they see it fall. They will soon cease to be surprised by this movement, and will no longer even pay attention to it: without knowing the causes, they will have integrated this phenomenon, which has become a factual truth, into their model of how they represent the world.

Let's take a second, operational example, this time from the tennis player Andre Agassi. He had just lost three times in a row to Boris Becker, a newcomer on the world circuit. Becker had an innovative and effective serve. Agassi decided to study this formidable opponent's serve closely, sitting among the spectators during his matches. He discovered that the German player positioned his tongue differently depending on his intention: when he wanted to serve to the right, he placed his tongue on the right side, and in the middle when he was aiming for the center of the court. This information was obviously invaluable, given the very short reaction time available to a tennis player to counter a serve. Having cracked his opponent's behavioral pattern—something Boris Becker himself was unaware of—[1] allowed Agassi to win nine of their next 11 matches. To avoid tipping him off, Agassi even chose to lose a few points deliberately, ensuring his opponent would not realize that his behavioral pattern had been cracked.[2]

My third example is a purchase I made recently in a Parisian chocolate shop. After listening carefully to the various choices offered by the saleswoman, I ordered an assortment of different kinds: pralines, dark, almond, liqueur, etc. As I paid for my purchase, the saleswoman slipped me a kind word, hoping that the gift would please its recipient. Intrigued, I asked her what made her think this purchase was a gift (which indeed it was). She replied that I had taken some time to think about it, and that she thought that if the chocolates had been for me, my decision would have been much quicker. What's more, I had made a choice that wasn't a choice at all: choosing an assortment meant that I didn't know the preferences of the person I wanted to please, and so I had minimized my risk. From my

---

1 https://www.youtube.com/watch?v=ja6HeLB3kwY.
2 The same problem is encountered in the film *The Imitation Game* when Alan Turing and his team, having cracked Enigma, the encryption machine used by German forces during the Second World War, sacrifice some of the Allied ships whose destruction they have decoded, so as not to alert their enemy and lose their decisive advantage.

signal—my hesitation and my choice of an assorted box—the saleswoman quickly inferred—correctly—that the chocolates were a gift.

These three examples show that the process of creating laws from observations is the very basis of learning, that it continues throughout life, and that once a model has been established we can anticipate behavior, or intention, which reinforces the effectiveness of action. When it comes to understanding how the brain works, one of the many theories that has recently come to the fore is "Bayesian cognitive inference."[3] Stanislas Dehaene, one of today's leading neuroscientists, has no hesitation in calling it a revolution in cognitive science, and has devoted a lecture to it at the Collège de France.[4]

Understanding Bayesian cognitive inference

Formally speaking, human cognition seeks to establish a model for representing the world based on observations, and constantly updates it according to the probability of a hypothesis.[5] The founding principle is based on a theory developed by an 18th-century English clergyman[6] and follows a simple, fundamental equation:

---

3 Some authors use the term *"causal inference"* (J. Pearl and D. Mackenzie (2018), *The Book of Why: The New Science of Cause and Effect* (New York: Basic Books)).

4 Available at https://www.college-de-france.fr/site/stanislas-dehaene/.

5 Thomas Bayes' theory differs from Boolean logic (G. Boole (1854), *An Investigation into the Laws of Thought, on which are Founded the Mathematical Theories of Logic and Probabilities* (London: Macmillan & Co.)). The latter consists in asking, on the basis of hypotheses, what the probability of an observation is. For example, if I establish the hypothesis that there are six black balls and four white balls in an urn, what is the probability of a black ball appearing on the first draw? This is the question Boolean logic seeks to answer: what will happen, based on our knowledge of what's going on in the urn?

   Conversely, Bayes' theory uses observations to establish the probability of a hypothesis (in the sense of its plausibility). For example, if I observe nine black balls coming out of an urn containing ten, what is the probability of the hypothesis that all ten balls are black? This, then, is the question that Bayesian inference seeks to answer: how does the urn work, given what it produces? In short, Bayesian inference looks for a law based on actual observations, whereas Boolean logic predicts future observations based on a law.

6 T. Bayes (1763), "An Essay Towards Solving a Problem in the Doctrine of Chances," *Philosophical Transactions of the Royal Society of London* 53: 370–418. And as Judea Pearl and Dana Mackenzie point out (J. Pearl and D. Mackenzie (2018), *The Book of*

$$p(H|D) = p(D|H)\ p(H)/p(D)$$

With:

$p(H)$ = *a priori* probability.

$p(H|D)$ = *a posteriori* probability of hypothesis H, given observation D.

$p(D|H)$ = *a posteriori* probability of observation D, given hypothesis H.

The formula reads as follows: the probability of hypothesis H, based on the observation of D, is equal to the probability of the observation of D given hypothesis H, multiplied by the probability of hypothesis H, divided by the probability of the observation of D.[7]

Thomas Griffiths, Charles Kemps, and Joshua Tenenbaum[8] use a concrete and familiar example to illustrate this law, which may seem abstruse at first glance: that of a coughing child. Given the child's cough, we ask: is it more likely to be lung cancer, influenza, or gastroenteritis? The probability $p(\text{flu}|\text{cough})$[9] is relatively high, since the probability $p(\text{cough}|\text{flu})$[10] is high and is multiplied by the probability $p(\text{flu})$, which is also high. This probability is higher than that of the child's having lung cancer, because although the probability of having $p(\text{cough}|\text{lung cancer})$[11] is high, the probability of having $p(\text{lung cancer})$ is low, so the product of the two is low. Similarly, the probability of having $p(\text{gastroenteritis})$ is high, but since the probability $p(\text{cough}|\text{gastroenteritis})$ is low, the product of the two is also low.

This thinking process requires very little cognitive effort, because, as Stanislas Dehaene explains,[12] with each observation the probabilities of a

---

Why: The New Science of Cause and Effect (New York: Basic Books)), Thomas Bayes' work was a response to David Hume's essay on miracles, which addressed the resurrection of Jesus Christ without making it explicit. The apostles adjusted their hypothesis on Jesus' divine nature after observing his resurrection. This update was made possible by the high correlation between the event (resurrection) and the hypothesis (Messiah).

7 To put it another way, the probability of hypothesis H, based on the observation of D, is proportional to the probability of the observation of D knowing hypothesis H, multiplied by the probability of hypothesis H.

8 T. Griffiths, C. Kemp and J.B. Tenenbaum (2018), "Bayesian Models of Cognition," in *The Cambridge Handbook of Computational Cognitive Modeling*, edited by R. Sun, 59–100 (Cambridge: Cambridge University Press).

9 This should be read as meaning: "the probability of getting the flu knowing that you have a cough."

10 Meaning "the probability of coughing knowing you have the flu."

11 Meaning "the probability of coughing knowing you have lung cancer."

12 Available at https://www.college-de-france.fr/site/stanislas-dehaene/.

hypothesis being proven multiply[13] and, as a result, the level of confidence in a given hypothesis very quickly becomes very high.[14] This is one of the reasons why this way of perceiving the world has been so widely adopted: the efficiency and speed of Bayesian cognitive inference reduces our energy expenditure and saves time, which is invaluable in many cases in the struggle for survival.[15] It is part of a more global framework in which natural selection has led to the privileging of all kinds of mechanisms corresponding to action in the world of solids, be it Euclidean geometry or its encoding within the brain itself, as shown by Alain Berthoz.[16]

Bayesian cognitive inference is also innate. It can be observed from an early age. For example, an eight-month-old baby was placed in front of an urn from which, at regular intervals, only red balls appeared. When, after a while, a black ball appeared, the baby, intrigued, looked more closely at the urn in question. By doing so, he was expressing his surprise at the occurrence of an event contrary to his representation of the world.[17]

---

13 In other words, P(H|D1, D2 ... Dw) is proportional to P(D|H)^w, where w is the number of observations.

14 H. Jeffreys (1939), *The Theory of Probability* (Oxford University Press).

15 This leads Noah Goodman, T. D. Ullman, and J. B. Tenenbaum to speak of a "blessing of abstraction," which offers a complementary explanation of nature's selection of this mechanism (N. D. Goodman, J. B. Tenenbaum, and T. D. Ullman (2011), "Learning a Theory of Causality," *Psychological Review* 118(1): 110–119).

16 A. Berthoz (2000), *The Brain's Sense of Movement (Perspectives in Cognitive Science)*, translated by G. Weiss (Cambridge, MA: Harvard University Press), quoting the French mathematician Henri Poincaré (H. Poincaré (1952), *Science and Hypothesis*, translation by W. J. Greenstreet (New York, NY: Dover) about the human species' selection of a Euclidean frame of reference:

> Our mind adapted itself to the conditions of the external world through natural selection; it adopted the geometry most advantageous or, to put it another way, most convenient to the species. Geometry is not true; it is advantageous [...] Euclidean geometry is, and will remain, the most convenient: 1st, because it is the simplest, [...] 2nd, because it sufficiently agrees with the properties of natural solids. (Kindle Edition, p. 64)

And Alain Berthoz shows that this representation of the world can be found in the very workings of the brain itself.

17 V. Garcia and F. Xu (2008), "Intuitive Statistics by 8-Month-Old Infants," *Proceedings of the National Academy of Sciences of the United States of America* 105 (13): 5012–5015.

Another feature of Bayesian cognitive inference is that it is encoded hier-archically in the brain:[18] the lowest level would be that of sensory data (or inputs—sight, touch, etc.) and the highest that of the most abstract models.[19] At any given moment, the brain is anticipating incoming signals based on its internal model of the world. If there is a "prediction error," in other words, if the observed signal does not corroborate the anticipation, the information about its inadequacy is passed on to a higher level so that a new explanatory framework can be sought, and so on.[20]

To establish these laws, Joshua Tenenbaum *et al.* show that Bayesian cog-nitive inference is constantly categorizing objects:[21] faced with a multitude of sensory inputs, the brain seeks to create categories so that it is always able to know whether or not it is likely that a particular specificity distinguishes one input from the others. There is an obvious energy gain here, because

---

18 As Herbert Simon had already explained, taking as his example the "resilience" (although he did not use this expression) of such systems, as illustrated by the con-struction of watches. Without an intermediate structure, any interruption in the manufacturing process is costly. If there is a hierarchy, the process is more robust (H. A. Simon (1962), "The Architecture of Complexity," *Proceedings of the American Philosophical Society* 106 (6) (Dec.): 467–482).

19 H-J. Park and K. Friston (2013), "Structural and Functional Brain Networks: From Connections to Cognition," *Science* 342: 1238411.

20 This hierarchy is also at work in the extreme case of the binocular experiment: the subject wears stereoscopic goggles, whose lenses are replaced on one side by the image of a house and on the other by the image of a human face. In prac-tice, the retina "sees" two different images simultaneously. We then observe that the brain will "see," alternately, for eight seconds, a house and then a face. This phenomenon stems from the fact that the brain is faced with an enigma: it perceives both images, even though it has learned that the probability of seeing them simultaneously is zero. The brain first tests the most probable hypothesis—i.e., the house—then the face. But since both have similar prob-abilities and are confirmed by the same sensory input—i.e., visual perception—the brain switches from one representation to the other, as it cannot find an explanatory framework. See K. Friston, J. Hohwy, and A. Roepstorff (2008), "Predictive Coding Explains Binocular Rivalry: An Epistemological Review," *Cognition* 108 (3): 687–701.

21 N. D. Goodman, T. L. Griffiths, C. Kemp, and J. B. Tenenbaum (2011), "How to Grow a Mind: Statistics, Structure, and Abstraction," *Science* 331 (6022): 1279–1285. In a table containing a multitude of shapes, when the subject sees that three of them are called a "Tufa," how do they identify which other shapes are also Tufas? The brain proceeds by categorizing the shapes using Bayesian cognitive inference.

once the category has been established and its specificities known, the cost of cognitive processing of any new similar "object" will be reduced.

The brain filters sensory input relentlessly, focusing only on signals that are vital to energy conservation and survival. Roger Shepard[22] postulates that the processing of any signal follows a Bayesian law of inference. Indeed, any significant new observation calls for a comparison with previous ones of the same nature, to estimate whether or not its effects are identical. He takes the example of a bird that swallows a caterpillar,[23] enjoys it, and then "wonders" whether objects similar in color and appearance will bring comparable satisfaction. Roger Shepard[24] considers that all animals process incoming signals within a "psychological space" that follows an exponential forgetting function: to optimize survival and access to resources, the brain favors the most recent signals and quickly discards the oldest.

Once the model has been established, the brain can then simulate the effects of an action that has yet to occur: for example, as in the case of an adult who is considering letting go of their yogurt. This ability to mentally simulate the consequences of an action offers another crucial advantage: the ability to consider different options and choose the one considered to be best.[25] The

---

22 R. Shepard (2004), "How a Cognitive Psychologist Came to Seek Universal Laws Psychonomic," *Psychonomic Bulletin & Review* 11 (1): 1–23.

23 R. Shepard (1987), "Toward a Universal Law of Generalization for Psychological Science," *Science New Series* 237 (4820) (Sept. 11): 1317–1323.

24 R. Shepard (1987), "Toward a Universal Law of Generalization for Psychological Science," *Science New Series* 237 (4820) (Sept. 11): 1317–1323 (pp. 1317–1319):

> A psychological space is established for any set of stimuli by determining metric distances between the stimuli such that the probability that a response learned to any stimulus will generalize to any other in an invariant monotonic function of the distance between them. [...] Yet, in every case, the decrease of generalization with psychological distance is monotonic, generally concave upward and more or less approximates a simple exponential decay function.

25 Some authors, such as Judea Pearl and Dana Mackenzie, make this a defining point of Bayesian cognitive inference (J. Pearl and D. Mackenzie (2018), *The Book of Why: The New Science of Cause and Effect* (New York: Basic Books)):

> One of the crowning achievements of the Causal Revolution has been to explain how to predict the effects of an intervention without actually enacting it. [...] When the scientific question of interest involves retrospective thinking, we call on another type of expression unique to causal reasoning called a counterfactual. For example, suppose that Joe took Drug D and died

human mind thus has the capacity to refine its model of representation of the world, not on the basis of observations or actions, but on the basis of simulations *in abstracto*—i.e., by asking itself questions. To illustrate this, Étienne Klein[26] uses the example of Galileo's attack on Aristotle's theory of gravitation. Aristotle had postulated that the heavier a body, the faster it falls. Galileo performed the following thought experiment: he pictured a large stone attached to a lighter one by a string. According to Aristotle's law, the whole object— i.e., the heavy stone attached to the lighter one—must be heavier than the heavy stone alone, and must fall faster than the latter. However, by applying the same law, the lighter stone should, because it is slower to fall, slow down the heavier stone; the whole object should therefore have a lower speed than the heavier stone falling alone. Galileo saw that applying the same law yielded two contradictory outcomes—so he concluded another force must be at work. His model of the world had just been modified.

Three cognitive strategies depending on the environment

According to Philip Schwartenbeck *et al.*,[27] all living beings seek to reduce surprise—i.e., unexpected situations—in order to optimize the use of their energy and their chances of survival. To this end, the human mind resorts to Bayesian cognitive inference according to three main families of possibilities: (1) a simple application of the model of world representation (which he calls "exploitation"); in this case, I decide to apply the established model without seeking to refine it in any way;[28] (2) a refinement of the model (which he calls "exploration"); in this case, I perfect my understanding of the world; (3) an "adaptation"; in this case, I act to bring the world into line with my mode of representation. The choice between these

---

a month later; our question of interest is whether the drug might have caused his death. To answer this question, we need to imagine a scenario in which Joe was about to take the drug but changed his mind. Would he have lived? (Kindle Edition, pp. 9–10)

26 E. Klein, "How Thought Experiments Advanced Science." Available at https://www.youtube.com/watch?v=V5oV3SVkbJE (in French). Accessed July 30, 2025.
27 R. Dolan, T. FitzGerald, K. Friston, and P. Schwartenbeck (2013), "Exploration, Novelty, Surprise, and Free Energy Minimization," *Frontiers in Psychology*, 4, article 710.
28 The level of confidence in the model is then such that the gain in refining it compared to the energy spent on this additional precision is not worthwhile. This threshold is certainly reached according to the mechanism described by Stanislas Dehaene above.

three possibilities depends on the environment in which I find myself, and my confidence in my representational model and possible actions.

To illustrate how this decision-making process works, consider three travelers—John, Emma, and Jake—preparing to pack for a trip. Their situations reflect the behaviors of exploitation, exploration, or adaptation—depending on their confidence in their model of the world.

I exploit: Confidence in an established model

Let's imagine John, who is preparing to leave for Miami on August 15. Confident in Florida's typically sunny weather at that time of year, he opens his closet, assesses his options to ensure he has everything that will be needed (for a party, for the beach, etc.), and chooses what to pack. He trusts his mental model (sunshine) and assumes his actions (accessing his clothes) are appropriate. Everything seems in order.

Disorganized, he can't find his sunglasses, but decides to leave without them. Since he doesn't believe his search will succeed, he abandons it—even though the sunglasses might prove useful.

With only minutes before his cab arrives, John grabs the first shirts he sees and stops packing. He prioritizes catching his flight over reviewing his packing list.

Even when he hears a rare weather alert predicting rain in Miami, John doesn't change his packing. His confidence in his original model—and his desire for it to remain true—prevent him from updating his assumptions.

I explore: Seeking information and questioning the model

Another traveler, Emma, has also been planning to head to Miami. Like John, she expects good weather, but having heard about climate change, she refines her model by considering climate anomalies like heatwaves or hurricanes—demonstrating exploratory behavior and abstract thinking.

Having always spent her vacations in Florida since childhood, however, Emma now thinks it is time to see something new, and she decides to explore the unfamiliar: Portland, Oregon. She packs sweaters and rain gear.

While she's always chosen Miami in the past, this time Emma gives extra value to trying something new—even convincing herself the weather should not be that bad. She distorts reality slightly in favor of exploration, which increases the likelihood that she will go to Portland.

Suppose she can't access the internet while packing, and instead asks friends who have seen the weather report. Since she can't reach the desired state (certainty) alone, she turns to cooperation—trusting their insights.

I adapt: Acting to modify or adjust to the environment

Jake had planned to visit Las Vegas, but hearing about an extreme heat-wave, he changes plans and books a trip to San Francisco instead—adjusting the environment to better match his comfort expectations.

However, that summer, San Francisco turns out to be unusually cold. Having only packed his usual light clothes, Jake is forced to buy a sweater on arrival—an adaptive strategy. But stores are sold out due to high tourist demand. He can't make the necessary adjustment.

If, before leaving, Jake had realized he couldn't predict the weather due to lack of reliable info, he would pack for multiple scenarios: T-shirts, swimwear, and sweaters. Unable to refine his model, he would adopt a strategy suited to uncertainty, accepting trade-offs—like heavier luggage and less space for books.

Alternatively, he might have packed only a T-shirt, planning to buy whatever else he needs upon arrival. In doing so, he would accept real-time adaptation and the risks that come with it—being unprepared and dependent on local resources.

As illustrated in these examples, the choices made by John, Emma, and Jake depend on the states they anticipate and the confidence they place in both their world model and the actions they consider.[29]

Depending on our sensitivities and the moment, we can be John, Emma, or Jake, which speaks to the complexity of a seemingly banal situation, beyond the broad categories. When it comes to the climate challenge, we think we're Jake, and that we'll always be able to adapt. But what if we were, in fact, collectively John, receiving the signal but unable to hear it?

---

29 Only the first, rare case is related to the school of Oskar Morgenstern and John Von Neumann (O. Morgenstern and J. Von Neumann (1944), *Theory of Games and Economic Behavior* (Princeton, NJ: Princeton University Press)); the second, consisting of taking only a few cases, to Herbert Simon's "Bounded Rationality" (H. A. Simon (1956), "Rational Choice and the Structure of the Environment," *Psychological Review* 63: 129–138); the third, the pullover added "just in case," à la Kahneman and Tversky (D. Kahneman and A. Tversky (1979), "Prospect Theory: An Analysis of Decision under Risk," *Econometrica* 47 (2): 263–291. Bayesian cognitive inference thus offers an (almost) global conceptual framework.

Selection criteria

If we now seek to model these decisions, we find that the brain constructs a generative model based on three pillars: "values," "states" to be occupied in order to satisfy these "values," and "actions" that achieve these "states."[30] Each of these pillars offers several alternatives, which can be classified according to the subject's degree of confidence in achieving the expected result (see Figure 2.1).

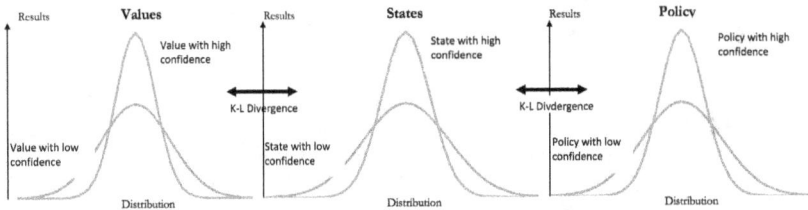

Figure 2.1 Three-pole graph of "values," "states," and "policy"

Source: Author.

Note: Every individual holds values that vary in certainty—illustrated by the example of the tennis player described below. The question will then be to know what policy to put in place, in order to reach a state that will itself lead to the satisfaction of these values. In each case, the question will be about confidence in the representation that will enable the next step to be reached: from right to left; confidence in the policy that will enable the state to be reached, confidence in the state that will enable the values to be reached, confidence in the values.

Consider a tennis player preparing for a major tournament just weeks away. Their "value" is clear: becoming rich and famous is their sole objective. De facto, other possible values (a family life, getting a higher degree, etc.) are set aside. The question is whether the next tournament they enter is an important step in their career. If they feel they have a good chance of winning it, it comes down to whether this tournament corresponds to a "state" that enables them to achieve their "value." The question then becomes whether—by training even harder ("action")—they will increase their chances of victory ("state"). To do this, the brain uses the same generative model to map out possible actions and their consequences.

The tennis player must therefore reduce the discrepancy between these two probability distributions:[31] the probability distribution of the "states" they think they can achieve—i.e., winning the tournament—and that of

---

30 Karl Friston merges values and states, using the term "desirable states."

31 This is equivalent to solving the Kullback–Leibler divergence between two probability distributions. In formal terms, this amounts to selecting an action by

the "states" that can be achieved by implementing an "action"—i.e., training. They select and implement the action that reduces this gap, and train hard as outlined by Karl Friston et al (see Figure 2.2).[32]

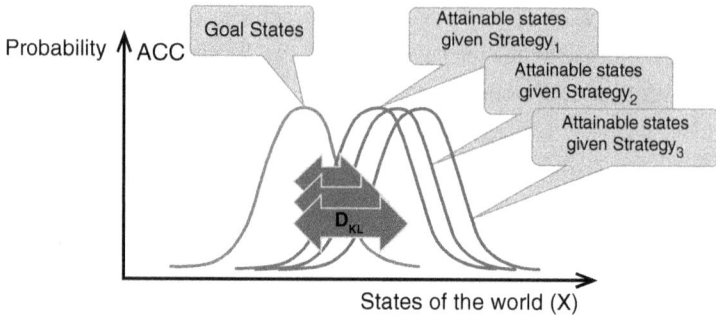

Figure 2.2 Plot of the reduction in distance between states as objectives and those that are attainable as a function of different strategies

Source: A. Peters, B. McEwen, and K. Friston (2017).[33]

Note: The brain constantly seeks to establish the highest probability of reducing the distance between a goal state and the states that can be reached, depending on the action policy that can be put in place.

---

estimating its consequences according to the generative model and the distance from the desired goal:

$$Q(\pi|st) = -DKL \left[P(s_{T}|s_{t},\pi) \;||\; P(s_{T}|m) \right]$$

Where:

Q is a given policy π from a specific state at time t $\in$,

DKL is the relative entropy between two probability distributions, P (sT|st,π) and P (sT|m),

P (sT|st,π) represents the probability distribution of states reached given an action π,

P (sT|m) represents the probability distribution of states corresponding to the agent's goals.

See R. Dolan, T. FitzGerald, K. Friston, and P. Schwartenbeck (2013), "Exploration, Novelty, Surprise, and Free Energy Minimization," Frontiers in Psychology 4, article 710.

32 T. Behrens, R. Dolan, T. FitzGerald, K. Friston, M. Moutoussis, and P. Schwartenbeck(2014), "The Anatomy of Choice: Dopamine and Decision Making," Philosophical Transactions of the Royal Society 369: 20130481:

[...] choices are based upon beliefs about alternative policies, where the most likely policy minimizes the difference between attainable and desired outcomes.

33 K. Friston, B. McEwen, and A. Peters. (2017), "Uncertainty and Stress: Why It Causes Diseases and How It Is Mastered by the Brain," Progress in Neurobiology 156: 164–188.

The tennis player operates in a clear, stable environment where their values, goals, and actions align: they have a representation model of reality that indicates a clear value (their personal fulfillment) that they believe they can achieve (winning a tournament), via an action that is also clearly defined (the more they train, the greater the probability of winning their tournament). They commit to this course of action without hesitation.

This simple, harmonious configuration of the three pillars is relatively exceptional. In everyday life, the respective weight of these pillars varies unevenly, influencing the action chosen. Thus, if we take a theoretical approach, according to Philipp Schwartenbeck et al.,[34] the decomposition of the value of an action highlights two dimensions: the first corresponds to the different "states" that the agent can achieve as a function of their actions; the second to the agent's goals, and their degree of confidence in their ability to achieve them. The relative contribution of the two depends on the current state of nature and the precision of the objectives, as illustrated in Figure 2.3 below:

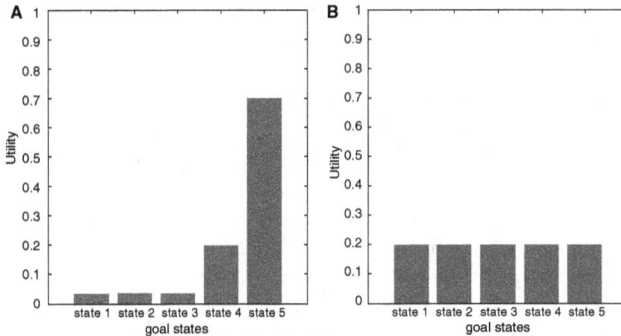

Figure 2.3 Graph of the accuracy profile of the desired states
Source: P. Schwartenbeck et al. (2013).[35]
Note: In case A, among the *goal states*, number 5 stands out as a priority, whereas in case B, all five are equivalent. This situation will lead to different choice-of-action policies being made in cases A and B.

34 R. Dolan, T. FitzGerald, K. Friston, and P. Schwartenbeck (2013), "Exploration, Novelty, Surprise, and Free Energy Minimization," *Frontiers in Psychology* 4, article 710.
35 R. Dolan, T. FitzGerald, K. Friston, and P. Schwartenbeck (2013), "Exploration, Novelty, Surprise, and Free Energy Minimization," *Frontiers in Psychology*, 4, article 710.

The confidence profile will then determine whether it is preferable to be in a logic of exploitation or exploration. Thus, according to Karl Friston et al.,[36] in case A (among the *goal states*, one stands out as a priority), we should choose exploitation; on the other hand, in case B (all the goal states are equivalent), we should choose exploration (or adaptation) and therefore allocate energy to reducing the surprise.[37]

However, what determines the level of confidence in a model? According to Arie Kruglanski, Katarzyna Jasko, and Karl Friston,[38] confidence is

---

36 T. Behrens, R. Dolan, T. FitzGerald, K. Friston, M. Moutoussis, and P. Schwartenbeck, P. (2014), "The Anatomy of Choice: Dopamine and Decision Making," *Philosophical Transactions of the Royal Society,* 369: 20130481:

> The relative contribution of entropy and expected utility depends upon the precision of prior beliefs about the final state or, equivalently, the relative utility of different states. If these beliefs are very precise (informative), they will dominate and the agent will (believe it will) maximize expected utility. Conversely, with imprecise (flat) prior beliefs that all final states are equally valuable, the agent will try to keep its options open and maximize the entropy over those states: in other words, it will explore.

37 Let's take the case of a student who is wondering about their future career. Either the student is in context A, where their goals are clearly defined and entropy is low. For example, if the student is totally confident that taking over their parents' medical practice will satisfy their medical drive, they can optimize the path to the identified goal and focus on the medical entrance exam. Or the student is in situation B, and has little confidence in their model of how the world is represented (due to their personal journey or due to an environment marked by high entropy, as was the case during the Covid). In this case, they should focus on exploration to refine their model, and travel the world; or put in place an adaptation strategy, and apply for as many internships as possible in a variety of fields, and see which sector picks up the fastest after the crisis.

38 K. Friston, K. Jasko, and A. Kruglanski (2020), "All Thinking Is 'Wishful' Thinking," *Trends in Cognitive Sciences* 24, (6): 413–424. The authors articulate a link between motivation and Bayesian inference. On the basis of these elements, we can hypothesize confidence in a model as a function of three essential dimensions: Motivation influences model acceptance (confirmation bias, avoidance of disturbing information, etc.), simplicity (minimization of energy consumption), and accuracy (a model must correctly reflect reality and enable reliable predictions to be made). Any nonalignment leads to reduced confidence (so an accurate model is not necessarily perceived as reliable if motivation or simplicity are not satisfied, or a simple and accurate model may be rejected if it is not aligned with motivations). Finally, as a living organism wants to remain

the result of the assessment of three factors: motivation (which influences model acceptance via confirmation bias, the avoidance of disturbing information, etc.), simplicity (minimization of energy consumption), and accuracy (a model must correctly reflect reality and enable reliable predictions to be made). Any nonalignment of these three dimensions leads to reduced confidence (so an accurate model is not necessarily perceived as reliable if motivation or simplicity are not satisfied, or a simple and accurate model can be rejected if it is not aligned with motivations). Finally, the drive to access resources is a fundamental force across all living organisms. From this, we can hypothesize that societies prefer models that allow access to resources and that are simple and accurate.

There is therefore a risk of selecting only those models that meet these criteria and failing to adopt an exploratory approach, which is inherently neither simple nor accurate, and in no way guarantees access to resources. And yet, exploration is sometimes necessary, because it leads to the refinement of a system of representation of the world and thereby reduced uncertainty. It does so either through the discovery of new states, or the perfection of knowledge about current states (e.g., precision, quality).[39] In other words, exploration and novelty bring about, first, a better understanding of the world and, second, a simplification of the model.[40] This is undoubtedly why, through the process of natural selection, the human brain has been built in such a way that

so, access to resources is a prime motivator. From this, we can hypothesize that societies prefer models that allow access to resources, and that are simple and exact.

39 R. Dolan, T. FitzGerald, K. Friston, and P. Schwartenbeck(2013), "Exploration, Novelty, Surprise, and Free Energy Minimization," *Frontiers in Psychology*, 4, article 710, 2013.

40 So it's not a question of increasing the complexity of the model, but rather of making it simpler and simpler (which goes back to Ockham's razor), or as Karl Friston *et al.* put it (K. Friston, C. Frith, A. Hobson, M. Lin, S. Ondobaka, and G. Pezzulo (2017), "Active Inference, Curiosity and Insight," *Neural Computation*, 29: 2633–2683):

[...] minimizing free energy is [...] equivalent to minimizing the complexity of accurate explanations for observed outcomes.

we have an inquisitive mind and an appetite for discovery:[41] the brain responds to novelty with a surge of dopamine, reinforcing curiosity and learning.[42] This has been observed in laboratory experiments: a monkey that is offered a little fruit juice has a dopamine spike. If the operation is repeated, the amount of dopamine drops. But if the monkey is offered two rations of fruit juice when it was only expecting one, it rises again. Dopamine is therefore released not in response to reward, but to surprise. Novelty is potentially a source of pleasure, which probably encourages us to seek and discover.[43]

However, exploration entails costs that must be considered—most notably, the time needed for analysis, which can conflict with the need to act quickly. This is the case of John, who grabs the first T-shirts he sees—better to leave for the airport, even if it means bringing the wrong clothes. Or, for example, when a doctor sees a patient arrive at the emergency room after a serious car accident, they could first carry out tests on the patient's diabetes or cholesterol, which would refine their medical diagnosis, but these analyses would endanger the individual's life due to their urgent need for an operation. The emergency physician must therefore halt further refinement of their mental model at a certain threshold—focused on essential symptoms—beyond which continued analysis could endanger the patient. The human being must therefore constantly decide whether or not to update their model of world representation, or whether they prefer to implement

---

41 Information that enhances our understanding of the world, and therefore our adaptability and chances of survival. From this perspective, freedom and money are also two possible vectors of adaptation and exploration, which, in addition to their own specificities, would also explain their societal value.

42 R. Adams, S. Bestmann, H. Brown, R. Dolan, T. FitzGerald, K. Friston, J. Galea, R. Moran, T. Shiner, and K. E. Stephan (2012), "Dopamine, Affordance and Active Inference," PLOS Computational Biology 8 (1): e1002327.

43 For similar reasons, we observe that human beings sometimes have a positively biased representation of the world (see N. Weinstein (1980), "Unrealistic Optimism about Future Life Events," Journal of Personality and Social Psychology 39 (5): 806–820). Moreover, this positive bias is reinforced the more important the envisaged state of the world is for the agent. In a way, reality is positively distorted to encourage human beings to occupy states that are favorable to them, which de facto increases their chances of survival or success. On the other side, the bias can also be negative, giving more weight to very negative events, again through the effect of natural selection, as this increases the chances of survival. The biases would then be at the extremes.

the existing model. Even evaluating whether to analyze further is, in itself, a cognitive action.[44]

Finally, in a high-entropy, high-threat world, rapid adaptation must prevail. In a world governed by chaos, there is no model to refine—because no stable model can be built to begin with. There are then two possible strategies: either to adapt, or to transform the world so that it adapts to us. In the first case, the most telling example is that of the soldier on the battlefield. Reality imposes its urgency: we must survive in the short term,[45] not try to understand and only act to adapt. In the second case, the aim is to influence the world in such a way as to reduce entropy.[46]

In summary, three primary scenarios emerge: in a low-entropy world where the agent trusts its world model, exploitation becomes the most efficient strategy. Energy will essentially be deployed to implement the identified action, since the value is clear, the state to be occupied to satisfy it is also clear, and the agent has confidence in the effectiveness of the actions it will perform to achieve it. In a complex world, energy will be allocated to exploration, either through a search for information or through a simulation of other possible worlds, bringing to light knowledge of the how the world's hidden forces interact. In a world of high entropy, the agent has no choice but to adapt: it must act to occupy the most favorable state (for example, dodging bullets on a battlefield), or, having identified the key points of these (positive) forces, focus its energy on bringing them to the surface.

Behaviors that change with confidence

At birth, the larva of the ascidian, an invertebrate marine animal that has populated all the world's oceans, has eyes and a small brain that enable it to

44 S. Gershman, E. Horvitz, and J. B. Tenenbaum (2015), "Computational Rationality: A Converging Paradigm for Intelligence in Brains, Minds, and Machines," *Science* 349 (6245), July 17.

45 Like Stendhal's Fabrice del Dongo at the Battle of Waterloo, who doesn't know what's at stake (Stendhal (1925), *The Charterhouse of Parma*, translated by C. K. Scott Moncrieff (New York: Boni and Liveright).

46 The broader process of domesticating nature can be seen from this perspective. Domestication is not unique to human beings, but is common to all animals. See R. Day, K. Laland, and J. Odling-Smee (2003), "Rethinking Adaptation: The Niche-Construction Perspective Perspectives in Biology and Medicine," *Perspectives in Biology and Medicine*, 46(1) (Winter): 80–95.

evolve. Once it has found a place to live, the ascidian eats its own eyes and brain. It then enlarges its stomach. In other words, the organ that enabled it to navigate and manage an unstable environment is no longer needed. Put simply: when exploring, the animal feeds its brain; when exploiting, it feeds its stomach.

To follow this evolution at a more granular level, let's take the case of a "synthetic" rat in a maze in search of food. At first, the rat wanders—it only has information, and not yet a representation model. As the rat gathers clues, it gradually constructs a model of its environment and gains confidence in its ability to locate the food. Once that confidence reaches a high threshold, it heads directly to the food source and stops exploring other possibilities.[47] If we follow Arie Kruglanski, Katarzyna Jasko, and Karl Friston,[48] we can clearly identify three states. Initially, there is no internal model of the world to guide behavior. The rat adopts a "quick and dirty" approach, wandering randomly through the maze. In the second situation, when it finds clues about the state of the world, the rat allocates its energy between accessing food and validating its internal model of the world. The optimal approach is, then, part exploitation and part exploration. In the third situation, when the model is perceived as reliable, the rat concentrates on the action that corresponds to its optimal internal model of the world. Exploration is no longer necessary to achieve the—now clearly identified—goal. The model is simple—the same path; accurate—the cheese is always in the same place; and corresponds to the motivation—the cheese, i.e., a resource. Ultimately, the rat gradually constructs a model of its environment, and once its confidence is high enough, it shifts to pure exploitation.

*

In conclusion, recent discoveries in cognitive science have uncovered the cognitive process by which we develop a representation of the world, and which we constantly update in response to new observations. It is based on

---

47 Note that if the rules are changed, the rat starts wandering the maze again, then rebuilds a new model. However, it now takes the rodent longer to trust its model (to switch to exploitation).

48 K. Friston, K. Jasko, and A. Kruglanski (2020), "All Thinking Is 'Wishful' Thinking," *Trends in Cognitive Sciences* 24 (6): 413–424.

the principle of inference as formulated by the Reverend Thomas Bayes in the 18th century.

Based on the laws thus established, the brain can anticipate and, depending on its confidence in the model, allocate resources in an optimal way, prompting exploratory, exploitative and/or adaptive behavior. The brain's ability to anticipate outcomes and allocate energy efficiently improves the agent's chances of survival.

This mechanism appears across species, suggesting a fundamental principle of cognitive evolution.

This raises a key question: Do similar mechanisms guide collective behavior in institutions like corporations and financial markets?

This is the subject of the next chapter.

3

MODERN COOPERATIVE STRUCTURES

Corporations and financial markets are modern coordination systems that operate across national and cultural boundaries. As intermediate-scale reductions of our complex societies, they offer a privileged field of observation for testing the hypothesis that human societies function like living organisms. If this hypothesis proves to be true, we should be able to discern structures geared toward the acquisition of resources, based on Bayesian cognitive inference mechanisms, as well as processes for optimizing the use of these same resources.

DOI: 10.4324/9781003638384-3

Is the corporation a living organism?

As Colin Mayer has shown,[1] the modern corporation is the fruit of a long evolutionary process with roots in the Roman Empire. At that time, structures appeared that were either flexible (such as those dedicated to the sale of clothing) or perennial (such as professional associations). Flexibility and durability gradually merged over the centuries to give rise to the corporation as we know it today.

Without lapsing into anthropomorphism, we can observe that a company functions much like a living organism. Its sales teams act as sensory organs, gathering information from the environment. General management serves as the nervous system, processing inputs, and coordinating responses. The corporation's legal identity forms a protective membrane, shielding it from external shocks. Together, these elements enable the company to model its surroundings, adapt to change, and emit signals that guide coordination—both internally and externally.

Sales teams function as sensory receptors, continuously relaying information about customer demands, market trends, and competitive pressures. General management performs three vital functions. First, it defines the corporation's core values, which shape its culture and align internal behaviors—facilitating cooperation through shared expectations, as explored in Chapter 2. These values also radiate outward, offering external

---

1 C. Mayer (2018), *Prosperity: Better Business Makes the Greater Good* (Oxford: Oxford University Press):

> The corporate enterprise has its origins in the parallel evolution of two institutions [...] The first institution is the corporation and the second is the partnership [...] the origin of both institutions can be traced back to Roman times. [...] The first was the societas and the second was the collegium. A societas was formed by the consent of the partners, socii, to undertake commercial and other activities. Examples include clothes, financial services, grain, maritime transport, and wine. The partners [...] were responsible for the liabilities of the societas and had a right to its claims. [...] The societas therefore lacked permanence and did not possess legal personality. [...] The collegium could hold property, employ and be employed, and sue and be sued. It was in particular associated with trade guilds of, for example, doctors, dyers, painters, shoemakers, and weavers, and religious associations. [...] such organizations could be legal entities in their own right with a legal personality that was distinct from the individuals who comprised them. (pp. 157–160)

partners a clear and consistent sense of how the corporation—and its representatives—will behave. Thanks to its legal continuity, or "eternity," the corporation establishes a lasting identity. When an Apple manager negotiates a deal, for example, their counterpart isn't merely assessing them as an individual but responding to a set of known behaviors and values associated with the Apple brand. This identity becomes a powerful asset in interactions across the corporation's ecosystem—whether with suppliers, regulators, or unions. That same "eternity" also enables the corporation to create products that function as recognizable signals for consumers.[2] Second, the management is continuously updating its internal model of the external world—tracking evolving customer expectations and competitive dynamics. This process informs updates to the corporation strategy, product development, and even the organizational structure. For instance, if the market consists of private consumers and large industrial clients, the corporation will often mirror this segmentation internally. Just as the brain restructures itself to reflect external realities—as we saw in Chapter 2—so too does a company reshape its architecture to align with its understanding of the environment. Third, in times of crisis, general management may halt updates to its worldview in order to focus on immediate action. Moreover, the corporation acts as a protective envelope—like a biological membrane—limiting the range of uncertain "states" its employees face, while ensuring stable access to essential resources. Think of the craftsman, directly exposed to the activity of his sector, or even obliged to relocate to keep up with the evolution of his customers. Conversely, the Apple engineer in Cupertino can count on the corporation's flexibility to adapt (for example, to a commercial craze in China). Similarly, the legal status conferred on the corporation's legal structure allows it to have separate assets and to take legal action, whereas the craftsman is on the front line. In parallel, the corporation grants its members access to resources they could not

---

2 The Vuitton bag and the iPhone are all signals of belonging to a group. Like religious signs, such signals enable everyone who is in the same group to identify each other, and thus encourage their cooperation. A traveler who has mislaid their Apple charger can hope for help from another traveler with a watch or phone from the same manufacturer. The modern enterprise creates communities of belonging, which also explains the importance given to brands.

obtain on their own. Individually, neither the accountant, the storekeeper, nor even the CEO could access the range of resources available through the firm. Finally, the company can also serve as a space for forming social bonds (see Figure 3.1).

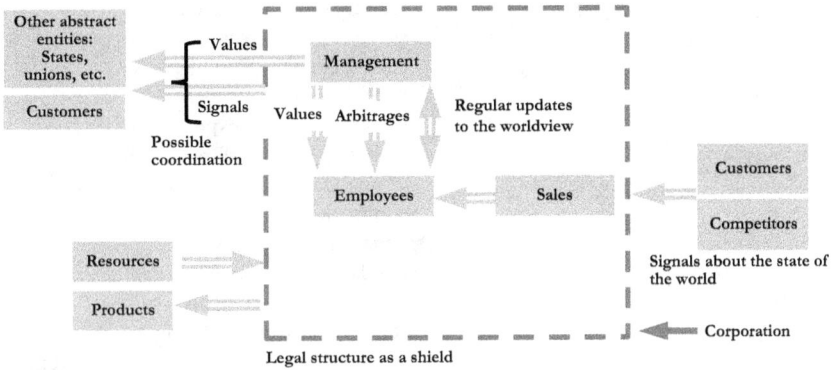

Figure 3.1 Graph drawing an analogy between a corporation and a living organism

Source: Author.

Note: The modern corporation stands as one of the most powerful expressions of large-scale human cooperation. Among the many possible explanations for its selection over other forms of organization—apart from the fact that it is a place where people belong to a group—is the fact that it provides access to more resources than its individual members could otherwise obtain. To this end, the corporation's structure can be likened to that of a living organism. A membrane (the legal entity status conferred on its legal structure) protects employees from changes in the environment. Sales teams, through their direct contact with customers and competitors, function as the corporation's sensory interface. General management also defines the corporation's core values, guiding coordination both internally and externally. This capacity is enabled by the corporation's indefinite lifespan. Shareholders and lenders provide capital with different risk and return profiles. Together, they provide privileged access to resources, and high adaptation/exploration capacities.

If we take a closer look at corporate strategy, we see that the Bayesian framework applies to organizations based on how they represent their environment.

Here are some examples.

Nature of the environment (and its perception)	Optimum energy allocation

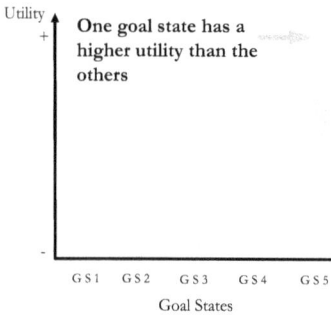

Figure 3.2 Graph of the goal states for a start-up

Source: Author.

Example: Start-up.

Modeling: High entropy and strategy built around a high-utility—i.e., precise and relevant—priority state objective: To survive. That is, to meet the urgent challenges posed by the market's variable nature, competition in that market, customer expectations, access to financing, etc.—failure to deal with any of which would endanger the life of the company.

Optimal organizational structure: One that favors maximum adaptability to a constantly changing environment. The speed with which the company moves from one state to another without error is of paramount importance. There's no need to try and refine the representation model of a world recognized as chaotic and intrinsically unpredictable.

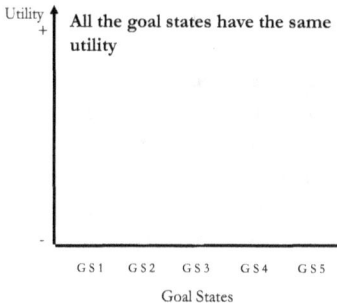

Figure 3.3 Graph of the goal states for Google and Android

Source: Author.

Example: Google for Android, which managed several versions of its operating system in parallel, each tailored to the requirements of a different phone manufacturer, as it could not predict which brands would come to dominate the market.

Modeling: High entropy and equally precise and relevant state objectives.

Optimal organizational structure: Maximum adaptation to an environment whose state within a known series cannot be predicted (the possible events are known, but the company does not know which one will occur) requires the simultaneous maintenance of several positions ("states"). The corporation should not waste resources on seeking to perfect its world model, recognizing that certainty is impossible.[3]

(Continued)

---

3 The model could be refined by introducing two additional variables: speed of adaptation when a company is forced to review its production, and adaptability when it is forced to change its range of products.

Nature of the environment (and its perception)	Optimum energy allocation
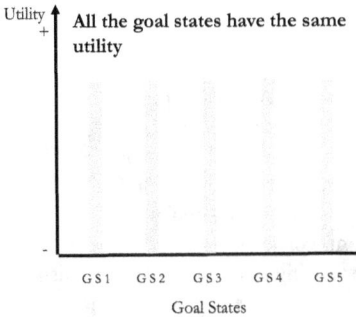

Figure 3.4 Graph of the goal states for Apple in the 2010s
Source: Author. | **Example**: Apple in the 2010s, when it set up the iTunes platform (enabling it to escape the specificities imposed by software publishers).

Situation: High entropy, multiplicity of possible states of equal relevance and likelihood, some of which may reduce the entropy of the environment.

Optimal organization structure: If the company has a sufficiently large market share, it can create its own ecosystem, thereby reducing the effects of market entropy. |
|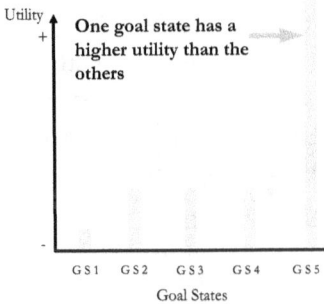

Figure 3.5 Graph of the goal states for ExxonMobil in the 1990s
Source: Author. | **Example**: ExxonMobil in the 1990s.

Situation: Low entropy and a strategy organized around a single high-utility state objective.

Optimal organizational structure: The aim here is not to refine the company's world model, as it is deemed reasonably accurate, but to apply it as effectively as possible. The exploitation strategy takes priority. |
|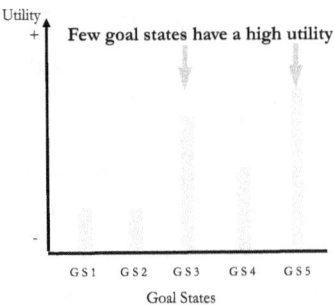

Figure 3.6 Graph of the goal states for most corporates
Source: Author. | **Example**: Most companies.

Situation: Average entropy and a few state objectives with higher utility than others.

Optimal organization structure: To meet the needs of a strategy that combines exploitation, adaptation, and exploration. |

(Continued)

Nature of the environment (and its perception)	Optimum energy allocation
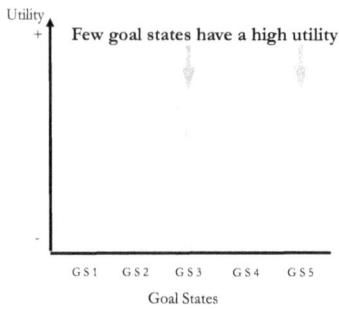 Figure 3.7 Graph of the goal states for Shell in the 1970s Source: Author.	**Example**: Shell in the 1970s. **Situation**: Low entropy, company with a few state objectives with higher utility than others, which anticipates possible changes in its environment. **Optimal organizational structure:** A combination of exploitation and exploration through simulating different scenarios, leading to a better understanding of the possible relationships between the forces identified in the environment.

The corporations have adopted distinct strategic approaches. Google tailors Android to fit diverse manufacturer needs; Apple enforces a tightly controlled iTunes ecosystem. ExxonMobil has pursued aggressive expansion in oil exploration, while Shell has focused on anticipating major shifts in the energy market. In each case, the corporation's strategy emerges from a form of environmental modeling—whether explicit or intuitive. However, they are all based on the same representation mechanism, which the study of Bayesian cognitive inference has enabled us to identify.

An equally striking observation is that corporations can model the world with a sophistication rivaling that of great thinkers. Is there a difference in nature between Galileo, testing Aristotle's principles in a pure thought experiment, and Shell's management simulating the evolution of its core values, business model, and organization in equally abstract scenarios? In the early 1970s, when oil markets were still stable, Shell's leadership could have relied on an exploitation strategy. Instead, they chose to explore possible future scenarios—methodically analyzing the forces that might trigger them. Their aim was not to predict probabilities, but to understand the dynamic forces that could shape radically different futures.[4] For them, it wasn't just a question of building statistical projections or carrying out impact analyses of new situations on the corporation, but also of developing scenarios that would model the forces that

---

4 P. Wack (1985), "Scenario: Shooting the Rapids," *Harvard Business Review* 63 (6): 139–150.

could lead to these states[5] and their dynamics, without worrying about the probability of these scenarios. Highlighting these possible interactions was the objective of the exercise. Shell's self-imposed approach was to explore the world's dynamics "in the laboratory."[6] By doing so, the corporation was able to anticipate and prepare for oil crises[7] and significantly reduce its adjustment costs.

These examples show how corporations, though composed of individuals, operate in ways that grant them access to far more resources than any one member could obtain alone. Corporations behave like living organisms, constructing structured models of the world and even performing abstract simulations. Their strategic behaviors—whether exploratory, exploitative, or adaptive—mirror the brain's approach to energy-efficient decision-making in complex environments.

The analogy between corporate functions and biological mechanisms appears to be both valid and illuminating.

---

5 P. Wack (1985), "Scenario: Shooting the Rapids," *Harvard Business Review* 63 (6): 139–150: "Scenario analysis demands first that managers understand the forces driving their business systems rather than rely on forecasts or alternatives."

6 P. Wack (1985), "Scenario: Shooting the Rapids," *Harvard Business Review* 63 (6): 139–150: "You will find little or no power by merely accepting expert information about an outcome like the future price of oil or the future level of demand; power comes with an understanding of the forces behind the outcome."

7 P. Wack (1985), "Scenario: Shooting the Rapids," *Harvard Business Review* 63 (6): 139–150:

> During stable times, the mental model of a successful decision maker and unfolding reality match. Some adjustment and fine tuning will do. Decision scenarios have little or no leverage. [...] In times of rapid change and increased complexity, however, the manager's mental model becomes a dangerously mixed bag: rich detail and understanding can coexist with dubious assumptions, selective inattention to alternative ways of interpreting evidence, and illusory projections. In these times, the scenario approach has leverage and can make a difference. [...] By presenting other ways of seeing the world, decision scenarios allow managers to break out of a one-eyed view. Scenarios give managers something very precious: the ability to reperceive reality. (My translation)

Financial markets: An experiment in Bayesian cognitive inference on a global scale?

Another major area of modern human cooperation is the financial markets.[8] Is this another example of a mechanism that mobilizes Bayesian cognitive inference mechanisms to access resources? Our findings confirm this and show that the process operates on several levels.

At the first level, the mission of the financial markets is to synthesize the qualitative information about a company that can be gathered from a variety of heterogeneous sources (sales, balance sheet, management personality, strategy, culture, etc.) to enable a simple and rapid judgment. This work is carried out by financial analysts, who transform the data into a key indicator reflecting the corporation's health: earnings per share. At the same time, civil society, by reducing the role of the corporation to that of profit maximization, is reinforcing the idea that this indicator is a relevant representation of the company's reality as a whole.

At the second level, largely based on earnings per share, market operators carry out transactions whose outcomes are made public through pricing signals. These stock market exchanges serve as a vehicle for asset transfers, which have a utility function in themselves, as they help establish the corporation's value.

At the third level, the public nature of these exchanges enables each agent to construct their own inferences from the point of view of the other agents, thus fulfilling an exploratory function thanks to its informational value. Let's take the example of an investor who sells their Apple shares, thinking that their value will fall, but finds, on the contrary, that the share price is rising. This suggests that other investors are clearly of a different opinion, since they are buying the shares. This leads the investor to reconsider their assumption about the corporation's valuation and to ask themselves why others have a different perception of the situation. Has Apple launched a new product? Deployed a new sales strategy? This process may lead them

---

8   F. Braudel (1985), *La Dynamique du Capitalisme* (Paris: Arthaud):

> The 15th century, especially after 1450, saw a general economic recovery, benefiting cities, which, favored by rising "industrial" prices while agricultural prices stagnated or fell, got off to a faster start than the countryside. [...] in the following century, the driving force was the international fairs [...] the working life of the 17th century [...] developed across the vast expanse of the Atlantic Ocean [...] the fairs gave way to the stock exchanges. [...] In the 18th century [...] the stock exchanges expanded their activities. (Kindle Edition, p. 28; my translation)

(although it may not do so) to question their own model or that of others based on a public signal—the stock market price.

At the fourth level, society can take advantage of this signal to ensure it optimizes the allocation of its resources (suppliers, bankers, etc.).[9]

Such implementations of the mechanism reflect those that take place in the brain: the transformation of a flow of input into a discrete signal and the construction of a space in which to collectively update an internal model of the world based on that signal, all at a low energy cost. Ultimately, this enables the mobilization of a vast number of resources worldwide, both intellectual (market players) and operational (companies), and the optimal allocation of resources within society. The combination of "access to resources/implementation of Bayesian cognitive inference mechanisms" that has been identified in the human brain is thus clearly in evidence (see Figure 3.8).

Before the rise of financial markets, similar mechanisms existed, though they operated with less efficiency. Consider the example of an apple merchant. After harvesting their apples, rather than setting up shop at the edge of their field, they choose to head to the village square—a visible, accessible location where the market is held. This decision is, in effect, the decision to join a marketplace. From the perspective of Bayesian cognitive inference, the placement of their apple stand grants them access to the other agents' world models—insights that would have otherwise remained out of reach. By observing the behavior of fellow sellers—who, like them, aim to sell their apples at the best possible price—they can update their assumptions about appropriate pricing. Though this mechanism functions to a degree, it remains constrained by several limitations: apples may vary in quality and variety; buyers may have differing preferences or objectives; and the physical location of a stall within the market square can influence sales. In short, while a price signal does emerge, a number of unknowns make the inference process far less efficient than it might be within a more structured, homogeneous system.

Modern financial markets have corrected these flaws, thereby greatly improving their members' ability to coordinate with one another: "apples" are now a standardized product (maximizing profits for shareholders), buyers share a common goal (maximizing profits), and "stalls" accurately reflect prices (in line with the theory of efficient markets). With the

---

9 Another example is found in the bond markets, where the pricing of long-term bonds serves as an indicator of inflation expectations. We can then try to identify its possible causes —a runaway economy? Tensions on the labor market? Scarcity of an essential resource? (etc.)—and adjust our understanding of how the world works on that basis.

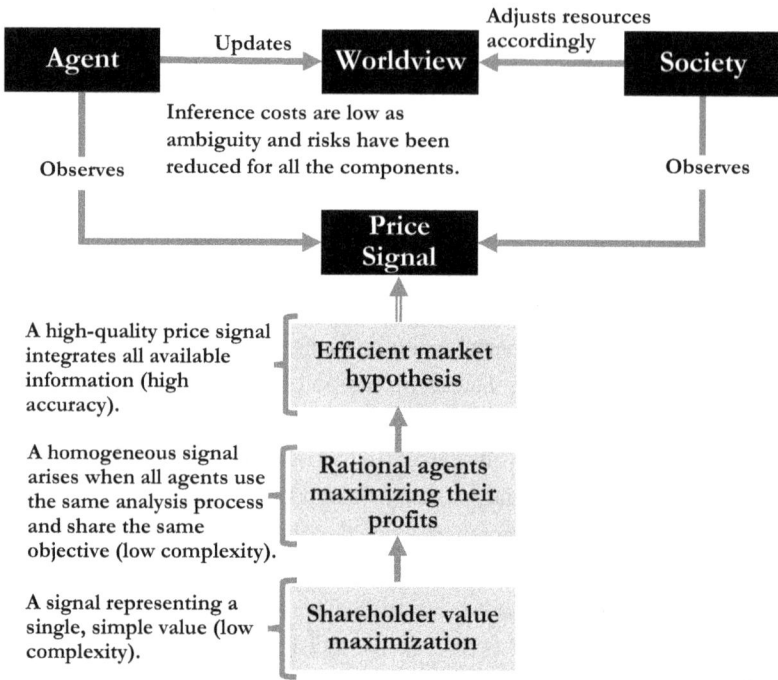

Figure 3.8 Graph showing how Bayesian cognitive inference is used to model the workings of financial markets

Source: Author.

Note: Financial markets can be read as a space in which large-scale Bayesian cognitive inference is deployed, with high informational quality and low discounting cost. The mechanism unifies all the various players' models of the world: considered as rational, they seek to maximize their profits by assessing the value of companies with the greatest possible relevance. Corporations are viewed as focused solely on one objective: maximizing shareholder profits. Markets are also perceived as efficient. The stock price signal corresponds to induced models that are simple, transparent, and shared by all. The potential for noise is therefore very low, and inference can be made at low cost. Moreover, the stock price signal enables the company to adjust its resource allocation (and possibly also its internal model of the world).

spectrum of assumptions thus reduced, inference becomes more efficient. This dynamic also illustrates the mechanism whereby collective intelligence is created, as highlighted in an experiment by Rafael Kaufmann, Pranav Gupta, and Jacob Taylor,[10] which explores the fundamental interac-

---

10 P. Gupta, R. Kaufmann, and J. Taylor (2021), "An Active Inference Model of Collective Intelligence," *Entropy* 23 (7): 830. In experience, first, there is the basic principle of inferring from the representational models of others to actualize one's

tions between agents who are engaging in Bayesian cognitive inference with a view to achieving collective intelligence. When a simulation is modeled that is close to the framework provided by financial markets (inference and common goals), the result is a remarkable overall efficiency, thanks in particular to the integration of the weakest agents' contributions, which other modeled approaches fail to include. Contrary to popular belief, markets are not just a competitive arena that rewards the strongest, but also a place for cooperation that benefits the group as a whole, and the weakest players in particular.

Could it be that, in inventing financial markets, the modern economy has devised a powerful mechanism for collective intelligence? A mechanism that allows each participant to access the asset valuations established by others and adjust their own assumptions about their mental models of the world, while in return disseminating up-to-date information throughout society, which enables worldviews to be updated via a continuous, collective process of Bayesian cognitive inference? Seen from this perspective, financial markets are, above all, a space for cooperation—centered on information sharing—that supports the ongoing refinement of each participant's perception of the state of the world. This approach follows in the footsteps of Friedrich Hayek:[11]

> Fundamentally, in a system in which the knowledge of the relevant facts is dispersed among many people, prices can act to coordinate the separate actions of different people in the same way as subjective values help the individual to coordinate the parts of his plan. [...] We must look at the price system as such a mechanism for communicating information if we want to understand its real function.

---

own, which falls under the concept of theory of mind. Second, the establishment of common goals or "Goal Alignment," which reduces the gaps between the desired states of each actor. The authors simulate two agents who are sensitive to a chemical signal whose highest concentration corresponds to food, and who can move and know the position of the other agent. The feeling that others are "similar" or the "otherness" criterion for inferring others' models is then varied, and the ambiguity of representation for goal sharing is reduced. Finally, agent B ("strong") is identified as being better able to perform the task than agent A ("weak"). The authors then model four situations. In the fourth (where A can make inferences about B and both share the same goals), A's individual performance and collective performance are the best.

11 F. von Hayek (1945), "The Use of Knowledge in Society," *American Economic Review* 35 (4) (September): 519–530.

From this perspective, Friedrich Hayek's economic analysis resonates with modern biological and cognitive processes.

*

In conclusion, these two forms of social organization—corporations and financial markets—allow their members to access more resources than they could individually. To achieve this, the modern company forms a kind of membrane through its legal identity, specializes its various functions in a manner reminiscent of the human body, and operates through a balance of exploration, exploitation, and adaptation, guided by its understanding of the environment—much like the human brain.

Financial markets mirror cerebral mechanisms by generating a discontinuous signal that reflects reality, enabling a large-scale process of Bayesian cognitive inference. Each participant gains access to the analytical resources of others, and, collectively, the market facilitates the optimal allocation of resources at the societal level, at least under steady-state conditions.

Through these various modes of resource access, both corporations and financial markets can be seen as implementing forms of Bayesian inference, bringing them conceptually closer to living systems. However, they remain localized and specialized structures. This raises the question of whether similar mechanisms are operating at the scale of entire societies. To explore that possibility, let's continue the journey—back to the very beginning of human history.

This is the subject of the next chapter.

4

COOPERATING TO ACCESS RESOURCES: A HUMAN STORY

There are many ways to approach the history of human societies. In this work, we explore the hypothesis that human societies derive a competitive advantage from privileged access to resources.[1] From this perspective, we will revisit the history of the past millennia—considering both direct access to material resources such as wheat or coal, and access to representations of the world that make such access possible.

With this lens, and from a Western perspective, we can identify three pivotal moments—three turning points in humanity's relationship to resource access. The first is the emergence of *Homo sapiens*, marked by the development of cooperative mechanisms both within groups and across

---

1 This does not necessarily mean a state of permanent competition between societies, because, as Daniel Milo puts it, as with all living things, the situation can reflect a "good enough" point of equilibrium (D. Milo (2019), *Good Enough: The Tolerance for Mediocrity in Nature and Society* (Cambridge, MA: Harvard University Press)).

DOI: 10.4324/9781003638384-4

group boundaries. The second is the era of the Greek city-states, which introduced collective forms of cooperation in a politically and socially diverse context. The third is the capitalist era, characterized by an unprecedented expansion of coordination processes within a diversity perceived as irreducible.

Homo sapiens: Cooperating within the group and abroad

Cooperation as a necessity

Following in the footsteps of Yuval Noah Harari,[2] let's retrace the steps of the first humans in the African savanna. How did our ancestors, bipeds lacking any remarkable physical assets in the face of much more powerful animals, manage to establish themselves as the dominant species? Cooperation played a decisive role in this evolutionary success story. As the abundant scientific literature underlines, cooperation is, above all else, a vital necessity for mankind. Pooling resources not only facilitates their acquisition (hunting), but also their protection once they have been acquired.[3] Our "cousins," the great apes—with whom we have so much in common, as Michael Tomasello reminds us—[4] do exhibit sociability, but it is mostly based on competition and marked by

---

2 Y. N. Harari (2015), *Sapiens: A Brief History of Humankind* (New York: Harper).

3 R. Dunbar (2016), "The Social Brain Hypothesis and Human Evolution," *Oxford Research Encyclopedia of Psychology*.

4 M. Tomasello (2019), *Becoming Human: A Theory of Ontogeny* (Cambridge, MA: Harvard University Press):

> [...] some great apes (1) make and use tools, (2) communicate intentionally (or even "linguistically"), (3) have a kind of "theory of mind", (4) acquire some behaviors via social learning (leading to "culture"), (5) hunt together in groups, (6) have "friends" with whom they preferentially groom and form alliances, (7) actively help others, and (8) evaluate and reciprocate one another's social actions. (Apple Books, p. 4)

strong individualism.[5] In contrast, the first human groups acquired food primarily through cooperation:[6]

> Humans diverged from other great apes around 6 million years ago. [...] then some early humans (the best guess is *Homo heidelbergensis* some 400,000 years ago) began obtaining the majority of their food through more active collaboration; indeed, the collaboration became obligate. This meant that individuals were interdependent with one another in much more urgent ways than before. An essential part of the process of obligate collaborative foraging was partner choice.

Our ancestors then selected those inclined to cooperate with them, and in particular, those with the ability to create shared values:[7]

> Individuals who were cognitively or otherwise incompetent at collaboration—for example, those incapable of forming a joint goal with others—were not chosen repeatedly as partners, and this meant no food. [...] The upshot was that there was strong and active social selection [...] for cooperatively competent and motivated individuals.

From the outset, therefore, cooperation was both a necessity and an opportunity, both within the group and for those outside it.

---

5 M. Tomasello (2019) *Becoming Human: A Theory of Ontogeny* (Cambridge, MA: Harvard University Press). LCA stands for Last Common Ancestor:

> Chimpanzees and bonobos—and thus the LCA—are and were very clever, but mainly or only as individuals [...]. In addition to kinship, their relationships were based mainly on (1) competition and dominance, and (2) cooperation and "friendship." [...] To cultivate good partners for these conflicts, they did various things to make friends (such as grooming and sharing food). [...] In general, the LCAs very likely had a special sympathy for kin and friends—especially those who supported them in competitive interactions—and thus cooperated with them in various ways. Their cooperation was grounded in competition. [...] Chimpanzees and bonobos, and so the LCAs, are and were very social, but only in an instrumental kind of way. (Apple Books, pp. 13–14)

6 M. Tomasello (2019), *Becoming Human: A Theory of Ontogeny* (Cambridge, MA: Harvard University Press), Apple Books, p. 15.

7 M. Tomasello (2019), *Becoming Human: A Theory of Ontogeny* (Cambridge, MA: Harvard University Press), Apple Books, p. 15.

Attention to the most vulnerable

The human newborn is unique within the animal order in that it is defenseless and fragile. Its brain is three times less developed than those of its primate cousins[8] and has yet to accommodate the development of the prefrontal lobe and the appearance of new cerebral zones, the bases and structures of learning during childhood and adolescence. It could even be said that, from this point of view, the human being, an exception in the animal kingdom, is always born premature.[9] Our newborns must therefore benefit from substantial and lasting protection and attention, which it is difficult for their mothers (or even their immediate family) to provide on their own. This is undoubtedly why human populations very early on adopted a group-rearing mode, which entailed caring for a defenseless being without the benefit of immediate reciprocity.[10] According to Charles Darwin, this attitude was the key to the success of the groups that developed it, even if it did not provide a real advantage at the individual level: "It must not be forgotten that although a high standard of morality gives but a slight or no advantage to each individual man and his children over the other men of the same tribe"[11] at the group level, there is an "immense advantage" because:[12]

---

8   K. Isler and C. Van Schaik (2014), "How Humans Evolved Large Brains: Comparative Evidence," *Evolutionary Anthropology* 23: 65–75.

9   Indeed, as Jean-Jacques Hublin (J-J. Hublin (2024), *La Tyrannie du Cerveau* (Paris: Robert Laffont)) points out, women's pelvises have not been able to keep up with the evolution of brain size, so it is "necessary" for newborns to be born prematurely to make their way. Furthermore, the newborn's brain, by continuing to grow, would have represented too high an energy cost for the mother.

10   As Patrick Tort points out (P. Tort (2008), *L'Effet Darwin: Sélection Naturelle, et Naissance de la Civilisation* (Paris: Éditions du Seuil)):

   As for learning itself, it is common between generations in both domestic and wild animals. Higher up the animal ladder, on the human level, it compensates for a kind of primary vulnerability, as the new being owes its survival only to the protection and education received from its environment, which are the clearest and most immediate manifestations of instincts and social feelings. (Kindle Edition, p. 74; my translation)

11   C. Darwin (1871), *The Descent of Man, and Selection in Relation to Sex* (London: John Murray), Apple Books, p. 245.

12   C. Darwin (1871), *The Descent of Man, and Selection in Relation to Sex* (London: John Murray), Apple Books, p. 245.

[...] an increase in the number of well-endowed men and an advancement in the standard of morality will certainly give an immense advantage to one tribe over another. A tribe including many members who, from possessing in a high degree the spirit of patriotism, fidelity, obedience, courage, and sympathy, were always ready to aid one another, and to sacrifice themselves for the common good, would be victorious over most other tribes; and this would be natural selection.

This led to the spread of morality:[13]

At all times throughout the world tribes have supplanted other tribes; and as morality is one important element in their success, the standard of morality and the number of well-endowed men will thus everywhere tend to rise and increase.

Ultimately, the practice of caring for others emerged through natural selection—but it also marks the beginning of civilization.[14]

Establishing shared values

Cooperation within the group enables you to find help when you are helpless or unsure how to do something, without expending excessive energy.[15] One way of doing this is to value what others do. Let's imagine, for example, one of our ancestors, whom we'll call "Eka," entering a clearing on a fine spring day. Despite an incessant flow of information—the emerald color of the grass, the melodious song of the birds, the furtive movements of insects—her attention is fixed on a large plant, laden with round red, yellow, or green shapes. She has sorted and categorized it, identifying an object of value—in this case, a nutrient: the "apple" category. One of her

---

13 C. Darwin (1871), *The Descent of Man, and Selection in Relation to Sex* (London: John Murray), Apple Books, p. 245.

14 Anecdotally, when anthropologist Margaret Mead was asked what the sign of civilization was, she replied "a repaired femur." In the animal world, a broken femur meant death, as the animal could not survive on its own. Here, a repaired femur meant that someone cared for that person, and helping someone in trouble was the beginning of civilization.

15 M. Iacoboni (2009), "Neurobiology of Imitation," *Current Opinion in Neurobiology* 19: 661–665.

congeners, whom we'll call "Dvi," joins her in the clearing. She sees Eka absorbed in contemplating the round red and green shapes. She is faced with two possible choices of action: either she can explore the nutritional possibilities of this place herself, or she can imitate Eka. If she chooses the latter, it's because she assumes that Eka shares the same values as she does ("Survive") and is aiming for the same state ("Access food"). She infers that Eka is following an effective strategy. In short, by focusing on the large plant, Eka immediately provides Dvi with a solution.[16] In situations of uncertainty, imitation is the most energy-efficient strategy. It's reasonable to think that this imitation process has been favored by natural selection, leading to a cultural reinforcement of the value "Observe others and what they observe"—based on the assumption: "this congener is most likely aiming for the same states as I am." The mere fact that someone else pays attention to an everyday object of no particular value (such as a kitchen utensil) increases its value in our eyes.

This fact becomes obvious if we observe young children: as soon as one of them takes hold of an object, it provokes the covetousness of the others, who immediately seek to seize it. Maël Lebreton et al.[17] show that the simple fact of our showing interest in an object, whether it's food, a toy, a piece of clothing, or a tool, increases its perceived value to others.[18] The brain will activate "mirror neurons" and change the area dedicated to

---

16 In Bayesian terms, the scene could be expressed as follows: Plausibility P(Eka found edible food |Eka has the same goal as me) is superior to plausibility P(I'll analyze it myself and find better food or quicker | Eka started before me and shares the same goal).

17 J. Daunizeau, B. Forgeot d'Arc, S. Kawa, M. Lebreton, and M. Pessiglione (2012), "Your Goal Is Mine: Unraveling Mimetic Desires in the Human Brain," The Journal of Neuroscience, 32(21), May 23:

> The novel finding is evidence that the influence of action observation on subjective values may involve MNS (mirror neuron system) activity modulating BVS (brain valuation system) [...] Indeed, VS activation has been consistently shown to represent expected rewards or subjective desirability, which can be seen as goal values [...] We further suggest that MNS–BVS interaction constitutes an important mechanism serving to propagate values across individuals [...] Escaping the necessity of trial-and-error experience, including time and risk saving, is a potential advantage of this mechanism.

18 A. Bayliss, P. Cannon, M. Paul, and S. Tipper (2006), "Gaze Cuing and Affective Judgments of Objects: I Like What You Look At," Psychonomic Bulletin & Review 13 (6): 1061–1066.

values, creating *de facto* (potential) nonverbal cooperation.[19] If Dvi directs her gaze toward the same object as Eka, this simple action establishes an implicit consensus between them on the value of the apple tree. From then on, by aligning their "states" (both are focused on the search for apple trees at this moment), they simultaneously reduce their search efforts toward other potential "states" (e.g., the search for mushrooms) and pave the way for potential cooperation.

This attention to others relies in part on the ability to understand and anticipate what others are thinking. In this respect, the neuroendocrine system seems to play a key role. The oxytocin released in the brain of the agent initiating an action, and the endorphin produced by the observer, help to reinforce the attraction of faces and stimulate the desire to observe them.[20] In short, scrutinizing others is energetically efficient and also potentially reinforces cooperation.

Cooperation, however, depends on specific conditions being met. It remains to be seen whether Eka and Dvi can achieve the desired state— i.e., access to the fruit-covered apple tree—on their own or in cooperation. Two scenarios are conceivable: either Eka seeks to defend her apples to prevent Dvi from accessing them, or she considers that Dvi can help her explore other clearings and, in so doing, increase her chances of discovering other apple trees. As we mentioned earlier, according to Bayesian logic, Eka's decision will depend on her estimation of the plausibility of reaching this state by her own means. If she believes she can, she will choose only one of two approaches: confrontation or competition. The opposite conviction will lead her to cooperation. As René Girard suggests, mimetic desire is key—but whether it leads to cooperation or

---

19 Moreover, the process of natural selection has reinforced the effectiveness of this mechanism, with the activation of areas in the brain system leading to greater empathy when imitating others. See M. Iacoboni (2009), "Neurobiology of Imitation," *Current Opinion in Neurobiology* 19: 661–665.

20 R. Dunbar (2016), "The Social Brain Hypothesis and Human Evolution," *Oxford Research Encyclopedia of Psychology.* By observing others, human beings constantly seek to assess their intentions. The more aligned these appear to be with their own, the stronger their confidence in the value of any form of cooperation, including imitation.

competition depends on whether the agent believes she can reach the goal alone.[21]

Human beings are also the only animals capable of sharing their attention with that of others while maintaining a capacity for individual attention. This specificity appears with *Homo sapiens*, and contributes to our species' evolutionary leap, as emphasized by Michael Tomasello:[22]

> The radically new psychological process that emerged at this time was what we may call joint intentionality based on joint agency. A joint agent comprises two individuals who have a joint goal, structured by joint attention, each of whom has at the same time her own individual role and perspective. This may be called the dual-level structure: simultaneous sharedness and individuality.

This leads to the emergence of something totally new:[23]

> The creation of a joint agent—while each partner maintains her own individual role and perspective at the same time—created a completely new human psychology, spawning new forms of both cognition and sociality. [...] these were not just any skills. These were skills that created a new kind of agent, one in which two distinct individuals, in a sense, perceived and understood the world together while still not losing their own individual perspectives.

This joint attention is apparent in babies from the age of nine months. From the age of three, children develop the ability to participate in collective attention. To illustrate this mechanism, let's return to our two ancestors, Eka and Dvi. Suppose they enter the clearing, this time simultaneously. Each explores the clearing on her own, at a certain distance from the other. Glancing at each other, they realize that they are both

---

21 This debate was later revisited by Adam Smith, who also addressed the specialization of tasks in cities. As the scope of each individual's activity becomes more limited, the likelihood of personal success increases, reducing the need for cooperation and allowing competition to emerge—something then seen as beneficial for society.

22 M. Tomasello (2019), *Becoming Human: A Theory of Ontogeny* (Cambridge, MA: Harvard University Press), Apple Books, p. 15.

23 M. Tomasello (2019), *Becoming Human: A Theory of Ontogeny* (Cambridge, MA: Harvard University Press), Apple Books, p. 15.

looking in the same direction, toward an apple tree. In so doing, they are implicitly communicating that the value of "surviving energetically" outweighs all other possible values. Once this shared value is recognized, cooperation can (potentially) begin. This rare psychological capacity enabled humans to synchronize individual and collective worldviews.[24] When Eka and Dvi meet in the clearing, they can't know right away whether they share the same values—and therefore whether cooperation is possible. But thanks to their joint attention, they have created an alignment of values that reduces the risk of conflict arising from potential divergences between their priorities.

The cognitive leaps of abstraction and modeling

As Jean-Jacques Hublin notes,[25] Neanderthal man's brain is larger than our own. The reason for this is that "natural selection pushed populations of African *Homo sapiens* down an alternative path to indefinite and ever more costly brain growth."[26] This alternative path is certainly that of abstraction.[27]

This ability has several possible "origins." It can be seen as a "natural" extension of the process of cognitive Bayesian inference, which enables us to conceptualize, model, and generalize complex situations while optimizing the available brain resources. Apples fall when they come off the tree, but also when they escape from your hand. Observing this phenomenon and deducing a common law from it is the very essence of a capacity for abstraction, which differentiates *Homo sapiens* from Neanderthal.

---

24 A New York dog resembles a Tibetan dog: they play with a ball in the same way, bury their bones with the same care, follow similar behaviors, etc. On the other hand, a New York trader has a very different representation of the world than a Tibetan monk.

25 J-J. Hublin (2022), *Homo Sapiens, une Espèce Invasive* (Paris: Librairie Arthème Fayard and Collège de France):

> An example among the Neanderthals is the Wadi Amud man in Israel, with his 1740 cm³ brain. Among the Denisovans, a sister group to the Neanderthals who lived in Asia, the Xuchang 1 man has a cranial capacity of 1800 cm³. In both cases, this is well above current averages. (p. 30; my translation)

26 J-J. Hublin (2022), *Homo Sapiens, une Espèce Invasive* (Paris: Librairie Arthème Fayard and Collège de France), p. 30; my translation.

27 As Yuval Noah Harari argues (Y. N. Harari (2015), *Sapiens, A Brief History of Humankind* (New York: Harper)).

It may also be the result of social density. Indeed, our ancestors, as Yuval Noah Harari suggests,[28] would have developed another faculty: the ability to spread gossip. It's hard to say exactly where this came from. Was it a genetic mutation?[29] A consequence of the massive increase in the amount of information exchanged between individuals, which could sometimes lead to errors and a gradual distancing from reality? Or the fact that, when applied to social ties, the observation of reality does not require such rigorous objectivity, opening the way, if not to lies, at least to a more flexible interpretation of what is "true"? The fact remains that information can be dissociated from direct, objective observation, or even intentionally falsified. Gossip is thus a formidable factor in accelerating the process of exchanging information at different levels: about the world, and about others. Gossip tells us as much about the reality being described as it does about the sender. Gossip not only conveys information (true or false), but also informs the receiver about the level of trust they can place in the sender. From this paradoxical point of view, gossip can considerably intensify human cooperation mechanisms.

Whatever its origins, our capacity for abstraction has certainly favored a tremendous acceleration in both cerebral and social development. Cerebral, because by sharing common values, each individual expends less energy and benefits from the work done by others to build and maintain a shared representation of the world. Social, because as Robin Dunbar explains,[30] abstraction enables us to overcome the limit of human group size, which for a long time could not exceed around 150 individuals; this is still the case with the many species that have not adopted strict and therefore rigid organizational forms. By exceeding this natural limit, Homo sapiens gained an essential competitive advantage over the Neanderthal.

The ability to model the world also appears at this point, perhaps stemming from our competitive advantage over other species: the ability to hunt for long periods in the heat.[31] This made it possible to exhaust the

---

28 Y. N. Harari (2015), *Sapiens, A Brief History of Humankind* (New York: Harper).

29 Y. N. Harari (2015), *Sapiens, A Brief History of Humankind* (New York: Harper).

30 R. Dunbar (2016), "The Social Brain Hypothesis and Human Evolution," *Oxford Research Encyclopedia of Psychology,* 2016.

31 L. Liebenberg (2014), *The Origin of Science: On the Evolutionary Roots of Science and its Implications for Self-Education and Citizen Science* (Cape Town: CyberTracker):

prey animals.[32] But it also meant developing the art of modeling the animal's location and state of fatigue using clues, such as step size, to identify whether an animal was male or female, its age, and level of fatigue, etc. In other words, it meant developing a model for representing the animal's behavior in relation to the terrain, as proposed by Louis Liebenberg:[33] "Speculative tracking involves the creation of a working hypothesis on the basis of initial interpretation of signs, knowledge of the animal's behaviour and knowledge of the terrain."

The model is then updated according to the clues collected:[34]

> With a hypothetical reconstruction of the animal's activities in mind, trackers then look for signs where they expect to find them. The emphasis is primarily on speculation, looking for signs only to confirm or refute their expectations. When their expectations are confirmed, their hypothetical reconstructions are reinforced.

This, then, makes it possible to "predict" the future, and thus increases the chances of catching the animal:[35] "The tracker creates an internal

---

The combination of well-developed sweat glands and the relative absence of body hair make it probable that running humans display very high thermal conductance, with maximal values well above those of most cursorial mammals. (Kindle Edition, p. 44)

32 L. Liebenberg (2014), *The Origin of Science: On the Evolutionary Roots of Science and Its Implications for Self-Education and Citizen Science* (Cape Town: CyberTracker):

[...] success of persistence hunting is the fact that humans cool their bodies by sweating while running. If an antelope is forced to run in the midday heat on an extremely hot day it overheats and eventually drops or simply stops running from hyperthermia, allowing the hunter to kill it with a spear or other weapons. (Kindle Edition, p. 43)

33 L. Liebenberg (2014), *The Origin of Science: On the Evolutionary Roots of Science and Its Implications for Self-Education and Citizen Science* (Cape Town: CyberTracker), Kindle Edition, p. 70.

34 L. Liebenberg (2014), *The Origin of Science: On the Evolutionary Roots of Science and Its Implications for Self-Education and Citizen Science* (Cape Town: CyberTracker), Kindle Edition, p. 70.

35 L. Liebenberg (2014), *The Origin of Science: On the Evolutionary Roots of Science and Its Implications for Self-Education and Citizen Science* (Cape Town: CyberTracker), Kindle Edition, p. 70.

simulation of different possibilities, thereby simulating and predicting the future." A Bayesian cognitive inference process is at work here.

In addition, the hunter's specialization in food access by the hunter— as opposed to gathering, which can be done individually—reinforced the necessary rules of socialization.[36]

Signals for cooperation

The challenge of the encounter with the stranger is the question: should we cooperate or fight?[37] To decide this, it is necessary to assess the competence and benevolence of the person encountered.[38] It is in this context that signals indicating a willingness to cooperate undoubtedly appeared, a

---

36 As Jean-Jacques Hublin points out (J-J. Hublin (2024), *La Tyrannie du Cerveau* (Paris: Robert Laffont)):

> Access to plant food or insects is an individual problem that each member of a troop must and can solve [...] Among hunter-gatherers, the redistribution of killed game and the sharing of food resources in general take on a much more vital and universal aspect, and generally follow elaborate rules [...] there is no doubt that the degree of food solidarity achieved by Homo erectus groups, and the social organization it implies, were also powerful motors for the evolution of the brain. (Kindle Edition, p. 94; my translation)

37 This is the primary, immemorial question, as Marcel Mauss reminds us (M. Mauss (1954), *The Gift: Forms and Functions of Exchange in Archaic Societies*, translated by I. Cunnison (London: Cohen & West)):

> [...] at these times men meet in a curious frame of mind, with exaggerated fear and an equally exaggerated generosity which appear stupid in no one eye's but our own [...] There is either complete trust of mistrust. One lays down one's arms, renounces magic and gives everything away, from casual hospitality to one's daughter or one's property. It is in such conditions that men, despite themselves, learnt to renounce what was theirs and made contracts to give and repay. (Apple Books, p. 154)

38 A. Cuddy, S. Fiske, P. Glick, and J. Xu (2002), "A Model of (Often Mixed) Stereotype Content: Competence and Warmth Respectively Follow From Perceived Status and Competition," *Journal of Personality and Social Psychology* 82 (6):

> When people meet others as individuals or group members, they want to know what the other's goals will be vis-à-vis the self or in-group and how effectively the other will pursue those goals. That is, perceivers want to know the other's intent (positive or negative) and capability; these characteristics correspond to perceptions of warmth and competence, respectively.

key moment in human history. We know that chimpanzees identify each other through smells, gestures, and attitudes, and that they accept each other through reciprocal procedures (such as mutual delousing). But chimpanzees do not use objects as tokens of their intentions toward others.[39] However, this specific use of objects proves very important when it comes to quickly understanding whether to flee, fight, or cooperate when meeting a stranger. This is illustrated, for example, by the encounter between an English explorer and an isolated forest tribe in New Guinea[40] at the beginning of the 20th century. For this community, the question was crucial: was this new arrival a human or one of the dead who had returned, those legendary pale-skinned cannibal ghosts? Their survival depended on it. After conferring, they decided to test the explorer's humanity by offering him pigs. The explorer, with intelligence and subtlety, reacted not by eating the animal, but by offering them precious shells in return. In this way, he helped to shape the Papua New Guineans' perception of him: he was a pacifist, not a cannibal. Thanks to this exchange of signals, these individuals, strangers to one another, were able to update their representation of the world and establish a basis for mutual understanding. The conditions for cooperation were in place.

More generally, when people from different communities and cultures discover each other for the first time, they often manage to communicate through the exchange of gifts, which enables them to identify and compare their respective representations of the world. Exchanges are the foundation of sociability.[41] Archaeological excavations have shown that in around

---

39 M. Hénaff (2009), "Repenser la Réciprocité et la Reconnaissance : Relecture de l'Essai sur le Don de Marcel Mauss," *Revista Portuguesa de Filosofia* 65: 5–26: "Apparently only humans adopt the procedure of committing themselves by giving something of their own as a token and substitute for themselves" (my translation). And Marcel Hénaff refers to Adam Smith (A. Smith (1776), *An Inquiry into the Nature and Causes of the Wealth of Nations*, London: Strahan and Cadell)): "Nobody ever saw a dog make a fair and deliberate exchange of one bone for another with another dog" (Kindle Edition, p. 26).

40 M. Hénaff (2009), "Repenser la Réciprocité et la Reconnaissance : Relecture de l'Essai sur le don de Marcel Mauss," *Revista Portuguesa de Filosofia* 65, citing Andrew Strathern (A. Strathern (1971), *The Rope of Moka: Big-Men and Ceremonial Exchange in Mount Hagen New Guinea* (Cambridge: Cambridge University Press, 1971)).

41 Not least because the exchange follows rules, and therefore opens the door to a regulation of human exchanges and thus to socialization.

150,000–140,000 BC, Homo sapiens (not the Neanderthal)[42] was already using nonutilitarian objects, such as the shells of small, colored, and pierced marine gastropods. Probably used as signals, these objects could express a willingness to cooperate and test the intentions of one's interlocutors.

Many natural and cultural features of the human species have undoubtedly contributed to the emergence of representations of the world that are likely to be widely shared, notably mass religions. Several of these mechanisms can easily be identified. First, a shared narrative based on abstraction brings together a large number of individuals and provides an explanatory framework for how the world works (origins, present, future). It takes the form of simple, unambiguous symbolic signals—a cross, a veil, a yarmulke—that, in an encounter with a stranger, reveal that person's worldview and signal their ability to cooperate as a participant in that shared representation. These powerful, low-energy signals encourage large-scale cooperation.

In conclusion, the human species has, no doubt through natural selection, reinforced Bayesian cognitive inference mechanisms: abstraction, which is its societal variation and enables a human group to coalesce beyond its natural limits; the alignment of values (or the creation of shared values), which generates the search for action policies that will lead to mutual aid if the task is too arduous for the individual; and the creation of signals that enable the individual, when faced with a stranger, to update her representation of the world and better define her intentions. All these mechanisms have led to a higher level of cooperation and, consequently, have optimized access to resources.

The Greek city: Cooperation beyond trust

Reason as a tool for social coordination

Reason as a tool for social coordination has a date and a place of birth—2,500 years ago, in Greece; although other forms of rationality were also at work, notably in China, as Jean-Pierre Vernant also reminds us.[43] Prior

---

42 J.-J. Hublin (2022), Homo Sapiens, une Espèce Invasive (Paris: Librairie Arthème Fayard and Collège de France): "In the world of Neanderthals, such objects are extremely rare." (p. 38; my translation)

43 J-P. Vernant (1996), Entre Mythe et Politique, La Librairie du XXe Siècle (Paris: Seuil): "In our scientific and rationalist tradition, reason is considered to have originated

to this extension to the social sphere, the question arises of its appearance in life's great adventure. Hugo Mercier and Dan Sperber[44] put forward the hypothesis that the emergence of reason is part of the process of natural selection:[45] "reason is not just a tool for individual reflection, but is above all a tool of communication that is adapted to the richness of human interaction. It overcomes the need for trust by giving each person the opportunity to present their arguments to the other and have them adopted."[46] Let's imagine that Eka indicates the presence of a lion to Dvi. Dvi must ask herself whether or not Eka is willing to protect her, what her mood is at the moment, and so on. If Eka limits her message to tangible elements (tracks, smell, etc.) and a "reasonable" discourse (such as the common observation of a fawn the day before), Dvi can quickly and confidently deduce

---

in Greece 2,500 years ago [...] Benefiting from a different type of rationality, they (the Chinese) were able to integrate these phenomena into a rational way of thinking." (Kindle Edition, p. 253; my translation)

44 H. Mercier and D. Sperber (2017), *The Enigma of Reason: A New Theory of Human Understanding* (Cambridge, MA: Harvard University Press).

45 H. Mercier and D. Sperber (2017), *The Enigma of Reason: A New Theory of Human Understanding* (Cambridge, MA: Harvard University Press):

> Reason, we argue, has two main functions: that of producing reasons for justifying oneself, and that of producing arguments to convince others. [...] A first function of reason is to provide tools for the kind of rich and versatile coordination that human cooperation requires. [...] Evaluating the reasons of others is uniquely relevant in deciding whom to trust and how to achieve coordination. [...] The second function of reason—a function carried out through reasoning and argumentation—is, we claim, to make communication effective even when the communicators lack sufficient credibility in the eyes of their audience to be believed on trust. Reason produces reasons that communicators use as arguments to persuade a reticent audience. Reason, by the same token, helps a cautious audience evaluate these reasons, accept good arguments, and reject bad ones. (Kindle Edition, p. 7)

46 From the perspective of Bayesian cognitive inference, if we privilege the information that others provide on the representation of the world in relation to the social link, we must reduce our uncertainty linked to the latter's values—i.e., the biases inherent in their model of the world—as much as possible. To illustrate this point further, we need only imagine a dialogue in which only emotional expressions were exchanged, in order to measure what this dialogue would say about the world: The "noise" would be high, due to the personal nature of the information given, and the adjustment of representations of the world would be made more difficult, as it would require a separation of what is emotional from information about how the world works.

the presence of the predator. Reason allows us to focus on the validity of information about how the world works, rather than on the reliability of the individual who provides it or their psychological peculiarities, thereby enabling more effective updating of our representation of the world.

With the Greek moment, this mechanism replaces that of the narrative. As Jean-Pierre Vernant notes, the latter began with a disorder that was organized by a sovereign:[47]

> And, first of all, what was the context of the civilization from which this new way of thinking was to emerge? It's an oral civilization, where poetry, which is a danced, rhythmic song, takes center stage intellectually. [...] The idea was to write a story showing that, in a world where powers, authorities and forces oppose and compete, at a given moment a sovereign more powerful than the others will impose his law. From this imposition, the order of the world would become constant.

Now, instead of a sovereign, we're looking for laws to govern the world:[48]

> Thus, instead of placing pure disorder at the origin and giving birth to a sovereign from this disorder who will impose order, we are looking for what are the principles, or the Principle that is at the basis of everything. [...] What we are looking for is the principle that finds them. [...] Finally, in this starting point, we see the idea that it is law that governs the world and not Zeus. Order is therefore first in relation to power.

And this search for principles is carried out in an argumentative debate that begins with the sharing of the spoils, which is organized by giving everyone a voice:[49]

> This ancient configuration unravels and changes with the emergence of the city. The *polis* takes shape when the hoplite reform institutes equality among warriors and designates a neutral place in the center

---

47 J-P. Vernant (1996), *Entre Mythe et Politique*, La Librairie du XXᵉ Siècle (Paris: Seuil), Kindle Edition, p. 254; my translation.

48 J-P. Vernant (1996), *Entre Mythe et Politique*, La Librairie du XXᵉ Siècle (Paris: Seuil), Kindle Edition, p. 256; my translation.

49 M. Hénaff (2010), *The Price of Truth: Gift, Money, and Philosophy*, translated by J-L. Morhange (Stanford, CA: Stanford University Press), p. 7.

of their circle for the common spoils that will be distributed by lot. This place becomes the center from which everyone must talk to everyone else. This is the origin of the public space that becomes the space of debate [...] Authoritarian discourse is replaced by the exchange of arguments.

A process of Bayesian cognitive inference is now at the heart of the model of the world in the Greek city: the search for the hidden causes of the world.

Shared perception of beauty to establish common values

At the same time, a shared perception of beauty is emerging, and in particular, that of buildings, according to Marcel Hénaff:[50]

The *meson*, the focal point of public space located at the core of the *agora* from which persuasive speech was exercised, was also the locus through which the city expressed its relationship to the citizens— hence the importance of monuments and, above all, of their beauty.

The civic bond

Finally, while in cities the structure itself creates an initial sense of belonging, the population is large, and proximity to strangers is common. A new mechanism of social cooperation is established. An intense and limited bond—parenthood—is replaced in democracy by a less intense but broader bond—citizenship.[51] It is the transition from solidarity based on proximity to a broader social bond:[52]

---

50 M. Hénaff (2010), *The Price of Truth: Gift, Money, and Philosophy*, translated by J-L. Morhange (Stanford, CA: Stanford University Press), p. 250. As Hénaff also points out, this shared perception of beauty and democratic debate are the two pillars of the asymmetrical gift, or *kharis* in Greek: "The city's *kharis* was [...] at the same time the requirement of democratic speech expected to convince and seduce, and public space in the sense of what was given to each citizen in the name of all" (p. 250).

51 J-P. Vernant (1996), *Entre Mythe et Politique*, La Librairie du XXe Siècle (Paris: Seuil): "Henceforth, every individual born an Athenian is, as a citizen and as by definition, a free man [...].": Kindle Edition, p. 271; my translation.

52 J-P. Vernant (1996), *Entre Mythe et Politique*, La Librairie du XXe Siècle (Paris: Seuil); Kindle Edition, pp. 265–266; my translation.

> It is no longer a question of trying to find out who one's ancestors were, whether real or fictitious: As long as one is born an Athenian, one has the right to take part in the government of the city and to be a member of the People's Assembly.

This equality among citizens harmonized with the new relationship with reason:[53]

> [...] with the advent of democracy, the old power to decide based on the authority of the sovereign's position alone came to an end. Between equal citizens—*isoi*—the only thing that could win the approval of the assembly was convincing discourse based on arguments.

Ultimately, in response to the challenge of cooperation within the city—where the size and cultural diversity of the population take precedence over the specific characteristics of the clan—a new form of organization takes shape, founded on two fundamental pillars. First, persuasion: this emphasizes the virtue of debate and the confrontation of arguments in the search for the law governing the world. Second, a shared perception of the beauty of buildings: the Greek city organizes the convergence of its citizens' gaze toward its public buildings, an aesthetic offering visible to, and shared by all. This experience, by promoting the creation of shared values, helps to strengthen cooperation between community members. These two pillars of emergent democracy trigger Bayesian cognitive inference.

Capitalism: Cooperating around the world

New opportunities, new mechanisms

In Europe, at the turn of the 18th century, capitalism emerged as a minority organizational system.[54] There are many reasons for this advent (notably the emergence of Protestantism, business, and then financial markets).[55]

---

53 M. Hénaff (2010), *The Price of Truth: Gift, Money, and Philosophy*, translated by J-L. Morhange (Stanford, CA: Stanford University Press), p. 249.

54 As Fernand Braudel reminds us (F. Braudel (1985), *La Dynamique du Capitalisme* (Paris: Arthaud)): "Market economy and capitalism [...] are, until the eighteenth century, minorities, [...] the mass of men's actions remains contained, swallowed up in the immense domain of material life." Kindle Edition, p. 32; my translation.

55 For the purposes of this book, we'll confine ourselves to the historical dimensions relevant to the survey.

These transformations coincided, in time and space, with access to new resources, notably energy, providing Europe with the conditions for a remarkable boom. As Kenneth Pomeranz shows, this continent, which at the time was no more developed than other regions of the world such as Japan or China,[56] but benefited from more abundant resources, especially coal, as well as plant and mineral resources from its colonies:[57]

> [...] Europe, too, could have wound up on an "east Asian," labor-intensive path. That it did not was the result of important and sharp discontinuities, based on both fossil fuels and access to New World resources, which, taken together, obviated the need to manage land intensively.

At the same time, maritime innovations appeared,[58] and discoveries of new territories contributed to reshaping Europeans' perception of the world.[59] As early as 1503, with Magellan's circumnavigation of the globe, they were

---

56 K. Pomeranz (2000), *The Great Divergence: China, Europe, and the Making of the Modern World Economy* (Princeton, NJ: Princeton University Press): "[...] core regions in China and Japan circa 1750 seem to resemble the most advanced parts of western Europe, combining sophisticated agriculture, commerce." Kindle Edition, p. 17.

57 K. Pomeranz (2000), *The Great Divergence: China, Europe, and the Making of the Modern World Economy* (Princeton, NJ: Princeton University Press), Kindle Edition, p. 13.

58 F. Braudel (2025), *L'Aube, la Terre, la Mer: La Méditerranée, une Histoire: Extrait de La Méditerranée: L'Espace et l'Histoire* (Paris: Éditions Flammarion):

> Three transformations marked the general evolution of ships in the Mediterranean before steam navigation and iron hulls: the stern rudder, which appeared around the 12th century; the clinker hull, which appeared around the 14th-15th centuries; and the ship of the line, which appeared in the 17th century. [...]The stern rudder, an oceanic invention, is the rudder we know today: a shaft that pierces the hull allows it to be maneuvered from inside the boat. (...) The second transformation concerns the clinker planking. [...] To be clinker-built means that the planks of the hull, instead of being joined together, overlap each other like the slates of a roof. [...] The last transformation was the replacement of the galley by the ship of the line. (Kindle Edition, pp. 61–64; my translation)

59 In the same perspective, see Fernand Braudel (F. Braudel (1985), *La Dynamique du Capitalisme* (Paris: Arthaud)):

> The great history of Europe says so emphatically, and no one thinks it wrong to highlight Vasco da Gama's arrival at Calicut in 1498, the Dutchman Cornelius Houtman's release at Bantam, the great city of Java, in 1595, Robert

aware of the existence of another continent, the Americas, which they had learned to differentiate from India. They also "discovered" China. Although known since the time of Marco Polo's tales, the country had remained largely ignored in the West. Its true discovery came as a profound shock. Its civilization seemed irreconcilable with Christianity, which was shaping Western thinking and values.[60] In economic terms, its weight was impressive: in 1600, China and India accounted for more than half the world's GDP, while Great Britain accounted for just 2% (see Figure 4.1).

	1 600	% of total	1 700	% of total	1 800	% of total
Britain	6 007	2	10 709	3	100 179	9
Western Europe	65 955	20	83 395	22	379 223	34
China	96 000	29	82 800	22	189 740	17
India	74 250	23	90 750	24	135 882	12
World	329 417		371 369		1 101 369	

Figure 4.1 The evolution of GDP through the ages

Source: A. Maddison (2003),[61] author.

Note: In 1600, China accounted for almost 30% of world GDP, compared with less than 2% for Great Britain.

Clive's victory at Plassey in 1757, which delivered Bengal to England. (Kindle Edition, p. 61; my translation)

60 F. Julien (2022), *Moïse ou la Chine: Quand ne se Déploie pas l'Idée de Dieu* (Paris: Éditions de l'Observatoire/Humensis), taking up a question posed by Blaise Pascal, "Which is the more believable of the two, Moses or China?," which is representative of European thought regarding China at that time:

[...].Pascal's thought strikes [...].by what it genially lets us see: that Christian Truth, universal as it is, could find itself, not denied, hastily contested, but peacefully ignored. Suddenly suspect, not because of arguments to the contrary, but because of the fact that there, elsewhere, for millennia, in a civilization apparently so developed, it was so well dispensed with ... (Kindle Edition, p. 22; my translation)

And there was no period of habituation: "This 'Chinese case' is both unique and exemplary. It is unique because, for once, civilizations with equal power are meeting without any previous mediation having prepared the way for it." Kindle Edition, p. 29; my translation.

61 A. Maddison (2003), *The World Economy: Historical Statistics* (Paris: OECD).

From the point of view of the English or Dutch at this time, the situation is relatively clear: significant economic resources are available, but they are far away, both geographically and culturally, and thus benefiting from them will require an adaptation of mentalities and strategies. At the same time, "world-economies" were emerging; their centers shifted over the centuries, from Venice to Antwerp, then Genoa, Amsterdam, London, and finally New York.[62] These are centers that attract multiple talents and cooperate with the periphery:[63] new resources are accessible, but new systems of cooperation are required to enable exchange with cultures based on heterogeneous values.

Indeed, China, the colonies, and the world-city pose the question for economic players—whether they put it in these terms or not—of the need for new modes of cooperation in a context where distance and/or heterogeneity make it difficult to operate the usual coordination mechanisms, which are generally based on proximity (and therefore trust).[64] Capitalism seems

---

62 F. Braudel (1985), *La Dynamique du Capitalisme* (Paris: Arthaud):

> By world-economy, a word I have coined from the German word *Weltwirtschaft*, I mean the economy of only a portion of our planet, insofar as it forms an economic whole [...]. A world economy can be defined as a triple reality. It occupies a given geographical space [...]. A world economy always accepts a pole, a center, represented by a dominant city [...]. Every world-economy is divided into successive zones [...] centring took place around 1380, to the benefit of Venice. Around 1500, there was a sudden and gigantic leap from Venice to Antwerp; then, around 1550–1560, a return to the Mediterranean, this time in favor of Genoa; finally, around 1590–1610, a transfer to Amsterdam, where the economic center of the European zone stabilized for almost two centuries. Between 1780 and 1815, it moved to London. In 1929, it crossed the Atlantic to New York. (Kindle Edition, p. 54; my translation)

63 Cooperation that can take the imposed form of slavery, because as Fernand Braudel reminds us (F. Braudel (1985), *La Dynamique du Capitalisme* (Paris: Arthaud)): "After all, it was Western Europe that transferred and, as it were, reinvented ancient-style slavery in the context of the New World" (Kindle Edition, p. 60; my translation).

64 To illustrate this impact, we can quote Avner Greif (A. Greif (1994), "Cultural Beliefs and the Organization of Society: a Historical and Theoretical Reflection on Collectivist and Individualist Societies," *The Journal of Political Economy* 102 (5): 912–950), which describes two groups of merchants, the Maghribi in the 11th century, who formed part of Muslim culture, and the Genoese in the 12th, part of the Latin world. Both face the same challenge:

> The efficiency of their trades depended, to a large extent, on their ability to mitigate an organizational problem related to a specific transaction, namely, the provision of the services required for handling a merchant's good abroad.

to provide a solution by introducing depersonalized coordination through objects. Indeed, it can be seen as the invention of a social bond, designed to foster cooperation with heterogeneous "resources." Introducing a logic of economic efficiency and task specialization, it is gradually replacing the social bonds founded on proximity[65] and reciprocity that were manifested through gifts. Previously, economic relations had been based on the mechanism of charity: if A lent B a sum of money, the latter would decide, in a gesture of counter-giving, to return this sum and add another sum corresponding to a rate of interest. This economic relationship therefore had an

---

A merchant could either provide these services himself by traveling between trade centers or hire *overseas* agents in trade centers abroad to handle his merchandise.

The former (the Maghribi) had a collective culture, exchanges about people's nature, partnerships, mechanisms of reciprocity, and barriers to entry into the activity due to initial wealth as an indicator of responsibility. The second group (the Genoese) had an individualistic culture, little information about people, legal structures, a form of organization similar to modern companies, and few barriers to entry within the firm, allowing for social mobility. When battles and political changes arose, both groups had the opportunity to seize opportunities for international growth. The Maghribi had to send their own people abroad, while the Genoese were able to recruit locally, giving them access to local knowledge and making them more adaptable.

65 A complementary reading would be the recognition of a fault line in Europe between civilized and "barbarian" peoples, as Marcel Hénaff points out (M. Hénaff (2017), "L'Europe, une Genèse Paradoxale," *Esprit* (440), December):

It could also be that the trauma of the loss or non-recognition of one's vernacular ("barbarian" or pre-Roman) identity never ceases to produce symptoms of resistance or forms of conflict between North and South [...] Europe, a Roman colony and Christian space, was culturally formed in a disappropriation of itself, in a constant eccentricity in relation to its past and vernacular culture and in a permanent appropriation of something from elsewhere. (My translation)

One possible reading of the Protestant moment is that, by reducing social ties, it reduces historical tensions between cultures.

eminently social dimension,[66] as Marcel Hénaff[67] comments on Bartolomé Clavero:

> This is why this order of charity is radically different from the legal relationship of the order of justice regulated by the category of contract: "The law of friendship (*jus amicitiae*) is prior to and superior to law proper. What is the purpose of friendship? It's to make friends," Aristotle was already saying, another way of saying that exchanges of goods have no other purpose than to maintain or strengthen the social bond. (My translation)

With the arrival of Protestantism, according to Marcel Hénaff,[68] this mechanism underwent a real upheaval:

> The rupture brought about by the Reformation is not just the religious valorization of the craft as a vocation. Perhaps more fundamentally, it is the devaluation of the generous gesture as essential to salvation, and ultimately its presentation as an economically irrational gesture. *What is at stake here is the very form of the social bond.* [...] This is supposed to arise from the complementarity of tasks rather than from the reciprocity of gifts. (My translation)

---

66 Charity calls for gratitude, which in turn helps to strengthen the social bond. The link between gratitude and social bonding has notably been studied by Glenn R. Fox *et al.* (A. Damasio, H. Damasio, G. Fox, and J. Kaplan (2015), "Neural Correlates of Gratitude," *Frontiers in Psychology* 6 (1491): 1–10; also see Glenn Fox's comments (G. R. Fox (2017), "What Can the Brain Reveal About Gratitude?," *Greater Good Magazine*): "[...] our data suggest that because gratitude relies on the brain networks associated with social bonding and stress relief, this may explain in part how grateful feelings lead to health benefits over time."

67 M. Hénaff (2000), "L'Éthique Catholique et l'Esprit du Non-capitalisme," *Revue du MAUSS* (15): 35–67.

68 M. Hénaff (2000), "L'Éthique Catholique et l'Esprit du Non-capitalisme," *Revue du MAUSS* (15): 35–67.

Henceforth, the economic relationship with the other is separate from a strong social attachment.[69] This, combined with a direct and unmediated relationship with God, leads to the individualism[70] that lies at the heart of the Protestant revolution, as Marcel Hénaff[71] reminds us, taking up Max Weber's thesis: "The disenchantment of the world [...] cannot be separated

---

69 More generally, a form of noneconomic exchange has been the rule in certain cultures, as Marcel Hénaff points out (M. Hénaff (2010), *The Price of Truth: Gift, Money, and Philosophy*, translated by J-L. Morhange (Stanford, CA: Stanford University Press)), referring to the work of Bronislaw Malinowski (B. Malinowski (1972), *Les Argonautes du Pacifique Occidental* (Paris: Gallimard)) on the exchanges carried out by the Melanesian coastal populations of the Trobriand Islands:

> This surprising *kula* circuit has several salient features. The exchanges have a glorious and festive character; It is essential for the participants to display their generosity and to behave in a noble fashion by giving their most beautiful *waygu'a*. This sets a rigorous distinction between *kula* exchange and another important type of exchange, *gimwali*, or useful exchange, which can be practiced concurrently with *kula* but with different partners, and which often involves fierce barter. As for *kula* exchange, it remains above all *a way to ensure reciprocal recognition and gain prestige*. [...] Finally, every *waygu'a* has a unique character: its provenance, former owners, and history are known [...] thus, an entire network of personal bonds is woven between partners. A variety of interwoven interpersonal networks symbolized by these precious goods thus develops throughout archipelago communities. (p. 118)

The Trobriand Islands thus show two circuits for two functions, one of which is the intention to cooperate and strengthen social ties. It can also be hypothesized that making the group's social structures public in this way allows everyone to observe them and update their representation of the world. This example shows that this social organization was not a form of proto-capitalism in which gift-giving was an archaic form of market exchange, but one in which the social (and nonmarket) bond was key.

70 At this point there were still strong socialization structures at the time, such as religion and the States; there was also the great emphasis on fraternity at the time of the French Revolution, as Joseph Stiglitz reminds us (J. Stiglitz (2024) *The Road to Freedom: Economics and the Good Society* (New York: W.W. Norton & Company)):

> "Liberté, égalité, fraternité" ("Liberty, equality, fraternity") was the rallying cry of the French Revolution. It connected equality and solidarity—social cohesion—closely with freedom and liberty, and rightly so. [...] The French revolutionaries realized that social solidarity is a virtue in its own right and is necessary for the well-functioning of society. (Kindle Edition, p. 72)

71 M. Hénaff (2000), "L'Éthique Catholique et l'Esprit du Non-capitalisme," *Revue du MAUSS* (15): 35–67.

from another consequence: the affirmation of a radical individualism. For each believer is alone before God in the matter of election" (my translation).

To measure the impact of this European-born revolution in individualism, we can use an experiment described by Joseph Heinrich to highlight the specificity of European individualism.[72] The descendants of Eka and Dvi, who have taken the names of their ancestors, meet in a crowded market with identical suitcases. Dvi inadvertently takes Eka's suitcase. Eka's judgment will depend on her representation of the world. Perhaps Eka internalizes the judgment and tries to understand Dvi's motives; she may assume that Dvi took her suitcase by mistake, without malicious intent. Or Eka makes a factual judgment, which she delegates to the group; as she doesn't try to interpret Dvi's motivations and sticks to the facts, in this case, she defers to the rules established by the group. Even today, some cultures place greater emphasis on individual motivations and the understanding of intentions, while others privilege the objectivity of facts and the application of collective rules.[73] In Fiji, for example, the loss of the suitcase would be judged to have been both accidental (due to local conditions) and intentional. Conversely, in Los Angeles, Dvi's intentions will be judged.

Capitalism and Protestantism together contributed to the rise of contractual systems that define the terms of exchange and the use of money, which play a central role in shaping people's relationships with one another. In this way, relationships with others themselves evolve[74] and escape the social norms of the group. In short, this marks a major break in human history: relationships become depersonalized through the intermediation of objects and money. By freeing themselves from mechanisms based on social proximity, relationships with others gain in potentiality, are extended to foreigners, and reach out to all social strata, fostering a dynamic of equity

---

72 J. Henrich (2020), *The Weirdest People in the World: How the West Became Psychologically Peculiar and Particularly Prosperous* (New York: Farrar, Straus and Giroux).

73 Interestingly, Judea Pearl and Dana Mackenzie (J. Pearl and D. Mackenzie (2018), *The Book of Why: The New Science of Cause and Effect* (New York: Basic Books)) note that in answer to God's question as to whether Adam has eaten the fruit of the tree of knowledge of good and evil, Adam—and then Eve—respond not with the facts, but with an explanation of the reasons for this act (the serpent, etc.). Their response to God is therefore based on intentionality, not on the action itself. This logic is close to that of individualism.

74 M. Hénaff (2003), "Religious Ethics, Gift Exchange and Capitalism," *European Journal of Sociology* 44 (3): 293–324.

that accompanies the rise of democracies and benefits in turn from their historical reinforcement.

This new merchant order had its roots in the Middle Ages, with the rise of cities,[75] fairs, and guilds. Over time, it challenged the religious and political structures that dominated Europe, and found a form of "congruence" with the emergence of Protestantism, as Max Weber argues.

Another reading of the capitalist revolution is proposed by Albert Hirschman,[76] who argues that it also came about from within, under the impetus of the ruling classes and elites. The latter developed governance mechanisms that were capable of preventing excesses of political instability and the ferment of permanent violence, and of responding to the incessant wars in Europe, which were largely the result of religious conflicts. In his analysis of the interwoven dynamics of philosophical, political, moral, and

---

75 Although this is not the place for a detailed comparison with Karl Marx's work, it
    is summarized by Isaiah Berlin (I. Berlin (1996), *Karl Marx: His Life and Environment*,
    4th ed. (Oxford: Oxford University Press)):

    No full or systematic exposition of historical materialism was ever published
    by Marx himself. [...] The framework of the new theory is undeviatingly
    Hegelian. [...] But whereas, according to Hegel, the single substance in the
    succession of whose states history consists is the eternal, self-developing, uni-
    versal Spirit, [...], Marx, following Feuerbach, denounces this as a piece of
    mystification on which no knowledge could be founded [...]. The history of
    society is the history of the inventive labours that alter man, alter his desires,
    habits, outlook, relationships both to other men and to physical nature, with
    which man is in perpetual physical and technological metabolism. Among
    man's inventions—conscious or unconscious—is the division of labour,
    which arises in primitive society, and vastly increases his productivity, creat-
    ing wealth beyond his immediate needs. [...] but thereby also of the use of
    this accumulation—of these hoarded necessities of life—as a means of with-
    holding benefits from others, and so of bullying them, of forcing them to
    work for the accumulators of wealth, of coercing, exploiting and thereby of
    dividing men into classes— into controllers and controlled. (p. 194)

    For Karl Marx, class struggle is the driving force of history. It's true that the crea-
    tion of the city created the division of labor, but this is only one (possible) con-
    sequence of a broader principle: The selection by certain cultures of mechanisms
    for gaining access to resources. Class struggle is therefore not the driving force, but
    the consequence, in a particular context, of a broader principle. It should also be
    noted that other cultures do not select such mechanisms for accessing resources,
    and therefore do not create class oppositions.

76 A. Hirschman (1977), *The Passions and the Interests: Political Arguments for Capitalism before Its
    Triumph* (Princeton, NJ: Princeton University Press).

economic thought in Europe, Albert Hirschman identifies several major forces at work. First, values. Initiated by Niccolò Machiavelli, who explored the conduct and governance of a state, these reflections were echoed by Baruch Spinoza, who focused on man's true nature, which was defined not only by reason and duty, but also by human passions. This line of reasoning leads to the paradoxical possibility of the consubstantiality of an individual vice and a public virtue, with a result that is not the fruit of the will or desire of the individuals.[77] For example, the pursuit of glory can indirectly serve the collective good.[78] A new axis then emerges, using these passions as opposing forces, like the laws of Galilean physics governing the movement of the planets.[79] Just as gravitational forces balance to form a stable universe, might not passions be capable of bringing about a socially

---

77 Hegel's notion of "the cunning of reason."

78 Albert Hirschman goes back to St. Augustine, for whom the only passion to be tolerated was the pursuit of glory, as it led to the good of the city; in this viewpoint he was following in the footsteps of the Roman Empire (A. Hirschman (1977), *The Passions and the Interests: Political Arguments for Capitalism before Its Triumph* (Princeton, NJ: Princeton University Press)), citing Herbert Deane (H. Deane (1963), *The Political and Social Ideas of St. Augustine* (New York: Columbia University Press)):

> Thus Augustine speaks of the "civil virtue" characterizing the early Romans "who have shown a Babylonian love for their earthly fatherland," and who were "suppressing the desire of wealth and many other vices for their one vice, namely, the love of praise. (p. 25)

79 Albert Hirschman identifies Spinoza as the source (although he points out that Spinoza does not give a utilitarian function to the opposition of forces) (A. Hirschman (1977), *The Passions and the Interests: Political Arguments for Capitalism before Its Triumph* (Princeton, NJ: Princeton University Press, p. 23)) and quotes Baruch Spinoza in the Ethics (Part IV, Prop. 7, 1927 translation by W. H. White, revised by A. H. Stirling (London: Oxford University Press)): "An affect cannot be restrained nor removed unless by an opposed and stronger affect"; p. 770 in the Curley edition (B. Spinoza (1985), *The Collected Works of Spinoza*, edited and translated by E. Curley (Princeton, NJ: Princeton University Press)).
     Passions can then be opposed according to a principle of "compensatory passions." Albert Hirschman refers to Hume: "Hume advocated restraining the 'love of pleasure' by the 'love of gain,' knowing that Galileo's approach to human affairs was spreading with Hobbes, "who based his theory of human nature on Galileo," as Albert Hirschman also points out (p. 13).

beneficial equilibrium?[80] This idea led to the development of the polyphonic notion of "interest," a synthesis of passion and reason, which gives human beings a certain predictability.[81] Thanks to the virtues thus demonstrated of pacification through trade—which was beneficial to nations and individuals alike, as Montesquieu emphasized—[82]the conceptual framework was established. It paved the way for Adam Smith's[83] argument that economic relations, founded on egoism, paradoxically lead to the collective good:

> In almost every other race of animals, each individual, when it is grown up to maturity, is entirely independent, and in its natural state has occasion for the assistance of no other living creature. But man

---

80 As Albert Hirschman notes (A. Hirschman (1977), *The Passions and the Interests: Political Arguments for Capitalism before Its Triumph* (Princeton, NJ: Princeton University Press), this thinking then moved up to the level of states, and in particular the United States, which drew inspiration from it when setting up its "checks and balances" governance system, which is still in place today.

81 Albert Hirschman devotes many pages to this term, which is transforming European thought (A. Hirschman (1977), *The Passions and the Interests: Political Arguments for Capitalism before Its Triumph* (Princeton, NJ: Princeton University Press)): "Interest was seen to partake in effect of the better nature of each, as the passion of self-love upgraded and contained by reason, and as reason given direction and force by that passion" (p. 43).

This new concept should provide a stable, realistic world: "The belief that interest could be considered a dominant motive of human behavior caused considerable intellectual excitement: at last a realistic basis for a viable social order had been discovered" (p. 48).

And, finally, the human being becomes predictable: "The most general of these assets was predictability" (p. 48).

82 Montesquieu (1989), *The Spirits of Law*, translated by T. Nugent, edited by A. Cohler, B. Miller, and H. Stone (Cambridge: Cambridge University Press): "Commerce cures destructive prejudices, and it is an almost general rule that everywhere there are gentle mores, there is commerce, that that everywhere there is commerce, there are gentle mores" (Kindle Edition, p. 337).

Yet he adds: "But, if the spirit of commerce unites nations, it does not unite individuals in the same way. We see that in countries where one is affected only by the spirit of commerce, there is traffic in all human activities and all moral virtues; the smallest things, those required by humanity, are done or given for money" (Kindle Edition, p. 338).

83 A. Smith (1776), *An Inquiry into the Nature and Causes of the Wealth of Nations* (Strahan and Cadell), Kindle Edition, p. 26.

has almost constant occasion for the help of his brethren, and it is in vain for him to expect it from their benevolence only. He will be more likely to prevail if he can interest their self-love in his favour, and show them that it is for their own advantage to do for him what he requires of them [...] It is not from the benevolence of the butcher, the brewer, or the baker that we expect our dinner, but from their regard to their own interest. We address ourselves, not to their humanity, but to their self-love, and never talk to them of our own necessities, but of their advantages.

Ultimately, capitalism, the fruit of the rise of the merchant class and the desire of the ruling classes to reduce war in Europe,[84] creates a new relationship with values: strong, ancient values (such as those stemming from religions), which led to local cooperation but also to potentially violent competition,[85] are replaced by a new value, neutral because shared by all; that of "interest." This approach has a dual effect. On the one hand, as a result of the agreement on values, the energy allocated can shift from the values/states/actions relationship to that of states/actions. In other words, as the struggle for values has disappeared, only the distance between states and the actions to achieve them needs to be reduced. On the other hand, the development of world cities or economies leads to a specialization of tasks, reducing the need for cooperation to achieve these states. As a result, a new mode of social cooperation may emerge: individual competition. We are certainly still in this European moment of the modern era (see Figure 4.2).

---

84 In the same perspective, modern states were born with the 1648 Treaty of Westphalia, and the observation, after the Thirty Years' War, of the irreconcilable differences between religions in Europe—a system based as well on the notion of national interest.

85 Because of the absoluteness of values and their inevitable competition in the case of monotheistic religions; also because of their common roots and successive discourses of substitution. See Gérard Haddad (G. Haddad (2021), À l'Origine de la Violence: D'Œdipe à Caïn, une Erreur de Freud? (Paris: Éditions Salvador)).

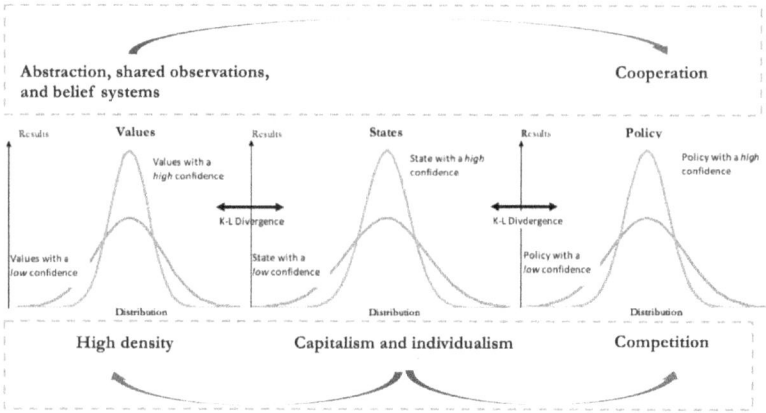

Figure 4.2 Graph showing the transition from local cooperation to global competition

Source: Author.

Note: Before the rise of capitalism, large-scale systems of societal coordination—such as abstraction, shared observation, and narrative—operated primarily at the level of values. Based on these values, a wide range of policies could be implemented to bring about states that corresponded to them. While this generated large-scale cooperation, it also led to global competition between groups attached to these values, due to their irreconcilable nature as absolute values. This is what capitalist thinkers emphasize.

With capitalism, values align with what all human beings have in common: their "interest." There is then, by design, no more competition between values. Attention can then shift to multiple states to be achieved, and violence is restricted. This reading echoes Montesquieu's thesis of "gentle commerce." And since these states can be achieved individually, particularly due to the specialization of tasks resulting from the growth of cities, the mechanism leads to competition between human beings.

In short, capitalism gives rise to competition within a large group, whereas previously cooperation prevailed within a small circle and competition, sometimes violent, between different groups.

The success of capitalism

This societal organization proved to be formidably efficient. Since then, human beings have found themselves in a situation of unparalleled material abundance. Economic growth has helped reduce extreme poverty from 85% in 1800 to less than 10% today (see Figure 4.3).

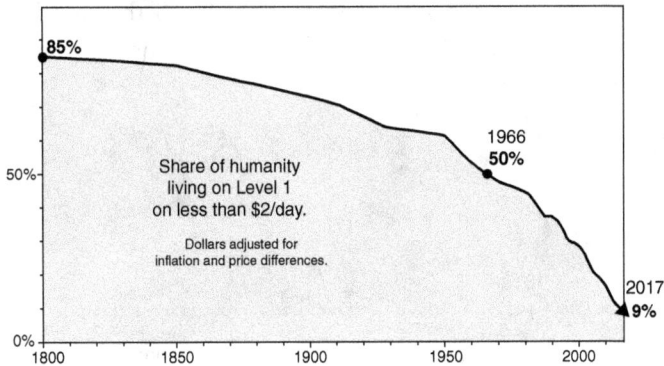

Figure 4.3 Graph showing the evolution of extreme poverty since 1800

Source: H. Rosling, O. Rosling, and A. Rosling Rönnlund (2018).[86]

Note: Extreme poverty (defined as living on less than $2 a day), has fallen steadily across the globe: while it represented 85% of the world's population in 1800 and still 50% in 1966, this rate was down to just 9% in 2017.

What's more, science has enabled us to make dazzling progress in medicine, increasing our average life expectancy from 31 to 72 years over the same period (see Figure 4.4).

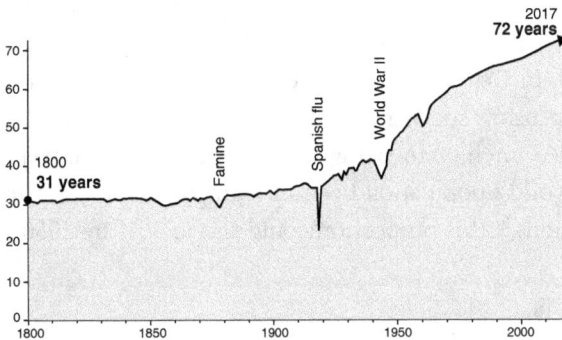

Figure 4.4 Graph showing the evolution of life expectancy since 1800

Source: H. Rosling, O. Rosling, and A. Rosling Rönnlund (2018).[87]

Note: Life expectancy has risen considerably worldwide. It has more than doubled since the early 20th century.

---

86 H. Rosling, O. Rosling, and A. Rosling Rönnlund (2018), *Factfulness: Ten Reasons We're Wrong About the World—and Why Things Are Better Than You Think*, translated by A. Rosling Rönnlund and O. Rosling (New York: Flatiron Books, 2018), p. 60.

87 H. Rosling, O. Rosling, and A. Rosling Rönnlund (2018), *Factfulness: Ten Reasons We're Wrong About the World—and Why Things Are Better Than You Think*, translated by A. Rosling Rönnlund and O. Rosling (New York: Flatiron Books, 2018), p. 62.

At the beginning of the 19th century, only 1% of the world's population lived in a democracy. Two centuries later, this proportion has risen to over 50% (see Figure 4.5).

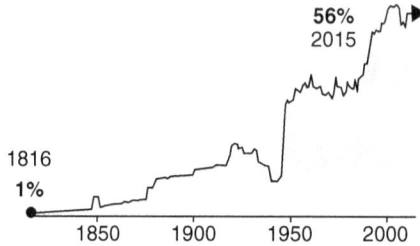

Figure 4.5 Graph showing the evolution of the proportion of humanity living in a democracy

Source: H. Rosling, O. Rosling, and A. Rosling Rönnlund (2018).[88]

Note: While the proportion of humanity living under a democratic regime was tiny in 1816 (1% of the population), it is now the majority.

Finally, over the same period, illiteracy has fallen, dropping from 90% of the world's population to less than 10%.[89]

In short, the world that existed when Adam Smith's societal doctrine dominated minds has now disappeared. At the same time, societal relations have evolved. In October 2024, there were over 5.5 billion Internet users, 90% of them using social networks.[90] The city has become the primary dwelling place for human beings, supplanting the countryside. Already, 56% of the world's population live in urban areas, and according to World Bank projections,[91] this proportion could rise to 70% by 2050.

*

88 H. Rosling, O. Rosling, and A. Rosling Rönnlund (2018), *Factfulness: Ten Reasons We're Wrong About the World—and Why Things Are Better Than You Think*, translated by A. Rosling Rönnlund and O. Rosling (New York: Flatiron Books, 2018), p. 69.

89 See "Literacy," *Our World in Data*. https://ourworldindata.org/literacy.

90 See B. Wong, "Top Social Media Statistics and Trends," https://www.forbes.com/advisor/business/social-media-statistics/.

91 See World Bank Group, "Urban Development," https://www.worldbank.org/en/topic/urbandevelopment/overview#1.

In conclusion, in the "Sapiens moment," the development of abstraction — the natural fruit of Bayesian cognitive inference—enabled a species with few assets to overcome natural constraints and gain access to considerable resources. It invented the symbol of willingness to cooperate, which facilitates exchanges with foreigners by inferring their intentions, or accesses nutritional resources through hunting, made possible by modeling the world. The "Greek moment" marks the use of reason as a tool for cooperation within the city, which faces an influx of individuals from diverse cultural backgrounds and seeks laws to explain the world instead of relying on sovereign rulers. Finally, in the modern era, capitalism established itself in Europe as a highly efficient system. Discoveries—such as coal, colonies, and China's integration into global trade—opened up new opportunities for access to resources. In response, new forms of cooperation emerged that enabled societies to fully exploit these resources and address the challenges of extended cooperation across both geographic and cultural boundaries. Thus, capitalism develops contracts and money, and posits a common value—interest—in response to morality and religions, which appear to be mutually immiscible. The social neutrality of the value "interest" enables cooperation across continents.

There have been many pivotal moments—whether for Homo sapiens, Greek, or capitalist—that have enabled societies to access more resources by generating new representations of the world. These moments all conformed to the rule of confidence in the selected model—simplicity, perceived "accuracy," and alignment with the motivation to access resources—and activated Bayesian cognitive inference mechanisms, such as abstraction in the case of Homo sapiens, or the search for governing laws in the Greek tradition.

Nevertheless, if Bayesian mechanisms are so effective, why do we now face such a catastrophic situation? Could they be deficient—and if so, under what conditions do those deficiencies arise?

This is the subject of the next chapter.

5

LIMITS TO OUR MECHANISMS FOR REPRESENTING THE WORLD

Bayesian cognitive inference, while a powerful mechanism for accessing resources and minimizing their overuse, can also give rise to three types of malfunctions. First, overconfidence in one's model: when an individual or organization places excessive confidence in their representation of the world, it limits their exploration and impairs their ability to update the model in response to environmental change, creating vulnerability. Second, poor assessment of coping capacities: failing to perceive or accurately evaluate available means of adjustment can result in an inability to respond effectively to challenges. Third, the nature of the signal itself: when signals are misleading or misinterpreted, they can distort situational understanding and lead to inappropriate decisions or misaligned policies.

In each of these cases, whether they apply to biological, economic, or societal entities, the risk of failure and endangerment is increased.

DOI: 10.4324/9781003638384-5

Overconfidence in the model

As we saw in Chapter 2, once (strong) confidence has been established in the model of world representation, exploitation takes precedence over exploration. A rat in a maze, for example, comes to believe that it knows exactly where the cheese is, and so gives up looking for other sources of food. This phenomenon can also be found among humans, whether individuals, corporations, or entire societies.

On an individual level, anger is an identified indicator of overconfidence. In their work on the categorization of emotions, Jennifer Dunn and Maurice Schweitzer[1] point out that although anger, sadness, and guilt all have a negative valence, the specificity of anger is that it is associated with the belief that we have control over things or people.[2] Thus, a world in which there is a high degree of confidence in models of understanding the world, which provides a sense of control, is also a world in which anger toward others can thrive.

This attitude of overconfidence can also be found at the corporate level, as shown by the example of ExxonMobil. In the 1990s, it was one of the most successful corporations in its sector. Its reputation was built on exceptional industrial expertise, and its contracts were considered industry benchmarks. What's more, its view of the world was so authoritative, particularly with regard to the geopolitical dynamics essential to its business, that it provided information to intelligence services. Armed with this confidence in its model, the company saw no need to explore other sources of information. This attitude was reflected in that of its CEO, who required journalists to pass a competency test before any meeting with him.[3]

---

1 J. Dunn and M. Schweitzer (2005), "Feeling and Believing: The Influence of Emotion on Trust," *Journal of Personality and Social Psychology* 88 (5): 736–748:

> In this work, we consider distinctions among emotions according to the secondary appraisal of control. For example, the emotions of anger, sadness, and guilt are all negative in valence, but they differ with respect to the appraisal of control. Anger is characterized by high other-person control, sadness by high situational control, and guilt by high personal control.

2 Whereas in the case of sadness, control is exercised over the situation, in the case of guilt, control is exercised over oneself.

3 S. Coll (2013), *Private Empire: ExxonMobil and American Power* (New York: The Penguin Press).

This approach illustrates an operating strategy taken to the extreme, and one that proved successful, as ExxonMobil became one of the world's largest market capitalizations. However, this strategy proved problematic from the 2010s onwards, when the issue of climate change took on increasing importance, bringing with it a complex and disruptive mix of new regulations and pressure from public opinion and investors. ExxonMobil, ill-prepared for this new context, saw its share price plummet. It also had to contend with stock market underperformance and massive asset write-downs.[4] The optimization strategy that had ensured the company's success in a stable environment had become a handicap in a world marked by increasing entropy and rapid transformation (see Figure 5.1).

Figure 5.1 Graph: ExxonMobil versus S&P 500

Source: Author.

Note: ExxonMobil (represented by the black curve) outperformed the S&P 500 (gray curve) in the 2000s. However, this dynamic reversed from 2015, coinciding with COP21, which for the first time marked an agreement between all the world's states to limit global warming.

Other examples of overconfidence can be found in states' representations of the world. Totalitarian regimes, for example, illustrate this phenomenon by exploiting an excessive demand for consistency in their models of representation, as Hannah Arendt points out.[5] These systems impose a rigid, monolithic worldview which, beyond its unacceptable

---

4 Bloomberg (2020), "Exxon Faces Historic Write-Down After Energy Markets Implode," November 30.

5 H. Arendt (1951), *The Origins of Totalitarianism* (New York: Harcourt, Brace & Company):

moral dimension, prevents any questioning or exploration of alternative perspectives.[6]

Ultimately, overconfidence in a model of world representation is a cornerstone for our understanding of inaction on climate issues.

Poorly assessed adaptability

Jared Diamond wonders why large animals (megafauna) have disappeared in Australia and New Guinea, but not Africa:[7]

> All of those Australian/New Guinean giants (the so-called megafauna) disappeared after the arrival of humans [...] In contrast, most big mammals of Africa and Eurasia survived into modern times, because they had coevolved with protohumans for hundreds of thousands or millions of years. They thereby enjoyed ample time to evolve a fear of humans, as our ancestors' initially poor hunting skills slowly improved. The dodo, moas, and perhaps the giants of Australia/New Guinea had the misfortune suddenly to be confronted, without any evolutionary preparation, by invading modern humans possessing fully developed hunting skills.

These animals disappeared because they lacked time to adapt to the sudden arrival of *Homo sapiens*—who were formidable hunters. This phenomenon highlights a contemporary paradox: today, humanity is in mortal peril because of its failure to adapt quickly enough to the environmental upheavals it has caused.

Like individuals and societies, companies must adapt to environmental changes driven by shifts in markets and consumption patterns. The

---

Only the mob and the elite can be attracted by the momentum of totalitarianism [...] What convinces masses are not facts, and not even invented facts, but only the consistency of the system of which they are presumably part. [...] Totalitarian propaganda thrives on this escape from reality into fiction, from coincidence into consistency. [...] their longing for fiction has some connection with those capacities of the human mind whose structural consistency is superior to mere occurrence. (p. 816)

6   See K. Popper (1945), *The Open Society and Its Enemies* (London: Routledge).
7   J. Diamond (1997), *Guns, Germs, and Steel: The Fates of Human Societies* (New York: W. W. Norton & Co, 1997), Kindle Edition, p. 56.

example of Alcatel illustrates the challenges and risks associated with such adaptation.

In the 1950s, Alcatel[8] was a flagship of French industry, with a diversified business portfolio (heavy industry, media, etc.) and a strategy that centered around its pivotal role in French society. At that time, the company operated in a low-entropy environment, characterized by a single profile of interlocutors, stable sales (long-term industrial projects), and low technological evolution.

However, in the 1990s, Alcatel—then the largest company in the CAC 40 index by market capitalization—made a strategic pivot, choosing to focus exclusively on telecommunications, and in particular, mobile phones. This repositioning involved withdrawing from other business lines and adopting a "fabless" business model by outsourcing manufacturing. The decision was made in a radically different context, one marked by high entropy, driven by at least four factors. First, globalization—Alcatel's customer base had become globally dispersed, with highly diverse needs and profiles. Second, rapid technological change—product life cycles had shortened considerably, demanding continuous innovation. Third, intensified competition—agile Californian start-ups, naturally oriented toward exploration, boasted younger workforces and more attractive compensation structures. Fourth, risky specialization—by concentrating on a single line of business, Alcatel increased its vulnerability to errors and market fluctuations, without the buffer of diversification.

The company, which had previously thrived in a relatively stable, low-entropy environment with a resilient organizational structure, was now struggling to adjust to the rising uncertainty and agility required by its new context. This difficulty persisted, despite the company's highly experienced management teams, who had proven track records in other sectors. In the 2000s, Alcatel quickly ran into serious difficulties, particularly with the bursting of the internet bubble, and had to be bought out by Nokia.

Similarly, in the 2010s, Fiat adopted a strategy centered on production efficiency, which naturally resulted in limited investment in green innovations such as hybrid and electric vehicles. This orientation reflected a desire to maximize short-term profitability while failing to take account

---

8   This example is not intended as a defense of conglomerates, but as an illustration of the need to ensure that a company's organization matches its environment.

of potential market developments and the regulatory requirements linked to the ecological transition. This choice proved problematic when the Dieselgate scandal broke. The European Commission then introduced ambitious new regulations on green vehicles, with very tight application deadlines. Fiat, which had not prepared for this transition, was faced with extremely high adjustment costs, as it had to catch up quickly on its technological lag by urgently accessing hybrid or electric engine technology. Faced with the scale of the challenge, Fiat, a century-old company, had to be put up for sale, and ultimately merged with Peugeot, giving birth to the Stellantis group.

The challenge of adaptation—and its constraints—can be insightfully compared to option management:[9] the goal of the options trader is to make their position as closely aligned as possible to fluctuations of the underlying share price.[10]

Let's take the concrete case of an options trader—the modern Eka—who has sold ten call options, with a strike price of 100 and a maturity date on D-Day. She receives an initial premium for these options. On the day of maturity (D-Day), the situation is as follows: if the stock is worth more than 100, Dvi, the option buyer, will exercise the option and request the delivery of ten shares, and pay the strike price[11]). Eka must therefore deliver these shares and must already hold them. If, however, the share price is below 100, Dvi has no reason to exercise the option, and Eka has no reason to hold the shares. In principle, the situation appears straightforward.

During the life of the option, Eka continuously adjusts the number of shares she holds. That number depends on the likelihood that the stock price will exceed the strike price of 100 at maturity, and obviously this probability is influenced by fluctuations in the share price. This leads to a dynamic

---

9 J. Hull (2018), *Options, Futures, and Other Derivatives*, 10th ed. (Boston: Pearson).

10 Over a century ago, Louis Bachelier (1900, "Théorie de la Spéculation," *Annales Scientifiques de l'ENS*, 3rd series, 7: 21–86)) described markets as following a Brownian, or random, process. Neoliberalism later reinforced the belief in market efficiency, suggesting that traders need not infer underlying rules (given the randomness of price movements) or question the reliability of signals (assuming efficient markets). Option management thus becomes an exercise in continually adjusting positions in response to price fluctuations.

11 If the share is worth 105, for example, Dvi will activate her right to buy (*call*) the share at 100, in return for payment of 100 and a gain of five (less the premium paid initially).

strategy characterized by continual adaptation to market conditions—an ongoing process of adjustment to a changing environment.

Let us consider Eka's position on the eve of expiration (D-1), when the stock price stands at precisely 100, and the market is scheduled to close at 4:00 p.m. the following day. Theoretically, Eka holds five shares, as the probability of the option expiring above or below the strike price is equal. She must therefore decide whether to increase her position in anticipation of delivering ten shares, or to sell the shares she currently holds. This decision will depend on how the share price evolves over the course of the next day.

If, on the following day (D-Day) at 3:00 p.m., the share price remains at 100, Eka faces the same decision—but now under greater time pressure: she has only one hour left to either buy or sell five shares.

If the price rises to 103, she purchases three additional shares, as the probability of the option expiring above 100 increases. Conversely, if the price suddenly drops to 99, she must sell four shares.[12] In other words, her vulnerability to price fluctuations—and the urgency of her adjustments—increase significantly as expiration approaches.[13]

If, at this point, Eka's purchase of the first two shares reduces market liquidity and pushes the price from 103 to 105, any subsequent purchases will be even more expensive. Her own actions have altered the environment, thereby increasing her adjustment cost. Furthermore, if the share price opens at 110 on D-Day following positive news announced overnight, she must immediately acquire four shares at this higher price.

In short, Eka is continually exposed to fluctuations in her environment, as reflected in changes to the market price of the underlying asset. The magnitude of these adjustments imposes significant costs, which can be exacerbated by sudden jumps in the stock price.

Options theory thus illustrates the risks faced by a company—or by society as a whole—when operating under a logic of exploitation. Pursuing efficiency alone resembles a form of temporal arbitrage, akin to selling

---

12 This is based on the estimate that at 99, the probability of exceeding the exercise price is only 40%, and that it is therefore only necessary to hold four shares, rather than the eight that were necessary when the share price was 103.

13 This sensitivity is linked to positioning (close to the strike price) and time (close to maturity). All other things being equal, the same change in share price occurring at option initiation would have had a limited impact.

options: an initial premium is gained, but it comes with deferred adaptation risk. This risk can translate into significant future costs, especially when decisions must be made under tight time constraints or in high-entropy environments.

ExxonMobil and Fiat had adopted primarily exploitation-based operating strategies, while Alcatel pursued an adaptation-focused approach. Despite these differing strategies, all three companies faced significant challenges, and some failed to adjust adequately in response to environmental changes. Alcatel and Fiat, in particular, were ultimately unable to avoid extinction.

These types of adjustments also reflect a core challenge posed by climate change, which demands large-scale adaptation within short time frames and under conditions of high entropy. This combination challenges the often-assumed confidence in society's capacity to adapt smoothly to emerging environmental constraints.

Misleading signals

It is reasonable to assume that investors' brains, when interpreting stock price signals, adjust their internal representations of the world—much like the bird in Roger Shepard's example, which narrows its cognitive focus when it sees a caterpillar, as we saw in Chapter 2.

This perspective lends itself particularly well to understanding financial bubbles, which can be interpreted as the emergence of a new explanatory model of the world—a widespread sense that "the world has changed"[14]—coupled with signals of asset appreciation, such as rising stock prices. These periods are typically characterized by high trading volumes, shortened memory spans, a sense of novelty, and relatively low volatility, all of which reinforce investor confidence.[15] While it is not the sole explanation, Bayesian cognitive inference offers a complementary framework for understanding these features, shedding additional light on how market participants update their beliefs and behaviors during bubble formation.

---

14 J. K. Galbraith (1990), *A Short History of Financial Euphoria: Financial Genius Is Before the Fall* (New York: Whittle Books).

15 P. Cauwels, G. Smilyanov, and D. Sornette (2017), "Can We Use Volatility to Diagnose Financial Bubbles? Lessons from 40 Historical Bubbles," *Swiss Finance Institute Research Paper Series* nos. 17–27.

Clearly, every financial bubble involves a significant appreciation in the value of an asset. Much like a bird evaluating a caterpillar, the trader adopts a restricted psychological space to process new, high-salience information. Recent signals perceived as critical take center stage, while prior knowledge or experience is relegated to the background (see Figure 5.2).

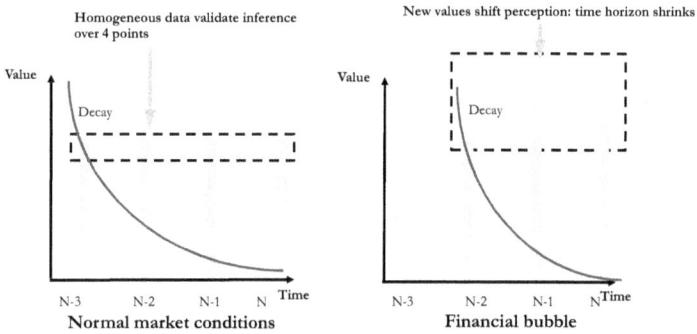

Figure 5.2 Graph of the impact of valuation on an attention space

Source: Author.

Note: Appreciating the value of an asset can create a "psychological space" similar to that of a bird faced with a caterpillar: its attention focuses on recent signals, which are perceived as having a high "nutritional" value, while seeking to confirm this perception with other positive signals.

Furthermore, trading volumes tend to be high during financial bubbles, as demonstrated by Harrison Hong and Jeremy Stein in their analysis of the dotcom bubble.[16] The increased velocity of market signals likely reduces the time interval between observations, which in turn may accelerate the natural phenomenon of exponential forgetting (see Figure 5.3).[17]

---

16 H. Hong and J. Stein (2007), "Disagreement and the Stock Market," *Journal of Economic Perspectives* 21 (2): 109–128. The authors point out that the monthly turnover (ratio of volume traded to total number of shares) of Internet companies was particularly high before the February 2000 peak. In 12 of the 24 months preceding this peak, they exceeded 50%, even peaking at 101% in 1998. By comparison, these same rotations on companies outside this sector were between 10 and 15% over the same period, with a single peak of 20%. A similar observation had already been made by John Kenneth Galbraith in the run-up to the 1929 crisis, highlighting the link between high volumes and the dynamics of financial bubbles (J.K. Galbraith (1979), *The Great Crash 1929*, 50th Anniversary Edition (Boston: Houghton Mifflin Company)).

17 This approach would also provide an explanation for the phenomenon observed by Maurice Allais of exponential forgetting in cases of hyperinflation (see in

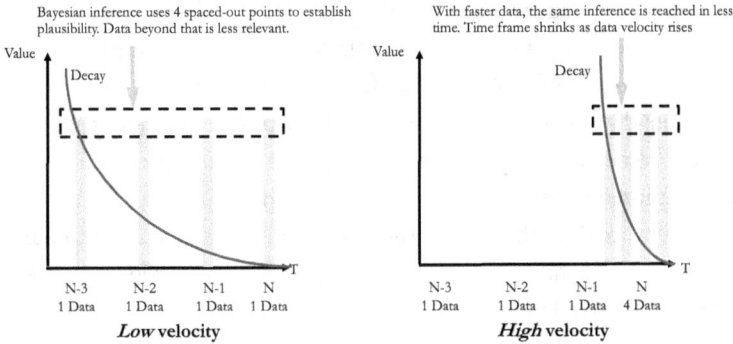

Figure 5.3 Graph of the impact of signal velocity on the time horizon

Source: Author.

Note: The velocity of exchanges also translates into a signal that accelerates its frequency of dissemination, with each transaction generating new information on that exchange. This multiplication of signals could lead to a reduction in memory depth by focusing attention on recent information, to the detriment of older data.[18]

Financial bubbles are often preceded by reduced asset volatility, comparable to a "calm before the storm." After studying 40 financial bubbles, Didier Sornette, Peter Cauwels, and Georgi Smilyanov[19] found this pattern in nearly two-thirds of cases. Lower volatility reinforces the agent's confidence in their model, as regular observations appear to confirm prior

---

particular E. Barthalon (2014), *Uncertainty, Expectations and Financial Instability: Reviving Allais's Lost Theory of Psychological Time* (New York: Columbia University Press)). This is another case of the velocity of asset valuation signals, although it occurs without wealth creation or low volatility, two other characteristics of financial bubbles. Financial bubbles and hyperinflation, through signal velocity, would create the conditions for exponential oblivion.

18 As may have been intuited by Roger Shepard (R. Shepard (1987), "Toward a Universal Law of Generalization for Psychological Science," *Science New Series* 237 (4820) (Sept. 11):

In a one-dimensional space, the distances must satisfy the following very strong additivity condition: For each subset of three points, the distance between the two most widely separated points equals the sum of the distances of those two points to the third point that lies between them.

19 P. Cauwels, G. Smilyanov, and D. Sornette (2017), "Can We Use Volatility to Diagnose Financial Bubbles? Lessons from 40 Historical Bubbles," *Swiss Finance Institute Research Paper Series*, nos. 17–27.

expectations. The resulting low level of surprise further consolidates this confidence, promoting a strategy of exploitation over exploration.

To extend the analogy of the bird: finding caterpillars in the same location day after day reshapes its model of the world, convincing it that the process will reliably recur. Its attention narrows to this space, and its inclination to explore elsewhere diminishes accordingly. Similarly, this consensus signal reinforces confidence in the financial bubble narrative, according to which the world has changed—and this is now regarded as an established fact by all (see Figure 5.4).

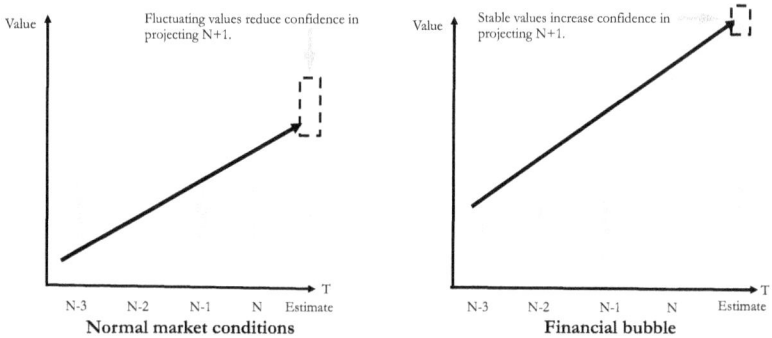

Figure 5.4 Graph of the impact of volatility on confidence

Source: Author.

Note: The low volatility observed during financial bubbles reinforces confidence in the perceived accuracy of the new representation of the world. It suggests a broad consensus among market participants regarding asset valuation, thereby implicitly validating the emerging model. Conversely, high volatility would signal substantial disagreement, casting doubt on the collective acceptance of the model's supposed "accuracy."

In short, a financial bubble can be interpreted as the result of a combination of factors which, alongside other explanations, align with the logic of Bayesian cognitive inference (see Figure 5.5).

This mindset is further reinforced by a signal with distinct characteristics: a bullish trend (which strengthens motivation and the perception of novelty), low volatility (interpreted as collective consensus around the new reality), and high signal velocity (which narrows the attention span, reinforcing the novelty narrative).

Moreover, because the signal is public—transmitted through the stock market—it contributes to widespread acceptance of the model. Rising

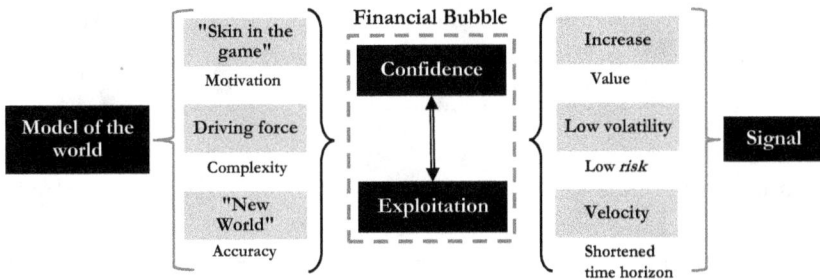

Figure 5.5 Graph of the forces at play in a financial bubble

Source: Author.

Note: A financial bubble can be understood as a situation of overconfidence in a particular model of world representation, reinforced by a specific type of signal. This overconfidence is supported by a triptych of cognitive features: motivation (the promoters of the bubble are also its participants), simplicity (a single factor is seen as sufficient to explain the situation), and exactitude (the belief in a "new world" that leaves no room for criticism).

prices signal a shift to the broader economy; low volatility reflects collective endorsement; and high velocity draws collective attention to the emerging paradigm. In this way, the signal plays a dual role: it strengthens confidence in the model and spreads this representation across society. At the same time, the authority displayed by key actors within the bubble contributes to the narrative's diffusion and social legitimacy.

As a result, these various factors interact to compress time horizons—both past and future—toward an intensified focus on the present. The past is obscured by the velocity of the signals, which accelerates forgetting, while the future is neglected due to ongoing value appreciation. This appreciation, coupled with the narrative of a transformative moment (such as the Internet revolution of the 2000s) and reinforced by low volatility, encourages a logic of exploitation. The outcome is a convergence of short-termism, anchoring attention in the immediate present.

Ultimately, financial bubbles offer a large-scale illustration of how the human brain processes signals in accordance with the principles of Bayesian cognitive inference. They underscore the decisive role that the nature of signals plays in shaping our representations of the world. In some cases, the form of the signal may lead us to perceive a situation as highly favorable and low risk, when in fact it is quite the opposite. More critically, the combination of such signals with overconfidence in our internal models of the world creates conditions that are ripe for a bubble—and with it, the risk of entrapment that can culminate in a burst.

*

In conclusion, while the Bayesian cognitive inference system is generally effective, it remains vulnerable to dysfunction. Such dysfunctions can stem from overconfidence in a particular model of world representation, from a misjudgment of available adjustment mechanisms, or from the misleading nature of the signal itself—each of which may lead to a distorted perception of the underlying "reality" of a situation.

These cognitive limits have shaped key episodes in human history, notably through the formation of societal bubbles.

This is the subject of the next chapter.

6

FORMATION OF SOCIETAL BUBBLES: REREADING HUMAN HISTORY

As we have seen with the *Homo sapiens*, Greek, and capitalist examples, societies create or select representations of the world that provide access to resources. However, the very success of these models can give rise to overconfidence in them.

What if the combination of these two phenomena produced "societal bubbles"? Like financial bubbles? What if, governed by their own logic and fueled by their success, these phenomena have shaped a way of relating to the world that has grown overconfident—and therefore increasingly rigid?

DOI: 10.4324/9781003638384-6

First societal bubble: Agriculture and modern science
Agriculture

Around 8,500 B.C., agriculture made its appearance: the cultivation of wheat developed in the Fertile Crescent.[1] This revolution transformed access to essential resources and brought relative opulence to part of humanity,[2] thanks in particular to the fact that wheat can be preserved. This is a crucial point, as the storing of food gives human beings stable access to food resources, thus guaranteeing a constant supply of nutrients to their brains.[3] What's more, the reduction in the number of journeys required to find

---

1 J. Diamond (1997), *Guns, Germs, and Steel: The Fates of Human Societies* (New York: W. W. Norton & Co.):

> [...] the earliest known cultivated emmer wheat comes from the Fertile Crescent around 8500 B.C. Soon thereafter, the crop appears progressively farther west, reaching Greece around 6500 B.C. and Germany around 5000 B.C. Those dates suggest domestication of emmer wheat in the Fertile Crescent, a conclusion supported by the fact that ancestral wild emmer wheat is confined to the area extending from Israel to western Iran and Turkey. (Kindle Edition, p. 110)

2 As Jared Diamond observes (J. Diamond (1997), *Guns, Germs, and Steel: The Fates of Human Societies* (New York: W. W. Norton & Co.)), this transition was not uniform, nor were the consequences:

> Until the end of the last Ice Age, around 11,000 B.C., all peoples on all continents were still hunter-gatherers. Different rates of development on different continents, from 11,000 B.C. to A.D. 1500, were what led to the technological and political inequalities of A.D. 1500. [...] While Aboriginal Australians and many Native Americans remained hunter-gatherers, most of Eurasia and much of the Americas and sub-Saharan Africa gradually developed agriculture, herding, metallurgy, and complex political organizations. (Kindle Edition, p. 8)

3 And this stability also allows for unequal societies, as Philippe Descola points out (P. Descola (2024), *Avec les Chasseurs-cueilleurs* (Paris: Bayard)):

> What counts in the accumulation of wealth is not so much subsistence techniques as the ability to store (Alain Testart is credited with drawing attention to storage in extraction economies, (A. Testart (1982), *Les Chasseurs-cueilleurs ou l'Origine des Inégalités*, Paris, Société d'Ethnologie). Storage eventually makes it possible to establish and maintain differences in social status. [...] This storage offered stability, permanence in the habitat and the possibility of developing unequal social structures based on a stable supply. (Kindle Edition, p. 46; my translation)

food, and the hazards that accompany them, encourages an increase in births.[4]

Then, at around the same time, rice cultivation emerges. These two resources each provide a natural example of social adaptability depending on their accessibility, as demonstrated by Thomas Talhelm:[5]

> The rice theory of culture is the idea that rice farming societies developed into more interdependent, tight cultures in response to the demands of the plant. [...] Paddy rice required twice as much labor per hectare as wheat farming. [...] Paddy rice also depended on irrigation systems to flood and drain the fields. Once farmers controlled water, they now had to coordinate how much water each farmer got, when to flood their fields, and how to divide the labor for repairing the canals.

And China offers a very interesting natural opportunity to observe the impact of wheat and rice on social construction, as shown by a study of the personality traits of students from regions growing either one or the other:[6]

> [...] students who grew up in rice-farming parts of China had more markers of interdependent culture than students who grew up in wheat-farming areas [...] students from wheat regions self-inflated;

---

4   J. Diamond (1997), *Guns, Germs, and Steel: The Fates of Human Societies* (New York: W. W. Norton & Co.):

> A hunter-gatherer mother who is shifting camp can carry only one child, along with her few possessions. She cannot afford to bear her next child until the previous toddler can walk fast enough to keep up with the tribe and not hold it back. [...] By contrast, sedentary people, unconstrained by problems of carrying young children on treks, can bear and raise as many children as they can feed. The birth interval for many farm peoples is around two years, half that of hunter-gatherers. (Kindle Edition, p. 100)

5   T. Talhelm (2022), "The Rice Theory of Culture," *Online Readings in Psychology and Culture* 4 (1): 1–18.
6   T. Talhelm (2022), "The Rice Theory of Culture," *Online Readings in Psychology and Culture* 4 (1): 1–18:

> China provides fertile ground for testing the rice theory because it is a large, relatively homogenous country that has farmed both rice and wheat for thousands of years. [...] China, the population is over 90% ethnic Han Chinese with a single government. Han China also shares a language family and religious history.

> students from rice regions did not [...] students from rice prov-
> inces of China thought more holistically than students from wheat
> provinces—even within the same university.

This also leads to different levels of social flexibility:[7] "Rice-farming societies tend to have less flexible, less mobile relationships. In contrast, wheat-farming and herding societies have more flexible relationships."

In other words, agricultural societies are socially structured according to the nature of the resource, supporting the hypothesis[8] that they function like living organisms.

Finally, the domestication of plants and animals also overturned existing representations of the world, placing man on an equal footing with the gods, as Marcel Hénaff explains:[9]

> It is a tremendous upheaval in the relationship between humans and the world around them, in that it represents a very new power acquired over life and, by the same token, over death. This power can be described as immense, in that it radically changes our relationship to the world as a whole [...]. This power [...] appears to them as almost stolen from the divinities. (My translation)

This paradigm shift is based on several new elements, but above all, sacrifice:[10]

> [...] what appeared to us as new dimensions in pastoralist-farmer societies: the emergence of ancestrality, the hierarchical structure of the world and social order, the primacy of filiation, the importance of debt, the

---

7 T. Talhelm (2022), "The Rice Theory of Culture," *Online Readings in Psychology and Culture* 4 (1): 1–18. This also leads to a different relationship to strangers:

> [...] people from rice regions of China treat strangers more harshly than people from wheat areas [...]. Rather being nicer or more pro-social, people from rice regions were more generous to friends but harsher toward strangers. In other words, relationships mattered more in rice areas than wheat areas.

8 And that cooperation or competition depends on the ability (or lack of it) to achieve the desired state alone, with rice in this case requiring more mutual aid than wheat. Thomas Talhelm shows, however, that growing rice also leads to competition, albeit more covert.

9 M. Hénaff (2008), "Repenser le Sacrifice: Nouvelles Approches Anthropologiques," *Archivio di Filosofia* 76(1/2) Il Sacrificio.

10 M. Hénaff (2008), "Repenser le Sacrifice: Nouvelles Approches Anthropologiques," *Archivio di Filosofia* 76(1/2) Il Sacrificio.

advent of an ontology dominated by analogism. In this agro-pastoral universe, the practice of sacrifice is the major institution. (My translation)

On this precise point, Marcel Hénaff[11] points out that when a farmer sacrifices some of their livestock in the hope of better conditions for the rest, their relationship with the world takes on a vertical dimension:

Instead of an egalitarian relationship of trust with the spirits of the forest, a relationship of dependence with the spirits of the world above takes over [...] the transmission of what has been acquired prevails over the encounter with the unexpected. (My translation)

Verticality, understood as the establishment of a hierarchical relationship, plays a central role in the new agro-pastoralist societies.[12] We may hypothesize that Bayesian cognitive inference mechanisms are at work here too. Human beings seem to have been motivated above all by the need to respond to their anxiety about the possible disappearance of food supplies, dreading an unpredictability that had, until then, been better tolerated.

In these societies, a new social order emerges, which also reinforces the desire to dominate other species.[13] There is also a new belief in the possibility of dialogue with the holders of the invisible forces that influence

---

11 M. Hénaff (2008), "Repenser le Sacrifice: Nouvelles Approches Anthropologiques," *Archivio di Filosofia* 76(1/2) Il Sacrificio.

12 M. Hénaff (2008), "Repenser le Sacrifice: Nouvelles Approches Anthropologiques," *Archivio di Filosofia* 76(1/2) Il Sacrificio.

13 As pointed out by Roberte Hamayon, who observed the change in representations of the world that took place during the transition from hunting to reindeer herding in Siberia (R. Hamayon (1990), *La Chasse à l'Âme: Esquisse d'une Théorie du Chamanisme Sibérien*, Société d'Ethnologie (Nanterre: Société d'Ethnologie)) quoted by Marcel Hénaff (M. Hénaff (2010), *The Price of Truth: Gift, Money, and Philosophy*, translated by J-L. Morhange (Stanford, CA: Stanford University Press)), taking up the example:

Then the conception of the supernatural as bestower of subsistence is overturned, and its status as the equal Order (the spirit of the game who is treated as a partner) becomes that of the superior Same (that is, the ancestors, from whom herds and pasture are inherited and, above them, the founder of the ethnic group. At the same time, the world order is overturned and shifts from a horizontal to a vertical organization. (p. 170)

And furthermore:

The supernatural becomes vertical and relationships with it become hierarchical; humankind no longer treats it as a partner; humans feel that their commitments to it are no longer based on exchange on an equal footing, but on a relationship of dependency. (pp. 170–171)

the harvest, through using sacrifice[14] to gain their favor. Indeed, sacrifice allows, on the one hand, the repayment of part of the debt associated with the monopolization of forces that control nature and, on the other hand, sends a signal of cooperation to those who hold these forces; a gift that calls for a counter-gift, in the form of rain or fodder for the buffalo, and thus additional resources. This model of world representation may also be the result of natural selection; strong confidence in the model leads to its wide-spread application and even greater access to resources, further reinforcing the success of the agro-pastoralists.[15]

In the absence of direct evidence, the impact of agriculture on our ances-tors' representation of the world can be assessed through the study of their rock paintings. The transition is clearly evident when comparing their rep-resentations of the world before and after this shift. As Philippe Grosos[16] shows, animals occupied a central place in Paleolithic art:

> [...] recent Paleolithic art [...] shows very clearly that [...] the dominant motif is that of the animal. [...] the bestiary of the Chauvet-Pont d'Arc cave in the Ardèche region [...] 430 representations, of which only one is likely to refer to a creature other than an exclusively animal one. (My translation)

---

14 As Marcel Hénaff notes, sacrifice, like ancestrality, only appears in agro-pastoralist societies (M. Hénaff (2008), "Repenser le Sacrifice: Nouvelles Approches Anthropologiques," *Archivio di Filosofia* 76(1/2) Il Sacrificio).

15 Indeed, from a Darwinian perspective of natural selection, belief in the control of invisible forces reinforces confidence in the model, encouraging continued efforts to apply it, thus optimizing access to available resources. In this precise context, overconfidence could play an adaptive role in promoting success: By consolidating commitment to the model, overconfidence maximizes the benefits provided.

16 Philippe Grosos' hypothesis (P. Grosos (2023), *La Philosophie au Risque de la Préhistoire* (Paris: Les Éditions du Cerf)) that Greek idealism came very late in the history of the domestication of nature is also interesting. It was not the starting point for a new representation of the world, but rather its formalization. With Greek philosophy, a discourse emerges in which man is perceived as the bearer of eternal truths, and the philosopher's job is to bring them to consciousness. This Greek moment is part of a broader trajectory, linking the invention of abstraction by *Homo sapiens* to the inven-tion of agriculture, which established a dialogue with the gods. Now endowed with access to eternal truths, humanity reached a new threshold of confidence in its models of world representation, consolidating a vision in which the human being occupies a central place in the universe and in our understanding of it.

Humans occupied a relatively marginal place compared to the animal world in the art of that time.[17] When humans are represented, they are generally female:[18]

> Metonymic, these representations of humans are also metonymic in terms of the representation of the sexes, [as they are] most often female. In the Cussac cave, for example, [...] only 5 out of 13 are male (which is already quite exceptional). (My translation)

The Neolithic period saw a complete reversal in artistic representations. The animal, once central, gradually gave way to the human. From then on, humans were no longer feminine, but masculine and warlike. They embodied values of domination, conquest, and control, in line with the new social and economic structures of agro-pastoral societies. This transformation reflects a profound change in the way humanity perceives itself and interacts with the world:[19]

> [...] a profound change in representations compared to what occurred during the Late Paleolithic [...] The number, and above all the quality, of human figures has changed completely. Where human figures were quantitatively in the minority and qualitatively marginalized in relation to animal figures, they are now not only slightly in the majority, but above all symbolically dominant. This symbolism is even highly gendered, since 2,978 of the 3,115 individuals represented are men, compared with just 137 women. [...] this art gives pride of place to archers, all of whom are male [...] this has consequences for the representation of the bestiary [...] it also shows 14% of wounded or dead animals. (My translation)

---

17 P. Grosos (2023), *La Philosophie au Risque de la Préhistoire* (Paris: Les Éditions du Cerf): "[...] Paleolithic art is not far from representing only animal diversity, to the point of almost never clearly showing humans themselves." (Kindle Edition, p. 46; my translation).

18 P. Grosos (2023), *La Philosophie au Risque de la Préhistoire* (Paris: Les Éditions du Cerf), Kindle Edition, p. 45.

19 P. Grosos (2023), *La Philosophie au Risque de la Préhistoire* (Paris: Les Éditions du Cerf), Kindle Edition, p. 51, referring to Lya Dams, who studied 7618 representations, including 3115 human figures and 2930 animals (L. Dams (1984), *Les Peintures Rupestres du Levant Espagnol* (Paris: Picard), p. 19.

Is a change in mental representations concomitant with a change in behavior? It's possible, but not necessarily generalizable. Jared Diamond's analysis of the war between the Maoris and Morioris in 1835 illustrates a possible link. Although these two peoples shared Polynesian roots, they followed distinct trajectories based on their respective access to the natural resources available in their environment. The Maoris, who had access to land suitable for agriculture, developed a warrior culture, stratified and organized around conquest and domination.[20] In contrast, the Morioris[21] remained hunter-gatherers, adopting a peaceful, technically rudimentary culture. When confrontation arose, it was violent, resulting in the massacre and enslavement of the Morioris.[22] This episode highlights how environmental and cultural changes, linked to access to resources, can influence behavior and mental representations, leading to profound divergences in social and political dynamics.

---

20 J. Diamond (1997), Guns, Germs, and Steel: The Fates of Human Societies (New York: W. W. Norton & Co.):

> Those Maori who remained in New Zealand increased in numbers until there were more than 100,000 of them. They developed locally dense populations chronically engaged in ferocious wars with neighboring populations. With the crop surpluses that they could grow and store, they fed craft specialists, chiefs, and part-time soldiers. They needed and developed varied tools for growing their crops, fighting, and making art. They erected elaborate ceremonial buildings and prodigious numbers of forts. (Kindle Edition, p. 59)

21 J. Diamond (1997), Guns, Germs, and Steel: The Fates of Human Societies (New York: W. W. Norton & Co.):

> With no other accessible islands to colonize, the Moriori had to remain in the Chathams, and to learn how to get along with each other. They did so by renouncing war, and they reduced potential conflicts from overpopulation by castrating some male infants. The result was a small, unwarlike population with simple technology and weapons, and without strong leadership or organization." (Kindle Edition, p. 59)

22 J. Diamond (1997), Guns, Germs, and Steel: The Fates of Human Societies (New York: W. W. Norton & Co.):

> Groups of Maori began to walk through Moriori settlements, announcing that the Moriori were now their slaves, and killing those who objected. An organized resistance by the Moriori could still then have defeated the Maori, who were outnumbered two to one. However, the Moriori had a tradition of resolving disputes peacefully. They decided in a council meeting not to fight back but to offer peace, friendship, and a division of resources. Before the Moriori could deliver that offer, the Maori attacked en masse. (Kindle Edition p. 56)

Ultimately, the emergence of agriculture marks a pivotal turning point in human history—one defined by an increasing control over natural resources. It also supports the hypothesis that societies function like living organisms. Social structures adapt to the characteristics of the dominant resource (as seen in wheat-based versus rice-based civilizations); access to those resources confers competitive advantages over other cultures (as in the case of the Maoris and Morioris); and belief systems are selected that contribute to the optimization of resource use—through practices such as sacrifice, the invocation of forces seen as controlling nature, and a cognitive distancing from the natural world that enables its domination.

Modern science

Modern science is part of this ongoing movement to develop tools that provide access to resources, enabling us to live. As the French philosopher Henri Bergson put it:[23]

> Our intelligence is the prolongation of our senses. Before we speculate we must live, and life demands that we make use of matter, either with our organs, which are natural tools, or with tools, properly so-called, which are artificial organs. Long before there was a philosophy and a science, the role of the intelligence was already that of manufacturing instruments and guiding the action of our body on surrounding bodies.

Science is an extension of this will to live, which leads to a desire to control matter:[24]

> Science has pushed this labor of the intelligence much further, but has not changed its direction. It aims above all at making us masters of matter. Even when science is speculating, it is still devoting its attention to acting, the value of scientific theories being gauged constantly by the solidity of the grip they give us upon reality.

---

23 H. Bergson (2007), *The Creative Mind: An Introduction to Metaphysics*, translation by M. Andison (Mineola, NY: Dover Publications), Kindle Edition, p. 25.

24 H. Bergson (2007), *The Creative Mind: An Introduction to Metaphysics*, translation by M. Andison (Mineola, NY: Dover Publications), Kindle Edition, pp. 25–26.

Modern science marked a fundamental acceleration in the history of mankind and a decisive shift toward certainty. With Galileo, a new relationship to the world was established, modifying the one the Greeks had established.[25] As Alexandre Koyré shows, the Tuscan scholar extended geometrization to nature and science,[26] introducing a framework in which natural phenomena could be measured, quantified, and viewed as governed by universal laws. This enabled man to dominate nature, rather than merely contemplating it:[27]

> Galileo Galilei's name is inextricably linked with the scientific revolution of the 16th century, one of the most profound, if not the most profound, revolutions in human thought since the discovery of the cosmos by Greek thought: a revolution that implied a radical intellectual "mutation," of which modern physical science is both the expression and the fruit [...]. Modern man seeks to dominate nature, whereas medieval or ancient man strove above all to contemplate it. (My translation)

This geometrization creates a profound rupture, calling into question the ancestral separation between Heaven and Earth.[28] This has several major

---

25 This continues the European adventure, since as François Julien points out (F. Julien (2022), *Moïse ou la Chine: Quand ne se Déploie pas l'Idée de Dieu* (Paris: Éditions de l'Observatoire/Humensis, 2022)): "Chinese civilization has promoted infinite knowledge, but not 'Science' as a demand for demonstrative, objective Truth [...]" (Kindle Edition, p. 63; my translation).

26 A. Koyré (1985), *Études d'Histoire de la Pensée Scientifique* (Paris: Gallimard): "These two characteristics can be summarized and expressed as follows: the mathematization (geometrization) of nature and, consequently, the mathematization (geometrization) of science," p. 170; my translation.

27 A. Koyré (1985), *Études d'Histoire de la Pensée Scientifique* (Paris: Gallimard), p. 166. And Alexandre Koyré underlines the break with Aristotle, whose physics rejected this same mathematization. Aristotle, in fact, believed that nature was essentially "qualitative and vague," and could not be reduced to mathematical exactitude. He saw such an approach not only as inadequate for grasping natural reality, but also potentially dangerous. In his view, the habit of thinking in precise, rigid terms risked leading to a vision disconnected from the complexity and qualitative richness of the natural world.

28 A. Koyré (1985), *Études d'Histoire de la Pensée Scientifique* (Paris: Gallimard):

> The dissolution of the Cosmos means the destruction of an idea: that of a world of finite structure, hierarchically ordered, a world qualitatively differentiated from the ontological point of view; it is replaced by that of an open, indefinite, even infinite Universe, unified and governed by the same universal laws [...]. The laws of Heaven and Earth are now fused together. (p. 170; my translation)

consequences. First, it puts an end to the idea of quality in nature, and to the search for truth through the senses. Abstract, mathematical reasoning now suffices.[29] Second, it breaks with the traditional conception of the cosmos as a static order, introducing a dynamic, mechanical vision of the universe.[30] Last but not least, modern science offers much more precise and reliable explanations of how the world "really" works. This intellectual advance paved the way for the appropriation of nature, a decisive step that was taken by René Descartes in his *Discourse on Method*:[31]

> But having no sooner acquired some general notions about physics [...] For these notions have made me see that it is possible to attain knowledge which is very useful in life, and that unlike the speculative philosophy that is taught in the schools, it can be turned into a practice by which, knowing the power and action of fire, water, air, stars, the heavens, and all the other bodies that are around us as distinctly as we know the different trades of our craftsmen, we could put them to all the uses for which they are suited and thus make ourselves as it were the masters and possessors of nature.

---

29 A. Koyré (1985), *Études d'Histoire de la Pensée Scientifique* (Paris: Gallimard):

> Galileo, like Descartes a little later [...] was obliged to do away with the notion of quality, to declare it subjective, to banish it from the realm of nature. This implies at the same time that he was obliged to do away with sense perception as the source of knowledge, and to declare that intellectual, even a priori, knowledge is our one and only means of apprehending the essence of reality. (p. 190; my translation)

30 A. Koyré (1985), *Études d'Histoire de la Pensée Scientifique* (Paris: Gallimard): "A place for everything and everything in its place: The concept of 'natural place' expresses this theoretical requirement of Aristotelian physics. The concept of 'natural place' is based on a purely static conception of order" (p. 174; my translation).

31 R. Descartes (2006), *A Discourse on the Method*, translated with an introduction and notes by I. MacLean (Oxford: Oxford World's Classics), p. 308. Another implication of his mechanistic worldview is the assumption that all problems can ultimately be decomposed into smaller, more manageable components: "The second was to divide all the difficulties under examination into as many parts as possible, and as many as were required to solve them in the best way" (p. 227).

This presents a significant challenge for modern science in conceptualizing complex systems, as noted by Philip W. Anderson (P. W. Anderson (1972), "More Is Different," *Science* 177 (4047): 393–396). This is particularly relevant in the context of climate change, which constitutes a system-level problem that cannot be adequately addressed at the local scale.

Coincidentally—though not entirely—[32]capitalism was simultaneously (re)developing legal property, weakening the social link:[33]

> Two major opposing systems of land appropriation have clashed in our history [...] At the origins of our law, and until the Revolution, there was a system of "simultaneous ownership" [...]Several owners worked side by side on the same land. None of them is the owner of the whole; [...] After the Revolution, a new form of appropriation emerged—one that had been long prepared for in theory and practice—based on the Roman model: exclusive ownership. (My translation)

Although it is not possible here to address all the links between capitalism, science, and democracy, this phenomenon can be interpreted from different angles. On the one hand, it reflects the rise of the bourgeoisie against the nobility, marking a gradual shift in power relations and economic influence. On the other hand, it can be seen as one of the effects of the growing individualism and erosion of social ties that are characteristic of capitalism, in that spaces that had previously been collective, such as

---

32 As Michel Serres points out (M. Serres (1995), *The Natural Contract*, translated by E. MacArthur and W. Paulson (Ann Arbor: University of Michigan Press)):

> Mastery and possession: There are the master words launched by Descartes at the dawn of the scientific and technological age, when our Western reason went off to conquer the universe. We dominate and appropriate it: Such is the shared philosophy underlying industrial enterprise as well as so-called disinterested science, which are indistinguishable in this respect [...] Our fundamental relationship with objects comes down to war and property. [...] Dominate, but also *possess*: The other fundamental relationship we have with the things of the world comes down to property rights. Descartes's master word amounts to the application of individual or collective property rights to scientific knowledge and technological intervention. (p. 32)

33 M-A. Patault (1989), *Introduction Historique au Droit des Biens* (Paris: Presses Universitaires de France). As Anne-Marie Patault explains, in Roman times, the juridical vision distinguished between material things that could be touched—such as trees, money, or fields—which were not distinct from property, and incorporeal things, which were governed by law. This vision faded in France with the franc regime, which introduced seizure; more specifically, "Having a right of possession means having the legitimate power to profit from it" (Kindle Edition, p. 21; my translation). And this power can be multiple: "men benefit jointly from the same land, each enjoying individually or collectively a different utility of the property" (Kindle Edition, p. 37; my translation).
In other words, the direct, individual relationship to Roman land contrasts with the multiple relationships to land use in the medieval world.

fields, forests, or meadows, cease to be places of social interaction and become private property. It is also conceivable that this evolution forms part of the broader aspirations for individual freedom driven by emerging democracies, where property becomes not only a fundamental right but also a symbol of autonomy and personal fulfillment.

Science and capitalism reinforce each other, driving profound societal transformation. Science provides an accurate and simple representation of the world, enabling rational understanding and increasing man's control over nature. At the same time, capitalism favors the effective possession of nature through technology, the generalization of individual private property, and increased access to resources. These include natural resources, including those from the colonies, and raw materials such as coal or the products of more intensive agriculture, but they also include human resources through the use of new coordination tools such as corporations, financial markets, or global trade networks (see Figure 6.1).

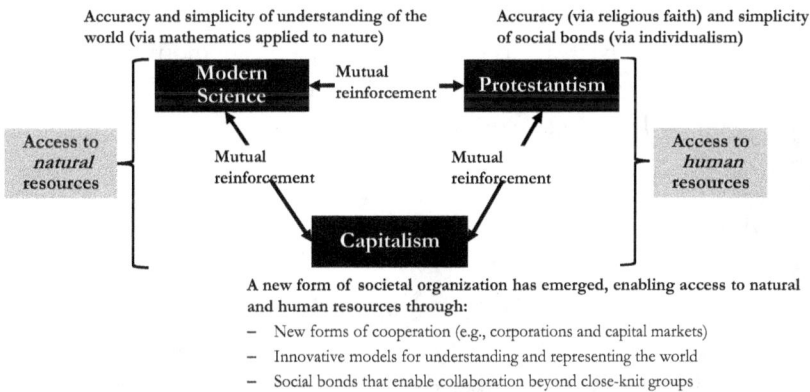

Figure 6.1 Ecosystem graph of modern science, capitalism, and Protestantism

Source: Author.

Note: Modern science responds to demands for high accuracy and reduced complexity, while at the same time providing increased access to natural resources. Capitalism, building on scientific advances, reinforces access to resources and strengthens belief in this new model of world representation. It draws on the mathematization of the world brought about by modern science, while shaping the concept of individual property. This innovation is echoed in the individualism promoted by Protestantism, which values autonomy and personal responsibility. Capitalism and modern science— these two worldviews—fit a world in perpetual motion. However, they also contribute to reducing the qualitative bonds both between humanity and nature, which was now perceived as an exploitable resource, and those between human beings, which were no longer based on relational but on contractual ties.

In return, modern science offers us a remarkable toolbox for improving the material conditions of humankind: health, food, access to knowledge, and so on. This evolution is accompanied by a growing overconfidence in the "veracity" of scientific models, which considerably reinforces the logic of control that was initiated with the advent of agriculture. This control finds a parallel in the appearance and generalization of the concept of private property, which is rooted in the emergence of individualism. Ownership becomes our economic foundation, redefining our relationships to land, resources, and even companies—which are now controlled by shareholders. The result is a world where everything is potentially knowable, controllable, and ownable, and where the spirit of exploitation reigns, at the risk of overconfidence.

Second societal bubble: Neoliberalism and the information society

As we saw in Chapter 2, overconfidence stems from the combination of a model perceived as accurate and simple, and motivation. These components are transformed under the influence of neoliberalism, here understood as the societal coordination provided primarily by financial markets.

The end of history

To better understand this evolution, let's look first at corporations. The emergence of the doctrine of profit maximization for shareholders[34] led to a reduction in the number of objectives pursued by corporations. In the 1960s, an American business leader generally had four or five objectives:[35] developing the company, producing quality goods, ensuring employee satisfaction, contributing to the development of the local communities in which the company operated, and, finally, satisfying shareholders. However, since the 1980s, with the rise of the doctrine

---

34 M. Friedman (1970), "The Social Responsibility of Business is to Increase Its Profits," *New York Times*, Sept. 13.

35 See L. Stout (2012), *The Shareholder Value Myth: How Putting Shareholders First Harms Investors, Corporations and the Public* (San Francisco: Berrett-Koehler Publishers).

of profit maximization for shareholders, this last objective has become predominant, often to the detriment of the others. Some even thought that this doctrinal model marked the "end of history"[36] in the analysis of economic life, since it was "exact" and therefore entirely reliable. This perception was reinforced, in the 1980s, by the emergence of executive compensation systems indexed to stock market prices. The facts speak for themselves: in 1984, equity-linked compensation accounted for none of the median compensation of S&P 500 executives; by 2001, it had risen to 66%.[37] This obviously created a powerful incentive to embrace the validity of the new model of coordination by financial markets. At the same time, the development of international trade—largely thanks to the container revolution, which dramatically reduced transport times, leading to a significant reduction in logistics costs,[38]and China's economic reforms under Deng Xiaoping—made China a low-cost production center for the consumer goods that fed the Western system. By refocusing their corporate objectives solely on maximizing profits for shareholders, and thereby reducing their social role—notably their contribution to local development—while reinforcing incentives for individual consumption, companies were now in a position to relocate their production facilities to low-cost locations, without incurring societal disapproval.

At the same time, governments were also adopting an approach designed to reduce complexity. From the 1980s onwards, neoliberalism promoted a simplification of the roles of the various players, pushing states—especially in the United States and England—to limit themselves to minimal functions.[39] In terms of motivation, beyond the confrontation with communist ideology, privatization—particularly in Europe—provided states with

---

36 H. Hansmann and R. Kraakman (2001), "The End of History for Corporate Law," *Georgetown Law Journal* 89 (2): 439–468.

37 L. Stout (2012), *The Shareholder Value Myth: How Putting Shareholders First Harms Investors, Corporations and the Public* (San Francisco: Berrett-Koehler Publishers), Kindle Edition, p. 20.

38 See https://historyandbusiness. fr/malcom-mclean-et-la-revolution-du-container/ or M. Levinson (2016), *The Box: How the Shipping Container Made the World Smaller and the World Economy Bigger*, 2nd ed. (Princeton, NJ: Princeton University Press).

39 Ronald Reagan in his inaugural address (R. Reagan (1981), "Inaugural Address," January 20, *The American Presidency Project*) famously said: "In this present crisis, government is not the solution to our problem; government is the problem."

new financial resources and civil servants with attractive career prospects and generous salaries. Another source of motivation was Western control of financial markets. The New York Stock Exchange (for finance) and the Chicago Stock Exchange (for natural resources and options) established themselves as global centers for the coordination of financial markets. This supremacy provided a powerful incentive to make these markets the primary means of coordinating society.

All these factors helped build total confidence in a model that is perceived as simple, definitive and therefore accurate, supported by powerful incentives. This confidence was so great that Francis Fukuyama spoke of the "end of history"[40] in the Hegelian sense—i.e., the end of competition between different systems of human coordination.

These two models—corporation and state—shared a common foundation: the theory of efficient financial markets. This theory led to the strengthening of these models and to their mutual weakening.

A self-reinforcing system

Indeed, the theory of efficient markets plays a central role for both companies and governments, and revolves around the same triptych introduced earlier: simplicity, accuracy, and motivation. It's simple, because it's based on a known physical process: random motion.[41] It is accurate, or at least perceived to be so, which seems to be "proven" if we observe the impact that an operation on a corporation's capital has on its share price.[42] Finally,

---

40 F. Fukuyama (1992), *The End of History and the Last Man* (New York: Free Press).

41 This random movement would well describe the movement of efficient markets, which reflect all known information. See P. Samuelson (1965), "Proof That Properly Anticipated Prices Fluctuate Randomly," *Industrial Management Review* 6 (2): 41–49.

42 E. Fama, L. Fisher, M. Jensen, and R. Roll (1969), "The Adjustment of Stock Prices to New Information," *International Economic Review* 10 (February): 1–21:

> [...] the evidence indicates that on the average the market's judgments concerning the information implications of a split are fully reflected in the price of a share at least by the end of the split month but most probably almost immediately after the announcement date. Thus the results of the study lend considerable support to the conclusion that the stock market is "efficient" in the sense that stock prices adjust very rapidly to new information.

it orchestrates a system of incentives for players in the world of finance and the economy in general, thanks to the development of financial instruments such as stock options, which apply a random process to the valuation of options.[43]

Moreover, the theory of efficient financial markets is based on a central concept: that of the rational agent seeking to maximize their interest.[44] This model is perceived as simple (since it reduces all human dimensions to one, however artificial[45]), accurate (since it is based on mathematical modeling), and as perfectly aligned with the representation of the world at that time.[46]

The theory of efficient markets legitimizes[47] profit maximization for shareholders, and seems to demonstrate the relevance of neoliberalism. By creating a common paradigm for the spheres of public and private

---

43 F. Black and M. Scholes (1973), "The Pricing of Options and Corporate Liabilities," *Journal of Political Economy* 81 (3): 637–654.

44 O. Morgenstern and J. Von Neumann (1944), *Theory of Games and Economic Behavior* (Princeton, NJ: Princeton University Press).

45 As Marcel Hénaff points out (M. Hénaff (2010), "La Valeur du Temps. Remarques sur le Destin Économique des Sociétés Modernes," *Esprit* 361 (January)):

> This rational actor, defined by his expectations and driven to maximize his interests, must be admitted to be a fiction [...] It has to be said: This character, outside the group, has never existed anywhere. [...] This actor is also outside a particular culture, outside history, outside religious beliefs, ageless and asexual [...] yet it is this absolute neutrality that makes it possible to (ideally) conceive of the market as the locus of perfect competition and to construct a rigorous mathematical theory of general equilibrium. (My translation)

46 In perfect synergy with the then-prevailing opposition of the Western economic system to communist doctrine.

47 As pointed out by Ronald Gilson and Reinier Kraakman (R. Gilson and R. Kraakman (1984), "The Mechanisms of Market Efficiency," *Virginia Law Review* (70): 549–644):

> Of all recent developments in financial economics, the efficient capital markets hypothesis ("ECMH") has achieved the widest acceptance by the legal culture. [...] the ECMH is now the context in which serious discussion of the regulation of financial markets takes place.

action, state action, and corporate action, it creates a mutually reinforcing mechanism,[48] making the mutual credibility of those models even higher.

Furthermore, proponents of the theory of efficient markets claim scientific status by using the tools and methods of physics. They develop models for representing the world that are supposed to reveal its reality, its objective truth. Under their influence, modern economics entered the age of certainty.

To summarize: a doctrine is emerging which claims to be a physical science, but which is not, because it is ill-suited to the complexity of life. It is based on these central postulates: the rationality of agents, the efficiency of financial markets, and the ownership of corporations by shareholders, which, while providing access to resources, are also erroneous or simplifying approaches to reality.

What's more, neoliberalism benefits from the reinforcement of individualism and the competitive spirit, while at the same time contributing to their consolidation. Indeed, as we saw in Chapter 2, for the agent, choosing between competition and coordination amounts to questioning what separates their actions from the state they are seeking. If they can achieve the latter by themselves, a competitive strategy will suffice. And confidence in the model is part and parcel of confidence in achieving the goal by one's own means. Consequently, the rise of individualism in the 1980s—promoted in particular by Ayn Rand,[49] whose ideas had a profound influence on Ronald Reagan—[50] can be interpreted as consistent with the strong belief in the effectiveness of the models proposed by neoliberalism (see Figure 6.2).

This self-sustaining mechanism is reinforced by the signals emitted by the economy and financial markets, which further bolster confidence in the model's validity. An example of this dynamic can be found in a 2004 speech[51] by US Federal Reserve Governor Ben Bernanke, who began his remarks with an observation on volatility:[52] "One of the most striking

---

48 At the same time, in 1992, the SEC strengthened shareholders' power over boards of directors. In 1993, the US Congress changed the tax rules on stock-price-linked executive compensation in a similar vein.

49 A. Rand (1943), The Fountainhead (Indianapolis: Bobbs-Merrill).

50 R. Reagan (2003), A Life in Letters (New York: New-York Free Press).

51 B. Bernanke (2004), "The Great Moderation," Meetings of the Eastern Economic Association, Washington, DC, Feb. 20.

52 Ben Bernanke then also refers to Christopher Sims (C. Sims (2003), "Implications of Rational Inattention," Journal of Monetary Economics, 50 (April), pp. 665–690), to

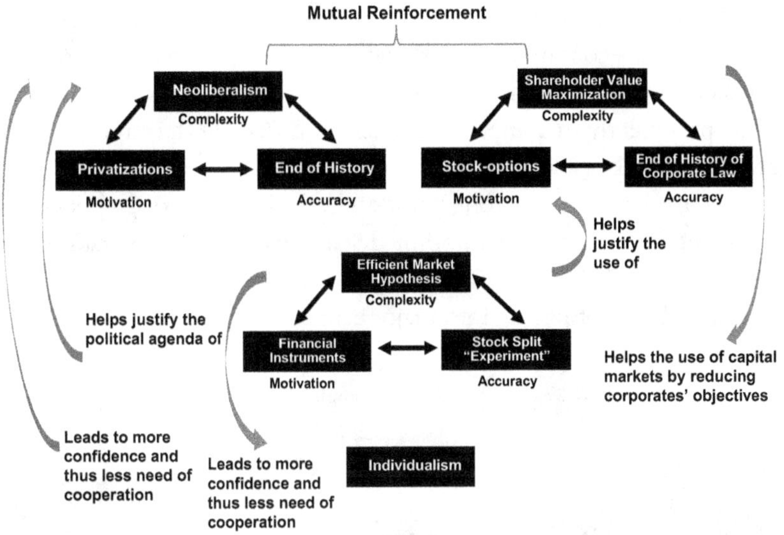

Figure 6.2 Mutual reinforcement graph for models

Source: Author.

Note: The representation of the world in Western economies in the 1980s is certainly the result of different models responding to each other: neoliberalism, profit maximization for shareholders, the theory of efficient markets, and individualism are all linked and interconnected. This architecture, perceived as "solid," has largely contributed to widespread overconfidence in this representation of the world.

features of the economic landscape over the past twenty years or so has been a substantial decline in macroeconomic volatility."

explain that this low volatility also allows for better growth, as economic agents then revise their decisions less and concentrate more on their activity:

> Theories of "rational inattention" (Sims, 2003), according to which people vary the frequency with which they re-examine economic decisions according to the underlying economic environment, imply that the dynamic behavior of the economy would change—probably in the direction of greater stability and persistence—in a more stable pricing environment, in which people reconsider their economic decisions less frequently. (B. Bernanke (2004), "The Great Moderation," Meetings of the Eastern Economic Association, Washington, DC, Feb. 20)

In other words, exploration was seen as costly to growth. And, contrary to Ben Bernanke's position, low volatility was not a sign of mastery, as Markus Brunnermeier also points out (M. Brunnermeier (2021), The Resilient Company (New York: Endeavor Literary Press)): "We should be most cautious when volatility is very low" (Kindle Edition, p. 24).

He listed three possible causes for this situation: *"structural change, improved macroeconomic policies, and good luck."* He went on to attribute this development mainly to a better understanding of economic mechanisms, particularly in comparison with the 1970s. On the strength of this analysis, Bernanke expressed great confidence in the future,[53] reinforcing the collective belief in the robustness and relevance of existing economic models. Yet three years later, the United States was facing its worst financial crisis since the 1930s. The financial system was on the brink of collapse, plunging millions of people into major economic hardship.

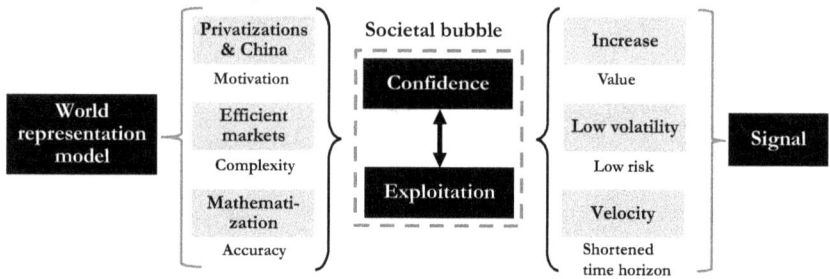

Figure 6.3 Graph summarizing the creation of a societal bubble with neoliberalism and the information society

Source: Author.

Note: The 1980s were marked by the conjunction of two distinct phenomena that led to the same effect: the creation of a "societal bubble." First, neoliberalism established itself as the definitive doctrine on which to base the organization of societies. This domination was based on several factors: belief in its validity, fueled by privatizations and access to new resources in emerging countries; its apparent accuracy, supported by the mathematization of models and its visible success; and its simplicity, stemming from postulates such as the efficiency of financial markets (an idea whose influence was further amplified by the latters' growing role as a tool for global coordination). Second, the emergence of an information society considerably accelerates the velocity of signals, shortening time horizons. At the same time, steadily rising financial markets provide access to value creation, while their low volatility reinforces confidence in a new understanding of the world. Combined, these two phenomena fuel overconfidence in the emerging model of world representation.

53 B. Bernanke (2004), "The Great Moderation," Meetings of the Eastern Economic Association, Washington, DC, Feb. 20: "This conclusion on my part makes me optimistic for the future, because I am confident that monetary policymakers will not forget the lessons of the 1970s."

During the same period, the information society rapidly expanded. Traditional media such as radio and television experienced significant growth, including the emergence of free radio, new broadcast networks, and 24-hour news channels. The rise of personal computers, an exponential increase in storage capacity and, above all, the emergence of the Web transformed the way information is disseminated and accessed. This transformation led to increased information velocity. Yet, as mentioned in Chapter 2, the application of signal processing rules in a "psychological space" suggests that this multiplicity of signals shortens the depth of memory, favoring the empire of immediacy, both individual and collective.

At the end of the 20th century, all the ingredients were in place for a new moment of overconfidence. Triumphant neoliberalism had led to a pure logic of exploitation, reinforced by signals of stability. At the same time, a new information society was emerging which, by shortening our memories, reinforced the idea that we had entered a new era. This coincidence created the conditions for a major "societal bubble," characterized by overconfidence in the dominant models and leading de facto to a logic of exploitation (see Figure 6.3).

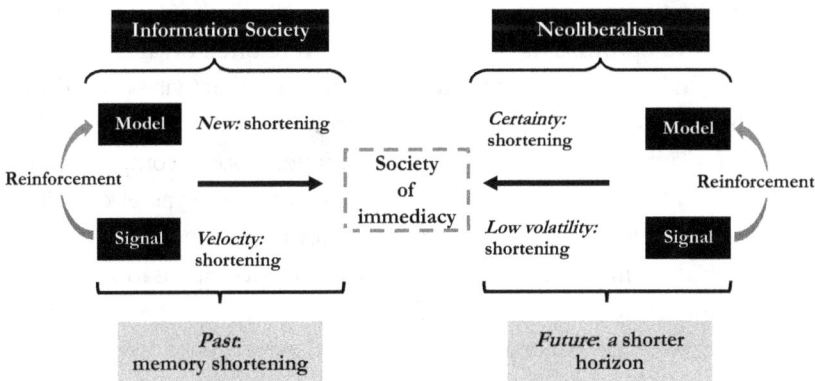

Figure 6.4 Graph showing the shortening of the time horizons
Source: Author.
Note: The information society, through the velocity of messages, generates exponential forgetting, which reduces the temporal horizon linked to the past. At the same time, the success of neoliberalism, reinforced by low-volatility social signals, leads society to a logic of exploitation, and thus to a shortening of future horizons. The convergence of these two phenomena is helping to create a society of immediacy, where the present takes precedence over past and future temporalities.

The second consequence is the creation of a society of immediacy, the fruit of this new informational structure and of the overconfidence born of neoliberalism; here, a logic of exploitation inevitably unfolds, reflecting a temporal arbitrage in favor of the present, to the detriment of possible futures (see Figure 6.4).

A system that weakens itself

Behind this apparent success lies a systemic fragility. We have organized both our corporations and our societies on the basis of a belief in a stable world. If this was the case in the 1950s, entropy has steadily increased since the 1970s, as evidenced by the growing number of financial crises. This mismatch between the structure of systems and the growing reality of instability has created an underlying fragility.

In the 1950s, corporations in the developed world were operating in a low-entropy environment: financial crises were rare, their interlocutors tended to correspond to a single profile, and industrial goods provided a certain stability. Just think of IBM selling a few large computer systems. From the Armonk firm's point of view, this meant production stability and a limited, homogeneous number of contacts. What's more, corporations did not seek to optimize their activities: they were often organized as conglomerates, which enabled them to carry out several activities simultaneously; this ensured them a certain overall economic solidity, and therefore a form of adaptability. In addition, as mentioned above, company directors were pursuing multiple objectives, particularly in terms of contributing to local development. Lastly, they were not primarily concerned with optimizing their financial structure, and executive compensation was not directly indexed to stock market performance. In short, the corporation was organized to be exploratory and adaptive, even though it was operating in a world of low entropy.

Since the 1970s, corporations have undergone a transformation: they have reduced the number of their activities—the end of conglomerates; narrowed their objectives—to concentrating solely on the maximization of profits for shareholders; sought to optimize their financial structure—via share buy-backs; and aligned the remuneration of their executives with a

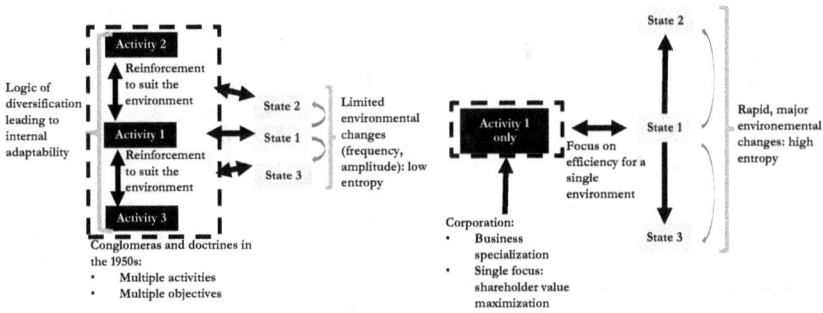

Figure 6.5 Graphs showing the transition from resilient organization in the 1950s to optimization from the 1970s onward

Source: Author.

Note: This graph illustrates the direction of change—from the 1950s, when corporate structures favored resilience through diversification, to the 1980s, when companies shifted toward exploitation, specialization, and a narrower set of objectives.

single objective—using stock options to align their interests with those of shareholders. Some companies have also shifted their focus to intangible fields, or launched consumer products used by a large and diverse global audience. Just think of Apple, selling phones to billions of culturally diverse people around the world (see Figure 6.5).

At the same time, financial crises were multiplying—the oil crisis of 1973–1974, the debt crisis in emerging countries in the 1980s, the stock market crash of 1987, the economic crisis in Japan in the 1990s, the Asian financial crisis of 1997, the Russian crisis of 1998, the bursting of the Internet bubble in 2000–2002, and the subprime crisis of 2007–2008, etc.—gradually transforming the corporate environment into a context of high entropy. Since the 1970s, two intersecting dynamics have emerged: while corporations have adopted an organizational structure that is based on exploitation, their environment has become increasingly unstable, a situation that should have favored a strategy of adaptation or exploration.

If we were to compare corporations to motor vehicles, we could say that they have gone from being off-road cars on a freeway to Formula 1 cars on increasingly dilapidated country roads. This transition has made their situation structurally fragile (see Figure 6.6).

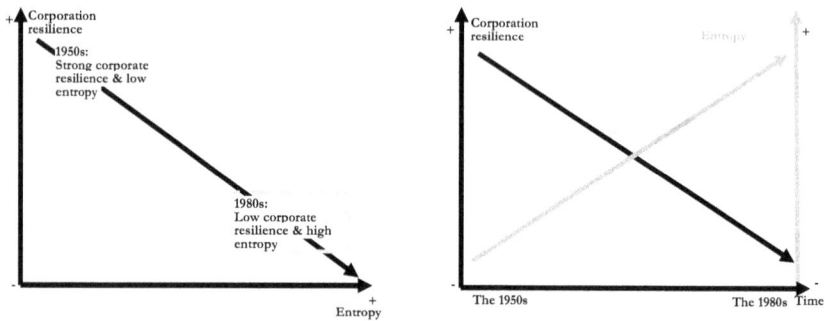

Figure 6.6 Graphs of systemic fragility

Source: Author.

Note: In the 1950s, corporations were organized in a resilient way, while the entropy of their environment was low. In the 1970s, they reorganized themselves along exploitative lines, while the entropy of their environment increased sharply. The crossing of the curves indicates an intrinsic fragility.

The Alcatel example seen in Chapter 5 is not an isolated case, as evidenced by the lengths of time that different American corporations have been in the S&P 500. This average length, which was 33 years in 1964, was 24 years in 2016, and is set to shrink to 12 years by 2027. At the current rate, half of all companies will be replaced in the next ten years.[54] This phenomenon is not confined to corporations with an "industrial" profile. It concerns all sectors.[55]

Moreover, over the last few decades, governments have also adopted policies focused on efficiency at the expense of resilience. This has been reflected in the enthusiasm for globalization, leading to the increased specialization of national economies—as in England, which has focused on finance; in waves of privatization—reducing public control over whole swathes of the economy; and in major deregulations—such as the repeal of the Glass–Steagall Act in the United States.

And these two systems are interdependent. Governments need the growth generated by business. Businesses are increasingly turning to governments for help, notably through bailouts—such as the bailout of

---

54 Innosight (2018), *2018 Corporate Longevity Forecast: Creative Destruction Is Accelerating.*

55 F. Candelon and M. Reeves, eds. (2021), *The Resilient Enterprise: Thriving amid Uncertainty* (Berlin/Boston: De Gruyter), Kindle Edition, p. 55.

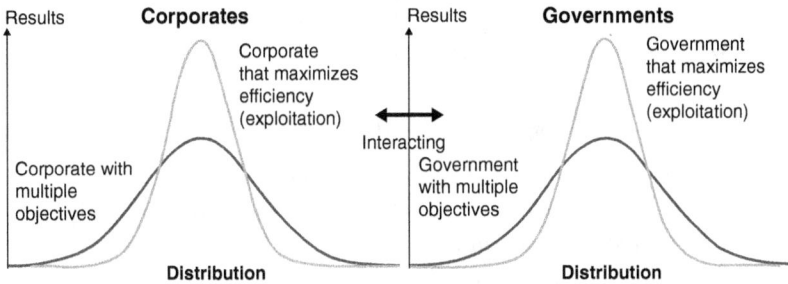

Figure 6.7 Two similar approaches leading to fragility and reinforcing each other

Source: Author.

Note: Since the 1970s and 1980s, corporations and governments have adopted strategies focused on exploitation, to the detriment of exploration and therefore of resilience objectives. At the same time, the entropy of their environments has steadily increased, marked by a proliferation of financial crises. This growing interdependence has accentuated systemic vulnerability, with each crisis in one area having repercussions on the other; for example, the financial crisis of 2007–2008 destabilized the entire global system, just as the crisis in Southeast Asia in 1997 weakened many companies.

the banks during the 2007–2008 crisis, or of entire sectors of the economy during the Covid crisis. This has led the global system, including both states and companies, to generate its own systemic fragility (see Figure 6.7).[56]

Using financial markets as the sole tool for coordination also weakened societies' capacity for exploration, since, as Marcel Hénaff points out,[57] in

---

56 As a result, central banks are playing an increasingly important role in ensuring the overall stability of economies.

57 M. Hénaff (2002), "De la Philosophie à l'Anthropologie: Comment Interpréter le Don? Entretien avec Marcel Hénaff," Esprit (February 2002) (no. 1):

The danger of universal commodification carries several risks [...]. The most serious threat is almost imperceptible. It stems from a kind of new normality that is taking shape around the very phenomenon of commodification, and can be summed up in this axiom: everything that concerns us (according to the order of desire) can and even must be bought. [...] important books that don't sell fast enough will be pummelled, profitable leisure activities will be stuck to, and only scholarly research capable of generating marketable

an extended market, in which everything is an object of transaction, only that which gives rise to a possible transaction has value. This necessarily leads to cultural homogenization and intellectual impoverishment—which leads to poorer models of world representation and, consequently, to reduced resilience. In short, although capitalism once demonstrated a formidable "desire" for exploration, which was often shared by science, it seems that this movement has recently, at least in part, taken the reverse direction, favoring logics and mechanisms that are focused on exploitation.

A system that weakens society

Third, this societal bubble has weakened society. As mentioned in Chapter 4, capitalism has extended the sphere of our relationships with others, which were hitherto limited to our immediate circle. Is it still possible today to find vestiges of these traditional forms of relating to others, as they existed before the spread of capitalism, in order to better understand their effects and, consequently, their transformations?

To illustrate this point, I'd like to share a personal experience. During the Covid pandemic, I fell seriously ill. My concierge learned of this, without my knowing how, and took the initiative of leaving food outside my door every day: a fruit salad she had prepared herself. As my condition worsened, receiving her daily text message announcing that my meal was ready was a valuable comfort, both nutritive and moral. Once I had recovered, I tried to thank her. I went to her house one morning and offered to reimburse her for the cost of the fruit salads and to give her a gift as a sign of my gratitude. In my mind, this was a fair and respectful attitude, which took care to separate the economic aspects from the gesture of gratitude. Yet, to my surprise, she curtly

---

products will be supported. The impasse is obvious: everything can be bought, but the market tends to offer and promote only what sells. Universal commodification (which claims unlimited openness) is giving birth to an increasingly restricted and narrow world, culturally homogeneous and intellectually flat. (My translation)

refused, explaining that she had acted without any expectation of quid pro quo. She even told me she would never speak to me again if I persisted in my idea of a gift. I left, sheepish and perplexed. With her refusal, my concierge had reminded me of some fundamental truths that are forgotten all too often. First, the sphere of responsibility toward others cannot be reduced to economic exchanges or transactional logic. Second, concern for others is not based on an expectation of reciprocity, but on an asymmetry that forms the very basis of ethics: giving without expecting something in return, especially when others are in a fragile situation.

The introduction of economic logics into social relations produces effects that are measurable but can run counter to the initial objectives, as shown by the work of Uri Gneezy and Aldo Rustichini.[58] These authors describe an experiment carried out in ten Israeli day-care centers: the late arrival of some parents forced one of the staff members to stay beyond normal working hours, without additional remuneration. To remedy this situation, a measure was introduced: a fine for latecomers, calculated at between 50 and 75% of the hourly rate for a babysitter. However, instead of reducing lateness, the fine had the opposite effect: parents arrived even later. By paying a penalty, they now perceived their lateness as a right, a service they could "buy." When the fine was finally suspended, their behavior did not return to normal: the late arrivals persisted.

The same researchers also studied the impact of financial incentives, revealing results that were just as surprising a priori.[59] In this experiment, three groups of students (A, B, and C) were asked to raise funds for causes of public interest, such as the fight against cancer. The three groups were given the same speech to encourage and motivate them. Groups B and C were informed that they would receive 1 and 10% of the funds raised, respectively. The results were revealing: although Group C (which received

---

58 U. Gneezy and A. Rustichini (2000), "A Fine Is a Price," *Journal of Legal Studies* 29 (1) (Jan.): 1–17.

59 U. Gneezy and A. Rustichini (2000), "Pay Enough or Don't Pay at All," *The Quarterly Journal of Economics* 115 (3): 791–810.

the highest reward) raised more than Group B, Group A (which received no reward) outperformed the other two. Introducing even a modest financial incentive can reduce the effectiveness of a commitment based on intrinsically societal motivations.

In another experiment conducted by Miranda Goode, Nicole Mead, and Kathleen Vohs,[60] the effect of the explicit or implicit presence of money on attitudes and forms of cooperation was studied. Three groups of participants (A, B, and C) were asked to construct meaningful sentences containing four of five mixed words. In group A, the words they were given were neutral; in group B, they contained explicit references to money; in group C, an unconscious reference to money was introduced by placing a Monopoly game in their visual field. Each of these groups had access to external help. The results showed that group A (with no money-related influence) was the first to seek cooperation, and B (whose thinking incorporated an explicit reference to money) the last, while C (whose influence was unconscious) was in between. In other words, the notion of money, whether consciously considered or not, tends to make behavior more individualistic and less cooperative.[61]

Similarly, the very structure of a market can influence moral behavior, as shown by the work of Armin Falk and Nora Szech. In their study, participants were faced with a moral choice: let a mouse live in good health, in excellent conditions, for another two years, or euthanize it and receive ten euros.[62] The results were striking: in a bilateral transaction situation, the mouse's chances of survival decreased significantly, and this trend became even more pronounced in a broader market context.[63] In

---

60 M. Goode, N. Mead, and K. Vohs (2006), "The Psychological Consequences of Money," *Science* 314 (5802): 1154–1156.

61 The situation was even more acute if group B had substantial financial resources at its disposal.

62 A. Falk and N. Szech (2013), "Morals and Markets," *Science* 340 (6133): 707–711. Three cases are then examined: either an individual decision, a bilateral decision, or the result of a market transaction. In the bilateral case, in the event of an agreement, the seller, who owned the mouse, received 20 euros less the price of the agreement (and killed the mouse), and the buyer received the price of the agreement. Otherwise, the mouse survived. The same mechanism applies to the fruit of a market, with prices displayed on a screen.

63 In the case of individual decisions, just under 50% of individuals kill mice in return for payment. In the case of bilateral negotiation, the rate rises to over 70%, and increases again slightly in the case of a deal.

other words, the confrontation of points of view in a market setting, combined with financial incentives, tends to reduce the weight of moral considerations.[64]

More generally, neoliberalism has encouraged the encroachment of economic mechanisms into spheres previously regulated by social dynamics, notably through the introduction of price-based coordination. This overconfidence in the economic models of the 1970s has had the effect of redefining relationships that would previously have been based on social ties;[65] this has had major consequences, including the increased fragmentation of society. As Michael Sandel shows,[66] this phenomenon is particularly evident in the rise of the meritocratic paradigm in the United States. *At first glance*, who could possibly oppose the idea that the most deserving should have their talents recognized by society? Yet putting this principle into practice has serious social implications. Michael Young, inventor of the notion of meritocracy, warned against the dangers of this model, which he saw as a destructive force for social cohesion.[67] Michael Sandel illustrates this critique with the bias in college admissions to the great American universities. Whereas in the 1950s, admission was largely dependent on the social status of applicants' families, today it remains unchanged, masked by the façade of a belief in individual merit.

---

64 Several explanations are put forward by the authors (diluted responsibility, awareness of new moral values, or shifting the stakes to negotiation). Another explanation may lie in what we saw with Joseph Heinrich in Chapter 4: in the West, unlike in many other parts of the world, the individual has internalized moral judgment, as opposed to relying on the moral standards of the group (family, clan, etc.). By positioning the question in a bilateral relationship, and even more so in a market, the internalization of moral judgment ceases and judgment is replaced in a collective structure, but one that does not possess norms. A final explanation is that this experiment illustrates the success of capitalism's initial attempt—via trade, and if we follow Albert Hirschman's lead, as we saw in Chapter 4—to establish relations between human beings outside the moral or religious sphere, since the latter had led to a great deal of tension.
In the end, the disappearance of morality through money within a collective structure should come as no surprise, since this was exactly what was intended.

65 Mark Carney also observes and deplores this shift from a market economy to a market society (M. Carney (2021), *Value(s): Building a Better World for All* (London: William Collins)).

66 M. Sandel (2020), *The Tyranny of Merit: What's Become of the Common Good?* (New York: Farrar, Straus and Giroux).

67 M. Young (1958), *The Rise of the Meritocracy* (London: Thames and Hudson).

Those who succeed in gaining entry to these prestigious institutions are then inclined to feel a form of condescension toward those who fail to do so. The latter, for their part, rather than attributing their failure to social factors—which are still profoundly active—are inclined to think that their failure is largely due to their lack of personal worth, which makes the situation particularly painful for them. More broadly speaking, this meritocratic conception is tantamount to considering society as a vast financial market, where everyone's social position is perceived as a measure of their "value" (see Figure 6.8).

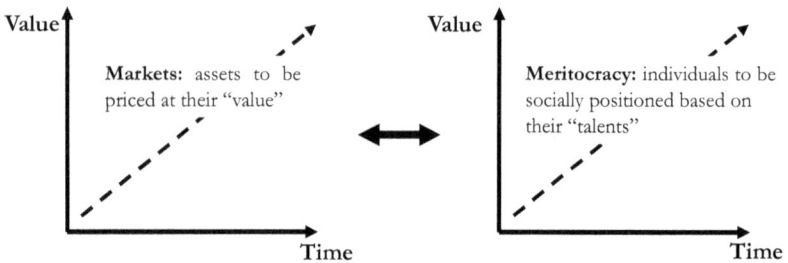

Figure 6.8 Graph of the parallel between financial markets and the meritocratic society

Source: Author.

Note: Meritocracy can be interpreted as the transposition to society as a whole of the idea that an individual's social value results from the recognition of their intrinsic value—just as a company's share price is seen as reflecting its true worth.

However, the "value" attributed to an individual in a meritocratic society does not necessarily stem from their actual contribution to the functioning of that society, but rather reflects what the society values at a given moment. For example, professions such as tennis player, lawyer, or Wall Street trader enjoy a high social status, even though their actual contributions to society may seem less than those of teachers, firefighters, garbage collectors, and so on. This dissociation between real contribution and perceived value to society contributes to the deepening of social divides, particularly in the United States. This dynamic may shed light on certain worrying phenomena, such as the decline in life expectancy for white men aged 45–54 since the late 1990s, which was highlighted by Anne Case and Angus Deaton[68] and is linked particularly to a loss of employability and social ties.[69]

World modeling bubble

As we have seen previously, the first mechanism for accessing resources was the group, which in the case of humans required attention to the weakest members. Then came *Homo sapiens'* invention of abstraction, which allowed access to a larger group, and the adjusted world model based around hunting; both of these created access to more resources. Then came agriculture, which offered greater control over nature, and the practice of making sacrifices, which established a symbolic and fruitful dialogue with higher forces; confidence in the existing models of world representation was thus reinforced. Then the Greeks introduced the idea of eternal truths (thanks in particular to Plato), and modern science elevated our representative modeling of the world to the level of discovering the laws of nature. Finally, neoliberalism led to the widespread use of financial markets, which can be seen as a model of the world that is constantly being adjusted;[70] the successive

---

68 A. Case and A. Deaton (2015), "Rising Morbidity and Mortality in Midlife among White Non-Hispanic Americans in the 21st Century," *Proceedings of the National Academy of Sciences of the United States of America* 112 (49): 15078–15083. Life expectancy for white men has been declining in the United States since the late 1990s. If the historical downward trend of 1.8% per year had been maintained, almost 500,000 lives could have been spared. The main causes of this reversal are attributed to an increase in "deaths of despair," including poisoning (notably overdoses), suicides, and diseases linked to excessive alcohol consumption.

69 A. Case and A. Deaton (2020), *Deaths of Despair and the Future of Capitalism* (Princeton, NJ: Princeton University Press): "Our story of deaths of despair; of pain; of addiction, alcoholism, and suicide; of worse jobs with lower wages; of declining marriage; and of declining religion is mostly a story of non-Hispanic white Americans without a four-year degree." (Kindle Edition, p. 4)

70 One question remains: does access to resources precede the model, which then consolidates that access through societal formalism—as was the case with agriculture? Or is it the model that opens up access to resources, emerging in a Darwinian logic—as was the case with *Homo sapiens'* invention of abstraction)? A third hypothesis could be that the model and access to resources are simply congruent with the forces at play, leading to a simultaneous and mutually reinforcing emergence.

successes of *Homo sapiens*, hunting, agriculture, science, and capitalism have solidified and reinforced confidence in our ability to model the world.

From then on, the law of overconfidence has applied.[71] The motivation behind our established model is always based on access to resources; its

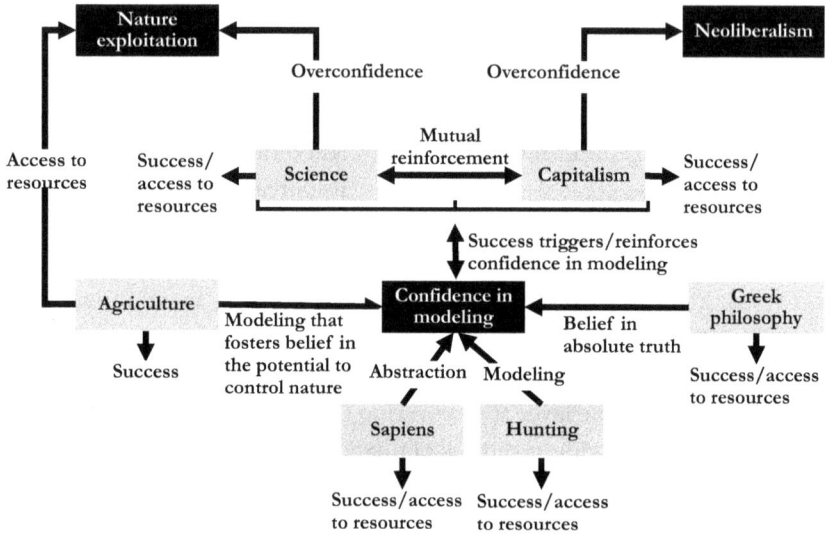

Figure 6.9 Graph of the growing development of confidence in models of world representation

Source: Author.

Note: While confidence in the models we used to represent the world gradually developed with *Homo sapiens* and persistence hunting, and were then reinforced with the advent of agriculture and Greek philosophy, our overconfidence probably stems from the massive access to new resources made possible by science and neoliberalism. This overconfidence has also been fueled by the success of these models over other representations of the world.

---

71 Since access to resources is a priority objective for all living organisms, it is quite obvious that any model of world representation that favors it creates a selection bias that distorts the perception of reality. A model that is simple or deemed accurate will thus be favored for its energy efficiency, even at the cost of over-simplifying reality. It is thus striking to observe that the foundations of modern science—which mathematizes nature—and neoliberalism—which reduces humans to egotistical beings—while incapable of grasping the entirety of reality, are proving particularly effective in gaining access to both natural and human

simplicity is ultimately that of reproducing the thought pattern derived from cognitive Bayesian inference; and its accuracy comes from its successful application down the ages.

Modeling the world has gradually become the preferred tool for humans to relate to the world (see Figure 6.9).

In short, while modern agriculture/science, and neoliberalism have created two societal bubbles, our way of representing the world has created a third bubble, a bubble within which we conceive of our entire system of modeling as an unsurpassable tool with which to relate to the world as a whole.

*

In conclusion, we can trace the whole biological pathway: where the adventure of the human species begins with attention to others, at the same time the brain's mechanisms of Bayesian inference enable us to anticipate and reduce energy consumption, two factors that increase our chances of survival. These mechanisms are then transposed to the societal level, both in our relationship with the world, e.g. via abstraction, modeling, agriculture, and modern science; or the signals we receive from others; or through cooperation platforms, such as companies and financial markets. These mechanisms are selected in accordance with the rule of trust—simplicity, accuracy, and motivation.[72] Then, when success is great enough, trust reaches a threshold beyond which there is no updating the model. We then enter into the societal bubbles of modern science/agriculture and neoliberalism, and into that of world modeling.

The rule of whether or not the model is updated—based on simplicity, accuracy, and motivation—also applies here, explaining the selection of these mechanisms. Another rule then comes into play: beyond a

---

resources. This underlines the central role played by the efficiency of access to resources in the selection of systems for representing the world. This is not to be taken as deterministic, as other cultures have not followed this path.

72 Sometimes, this involves a distortion of reality, such as the belief that financial markets are perfectly efficient or that science discovers eternal truths. These reinforce the perception of accuracy and therefore the level of trust, which in turn increases the access to resources made possible by this model and thus the success of this representation of the world.

certain point, due to their success, the adjustment of the model ceases. This leads to societal bubbles, such as those of agriculture/modern science and neoliberalism.

Finally, the same mechanism (selection followed by a shift toward exploitation due to success) also applies at a higher level of abstraction—just as it does in the brain—namely, to the very act of modeling the world (see Figure 6.10).

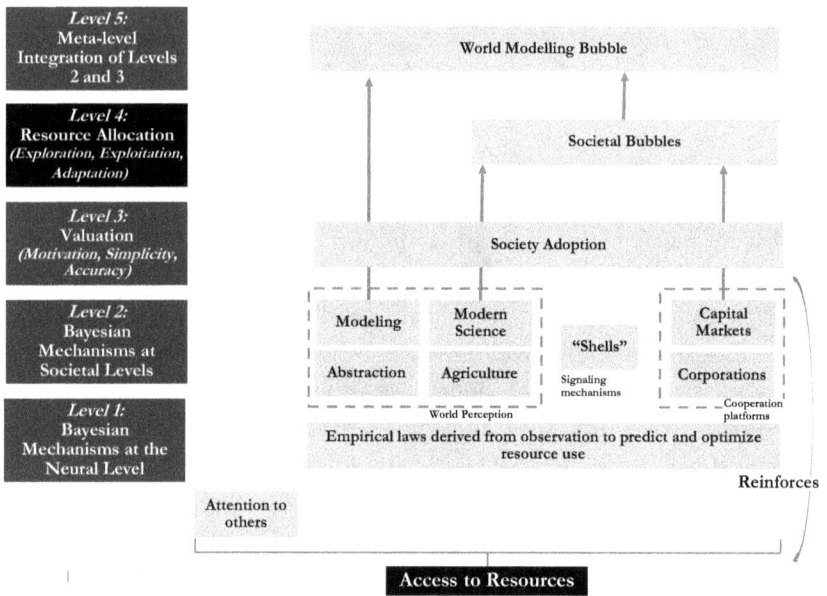

Figure 6.10 Graph of a Bayesian process operating at the societal level to select worldviews

Source: Author.

Note: One can read in human history—and from a Darwinian perspective—the spread of a brain-based mechanism for anticipation and resource allocation at the societal level. The process begins within the brain itself through Bayesian cognitive inference, which serves to anticipate and reduce energy consumption. It then externalizes at the societal level, either through representations of the world (world modeling for hunting, abstraction enabling large groups, modern science, and agriculture), through the creation of signals that allow for the updating of representations of the "other," and finally through companies and financial markets as modern mechanisms for accessing resources.

Now that our journey has taken us deep into the workings of the brain and societies since the time of *Homo sapiens*, perhaps it can help us answer our initial question: so, do we now have all the cards we need to solve the puzzle of inaction in the face of climate change? Can we bring these societal bubbles closer to the specific characteristics of climate change?

This is the subject of the next chapter.

7

SOLVING THE RIDDLE OF OUR COLLECTIVE INACTION

Our investigation is now coming to an end. What can we learn from it? An essential lesson: the human adventure is a biological one. Throughout history, societies have developed various mechanisms to access resources—through trial and error, chance, and selection—with those adopting the most efficient approaches becoming dominant over others. But the very success of these mechanisms can create societal bubbles of overconfidence.

It is therefore necessary to compare these bubbles point by point with the specific characteristics of the climate challenge as described in Chapter 1.

Inadequacy of societal bubbles with climate specificities

We can see this as a triptych made up of three distinct strands: first, the three bubbles; then the specificities of the climate challenge we saw in Chapter 1; and, finally, a societal governance issue. The latter can be broken

DOI: 10.4324/9781003638384-7

down into three main categories: access to resources, tools for social coordination, and the instruments we use to represent the world.

A mismatch between our societal bubbles and the unique features of the climate crisis then emerges, point by point (see Figure 7.1).

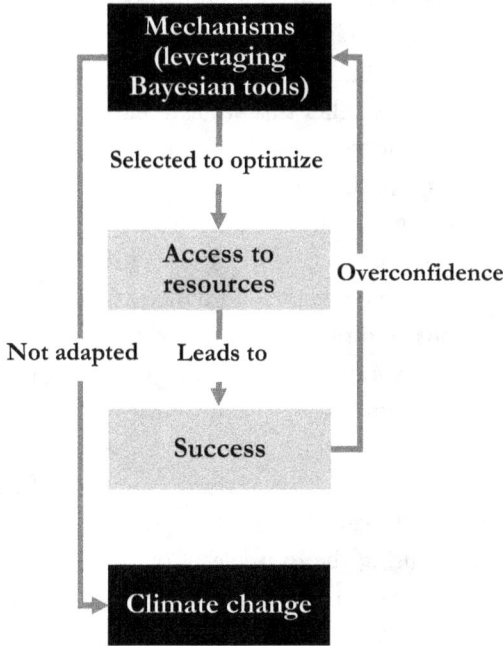

Figure 7.1 Graph showing the inadequacy of current human cooperation mechanisms to meet the specific challenges of climate change

Source: Author

Note: The various mechanisms of human cooperation can be read as having been selected because they have enabled ever-greater access to resources. However, they are not adapted to the unique features of the climate change challenge. What's more, their success has created a high level of societal confidence in them, making them difficult to adjust.

Inadequacy of the bubble of agriculture and modern science

As we have seen, there is a common thread that leads from Homo sapiens to neoliberalism: cultures that set up mechanisms to access resources first gain an advantage over other cultures, and then come to dominate them.

Thus, agriculture—and later modern science—made it possible to first control and then own natural resources, securing dominance over nomads at first, and eventually over much of the world. Suddenly, for the first time in human history, a limit has been placed on this access to resources, since their exploitation—whether fossil fuels or natural resources—now conflicts with the conditions necessary for human beings to survive on earth. This amounts to putting a brake on what has been the very engine of cultural success since the origin of human civilization.

Furthermore, this same belief that we can master nature leads us to be confident in our ability to control it, by building dams to combat rising water levels, bunkers, etc. In other words, the current belief is that, as we've been able to shape the earth to our will for millennia, this situation can be expected to continue. Yet, as we saw in Chapter 1, climate change is taking place at an unprecedented rate, with increasingly intense heat waves, more violent typhoons, and other extreme weather events. Faced with the violence of the elements, our ability to control them is illusory. At 50°C, human beings are in mortal danger, and nothing can really protect them from a typhoon.

What's more, this same belief has also led us to be confident in our ability to adapt. However, climate change corresponds to high entropy. As we showed in Chapter 5, using the example of options traders, a strategy for adapting to different situations can sometimes prove impossible to implement, given the short time frames and the scale of the adjustments required.

In other words, how do we adapt when the environment is constantly changing in unpredictable and seismic ways, forcing us to move from one unstable state to another? How do we adjust when the ice caps melt and then the Gulf Stream is disrupted, two events that will trigger shifts in the balance of nature? How to transfer the billions of people who, in the worst-case climate scenario, will have no other option but to fight for their survival at the end of the century?[1] If greenhouse gas concentration thresh-

---

1 As Günther Thallinger, Member of the Board of Management of Allianz, one of the largest insurance companies, points out (G. Thallinger (2025), "Climate, Risk, Insurance: The Future of Capitalism," LinkedIn, 2025) who, after emphasizing that critical points are being reached: "The insurance industry has historically managed these risks. But we are fast approaching temperature levels—1.5°C, 2°C, 3°C—where insurers will no longer be able to offer coverage for many of these risks."
He highlights overconfidence in the ability to adapt as well:

There is also the false comfort of "adaptation," as many risks do not lend themselves to meaningful adaptation. There is no way to "adapt" to temperatures

olds are exceeded, adaptation will become difficult—if not impossible—for much of humanity. We must come to terms with a sobering reality: we now face a situation over which we have little control.

In short, human beings succeeded in mastering a stable environment and, in the process, became overconfident—just as a new, unstable environment of their own making was beginning to emerge. This mirrors the systemic economic fragility explored in Chapter 6.

Finally, these societal mechanisms were selected because they provided access to resources. However, that very access is now being challenged by the climate crisis, which can be a source of violence.[2]

Inadequacy of the neoliberal bubble

Neoliberalism—in the sense of coordination by financial markets—has become our dominant model, after a long search for the optimum method of social organization. However, this approach is ill-suited to the specific challenges posed by global warming.

First of all, for agents to adjust, they need to receive a signal. But as we have seen, the signals coming from nature itself are too weak or too diffuse to bring about significant changes in strategy. Governments are trying to overcome this difficulty with new mechanisms such as carbon taxes. However, although they exist in some countries, they are often inadequate or even contribute to effects that are contrary to the desired objective. They do not take into account the physical risks associated with climate change, and are hampered by the financialization of societal issues, which tends to reduce the sense of responsibility felt by stakeholders.

---

beyond human tolerance. There is limited adaptation to megafires, other than not building near forests. Whole cities built on flood plains cannot simply pick up and move uphill. And as temperatures continue to rise, adaptation itself becomes economically unviable.

2   In the past, there has been at least one example where access to resources previously regarded as nearly free and "natural" was limited or removed: the abolition of slavery. We remember what followed: the American Civil War. As Karla Hoff and Joseph Stiglitz recall (K. Hoff and J. Stiglitz (2010), "Equilibrium Fictions: A Cognitive Approach to Societal Rigidity," Policy Research Working Paper 5219, World Bank), this violent reaction occurred because abolition contradicted a racist ideology that had emerged to justify the institutionalized exploitation of these human resources.

Agents could theoretically integrate the consequences of climate disruption into their decision-making models, but they lack three essential elements: societal values to guide their choices, clear incentives to take this kind of action, and a time horizon that matches the challenge at hand. What's more, they face the difficulty of modeling a highly complex issue that is marked by increasing entropy.

Furthermore, the financial markets are not designed to foster cooperation between companies on such issues, as they lack a decision-making center capable of coordinating the necessary collective effort. This is why, in situations of extreme crisis, market mechanisms have been suspended in favor of centralized decision-making; this is because, as Alan Milward has pointed out with the example of the Second World War,[3] the simple process of adjustment through prices was no longer working (see Figure 7.2).

What is more, as we saw earlier, overconfidence in neoliberalism in the context of an information society is leading to a shortening of time horizons, at a time when the climate crisis requires us to engage in industrial innovation to explore new ways of cooperating, new societal roles for companies, and so on. Furthermore, the essential tools of economics are rooted in the everyday laws of physics, a foundation that has given rise to a modeling bubble. While such laws may apply well to the world of solids, they are ill-suited to environments with high levels of entropy or to the specificities of living systems. Finally, both the mechanism of the financial markets and the ideology of individualism[4] weaken social bonds, whereas the climate is

---

3 A. Milward (1977), *War, Economy, and Society, 1939–1945* (Berkeley: University of California Press): "Everywhere the price mechanism came to be regarded as a method of allocating resources which was too slow and too risky" (p. 100).

4 Although not the main focus of this survey, the impact of social networks is worth mentioning. Their unprecedented rate of development is taking place against a backdrop of growing demand for social recognition in a fragmented world, combined with a deep-seated tendency in the West to distance ourselves from others. These trends are producing social bonds that, while gaining in quantity, are losing in quality. Moreover, the overabundance of signals produced by social networks stimulates the release of dopamine in the brain, reinforcing the appeal of digital interactions. The consequences are manifold, especially for cooperation: Social networks reduce opportunities to have our perceptions challenged (which is essential to our capacity for cooperation and understanding of the world); they also tend to reinforce our certainties (which reduces the motivation to cooperate) and erode the collective trust that is a key condition for cooperation to be

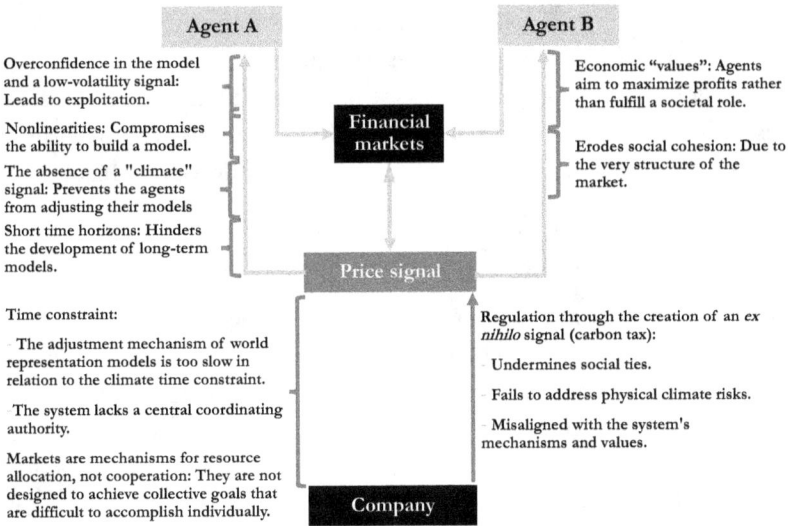

Agent A

Overconfidence in the model
and a low-volatility signal:
Leads to exploitation.

Nonlinearities: Compromises
the ability to build a model.

The absence of a "climate"
signal: Prevents the agents
from adjusting their models

Short time horizons: Hinders
the development of long-term
models.

Financial
markets

Agent B

Economic "values": Agents
aim to maximize profits rather
than fulfill a societal role.

Erodes social cohesion: Due to
the very structure of the
market.

Price signal

Time constraint:

  The adjustment mechanism of world
representation models is too slow in
relation to the climate time constraint.

  The system lacks a central coordinating
authority.

Markets are mechanisms for resource
allocation, not cooperation: They are not
designed to achieve collective goals that
are difficult to accomplish individually.

Regulation through the creation of an *ex
nihilo* signal (carbon tax):

  Undermines social ties.

  Fails to address physical climate risks.

  Misaligned with the system's
mechanisms and values.

Company

Figure 7.2 Graph showing the dysfunctional coordination of the financial markets'
response to the climate challenge

Source: Author.

Note: In the absence of a signal from the climate, society could consider adopting
a carbon tax, which would act both as a correction for a "negative externality"—
an economist's term for a behavior by an economic agent that leads to a cost for
society—and as a signal to adjust the way the world is represented.

However, this approach comes up against four blocks of constraints that can be
divided into two categories, represented here by agents A and B, with A dealing
with the technical specifics of the climate problem and B essentially with its moral
dimension.

First, agent A has overconfidence in the model, reinforced by the low volatility of
the climate signal. It is therefore possible that they are not paying enough attention
to the new signal—among others. Also, the nonlinearities inherent in climate make
the task of modeling very arduous for operators.

Second, agent B is motivated by profit-maximizing values—and not moral
stakes. This is reinforced by the inherent structure of markets, which reduces
moral sentiment. Furthermore, the financial markets themselves do not encourage cooperation—other than allowing actors to update their representations of
the world—and do not have a command center with which to implement rapid
large-scale, adjustments. Finally, by placing a value on the climate, agent B's
approach focuses on transitional rather than physical risks, and places an economic value on a societal issue, at the risk of obtaining a result that is the opposite
of the desired objective.

essentially a challenge of solidarity with the poorest in developed countries, the inhabitants of developing countries, and future generations.

Ultimately, our main tool of societal coordination—the financial markets—is ill-suited to the specificities of climate change. Furthermore, the information society and individualism both reinforce this inadequacy.

Inadequacy of the world modeling bubble

As we saw in the previous chapter, modeling the world has gradually become humanity's tool of choice for accessing resources—from running in the hunt to modern science and financial markets. This approach has three major incompatibilities with the specific characteristics of climate.

The first fundamental mismatch is rooted in how the brain functions: while signals are essential for updating our representation of the world, the climate signal is too weak relative to the scale of adjustment required. The fact that model updates rely on observations—rather than on leaders' speeches that can generate new values and, in turn, major societal adjustments—is therefore an obstacle to mobilization in the face of climate change. This lack of strong signals is therefore a primary obstacle to mobilizing an effective societal response to climate change.

Secondly, the very tool humans have developed to model the world is ill-suited to the climate challenge, which—depending on one's perspective—is defined by entropy, tipping points, or the specificities of living organisms.

Indeed, as Henri Bergson[5] intuitively understood—and as he explains here, without referring to the Bayesian approach—science is based on this mechanism of searching for invariants, in order to derive laws that enable us to act:

> The essential function of our intellect, such as it has been shaped by the evolution of life, is to light the way for our behavior, to prepare for our action upon things, and to predict, for a given situation, the favorable or unfavorable events that might follow. As such, the intellect instinctively picks out, within a given situation, that which resembles

---

effective. Ultimately, these social dynamics reduce our adaptability, an essential quality in the face of climate change.

5   H. Bergson (2023), *Creative Evolution*, translation by D. Landes (London: Routledge), Kindle Edition, p. 33.

However, since the advent of quantum physics, it has been mathematics—not the search for physical invariants—that has increasingly driven discovery, often yielding results that challenge our everyday perceptions of the world.

what is already known; it looks for what is alike, so as to be able to apply its principle that "like produces like." [...] Just like ordinary knowledge, science only retains the aspect of *repetition* that it finds in things.

From this point onward, three problems arise, each linked to the specific characteristics of climate for human beings: entropy, novelty, and the radical, irreversible nature of death.

When it comes to entropy, physical models often struggle to account for situations that lack clear organizational rules—such as the unfolding of war. A striking example is the six-week plan devised by Secretary of Defense Donald Rumsfeld for the 2003 invasion of Iraq: events quickly diverged from the expected trajectory. Such "planning" creates an illusion of control, obscuring the fundamentally unpredictable and chaotic nature of phenomena like armed conflict and climate change. Likewise, physics-based models have difficulty grappling with tipping points, since these moments, by definition, do not correspond to stable invariants. Consider, for instance, the melting of ice: a singular, irreversible event with far-reaching and permanent consequences.

Rooted in Bayesian inference, science is inherently constrained by its search for patterns in past observations, which limits its ability to apprehend genuinely novel or emergent phenomena. However, novelty is precisely what makes living beings unique, as Henri Bergson also points out:[6]

> That which is irreducible and irreversible in the successive moments of a history escapes science. In order to conceive of this irreducibility and irreversibility, we must break with the habits of science, adapted as they are to the fundamental requirements of thought; [...] This is why, despite the fact that life evolves before our very eyes in a continuous creation of unforeseeable form, the idea still persists that form, unforeseeability, and continuity are nothing but pure appearances, reflecting so many gaps in our knowledge.

In other words, where physics is repetition, life is constant novelty. Henri Bergson gave the example of the creation of a work of art: no law can predict what an artist will create, and they themselves do not know it when they begin the creative process.

---

6 H. Bergson (2023), *Creative Evolution*, translation by D. Landes (London: Routledge), Kindle Edition, pp. 33–34.

With regard to the radical, irreversible nature of death, physical models of nature are largely based on statistics that cannot incorporate sudden qualitative breaks such as the disappearance of a species. Indeed, unlike the hazard games that gave rise to statistics, where the outcomes may have different values but are homogeneous (in that they are essentially similar in nature), in the case of climate disruption, the consequences may include massive human losses or irreversible catastrophes. These are states of a qualitatively different nature. No probability can account for this situation. What's the value of playing Russian roulette, in terms of the odds? There is none. No rational mind should play such a game, quite simply because one's very survival would be at stake. In short, physics is the search for invariants and is therefore, by definition, homogeneous, whereas the living world is essentially driven by novelty and heterogeneity—especially in its essential, irreversible dimension: death.

In short, by modeling the world, the human being has been able to access resources that were hitherto unknown, but this mechanism, specific to action in the physical world, is unsuited to a situation marked by high entropy and shaped by the specificities of the living world.[7] Therefore, as Henri Bergson puts it, "our whole intellect rebels against this idea of the absolute originality and unforeseeability of forms,"[8] but "we must do violence to the mind and go counter to the natural inclination [pente] of the intellect."[9] And, he adds: "[...] that is precisely philosophy's role."[10]

Finally, the rise of world modeling as the dominant way of relating to it has coincided with a shift in our relationships with others—increasing in quantity but diminishing in quality. From agriculture, the hierarchization of

---

7 Although AI is not the focus of this book, and would require a detailed analysis on its own, a parallel can be drawn between the challenge it presents and that of the climate. AI continues the historical quest for resources—this time intellectual—following natural resources through agriculture and modern science, and human resources through neoliberalism, while also being part of the bubble of world modeling. Consequently, putting the brakes on this process is bound to run into the same difficulties as with climate change. Curbing AI would mean accepting a limitation on our access to resources. And that would mean acknowledging the modeling bubble and subordinating knowledge to the objective of life itself. We might therefore adopt the same reversal of perspective, remembering that the ultimate goal is life itself, and that knowledge is merely a means—albeit an effective one—of achieving it.

8 H. Bergson (2023), *Creative Evolution*, translation by D. Landes (London: Routledge), Kindle Edition, p. 33.

9 H. Bergson (2023), *Creative Evolution*, translation by D. Landes (London: Routledge), Kindle Edition, p. 34.

10 H. Bergson (2023), *Creative Evolution*, translation by D. Landes (London: Routledge), Kindle Edition, p. 34.

society, and the loss of gender equality; to the replacement of trust by reason; to capitalism, where money and objects mediate human connections—social bonds have gradually given way to individualism (see Figure 7.3).[11]

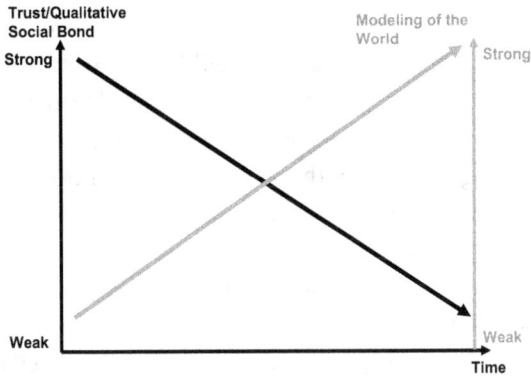

Figure 7.3 Graph showing the gradual domination of world modeling as the primary mechanism for accessing resources, as opposed to relationships with others
Source: Author.
Note: For humans—lacking physical traits that give an advantage in accessing resources and coping with premature birth—cooperation with the weakest was key, giving rise to ethics. Over time, another resource-access mechanism evolved from secondary to dominant: the modeling of the world, while relationship quality declined in favor of quantity. However, as we have seen, in the case of climate change, weakened social ties confront a necessary concern for others—in developing countries, among the most disadvantaged in developed countries, and for future generations.

Furthermore, the shift from attachment to others to a modeling approach was experienced during the French Revolution, with poor consequences as underscored by Claude Lévi-Strauss,[12] and more globally marked by periods of

---

11 Although Charles Darwin, as we saw in Chapter 4, saw this attention to others as a deciding factor that made those tribes who implemented it more successful than others.

12 C. Lévi-Strauss and D. Eribon (1991), *Conversations with Claude Lévi-Strauss*. Translated by Paula Wissing (Chicago: The University of Chicago Press):

> The Revolution put ideas and values into circulation that have fascinated first Europe and then the world [...] However, one may wonder if the catastrophes that have struck the West may also find their origin there. [...] it has given people the idea that society is to be ruled by abstract thought, when instead it is formed of habits and customs; by crushing these in the mortar of reason, one pulverizes ways of life founded on a long tradition, reducing individuals to the state of interchangeable and anonymous atoms. True freedom can

violence and conflict. Karl Polanyi, for example, observed that civilization in the 20th century did not collapse as a result of external attacks,[13] but because social ties based on work and the relationship to the land had been reduced in the 19th.[14] This in turn created a pull toward very rigid societal structures, notably the fascist movements of the 20th century.[15] Here too, beyond the inarguable moral considerations, such a rigidification of social ties is at odds with the solidarity needed to support the most vulnerable members of society.

Ultimately, all three bubbles—agriculture/modern science, neoliberalism, and world modeling—collide with the specific dynamics of climate change. They emerged from the gradual rigidification of systems that once enabled extraordinary leaps of human development: mechanisms of societal coordination (e.g., capitalism, financial markets); access to resources (e.g., agriculture, modern science); and our cognitive relationship with the world (e.g., world modeling). However, these systems are ill-suited to the specific demands of climate change: limited resources, urgent action, cooperation, care for the most vulnerable, weak signals, and our relationship with the living world. It is not surprising that tools designed to facilitate resource extraction prove inadequate when the objective shifts to long-term resilience and ecological balance. It's not strange that tools that were selected for one purpose—access to resources—should be ineffective for another (see Figure 7.4).

---

be based only on a concrete foundation and is made up of a balance among small adherences, little solidarities. Pitted against these are theoretical ideas proclaimed as rational. When they have achieved their goals, there is nothing left for them but to destroy each other. (p. 117)

13 K. Polanyi (1944), *The Great Transformation: The Political and Economic Origins of Our Time* (New York: Farrar & Rinehart): "Nineteenth-century civilization was not destroyed by the external or internal attack of barbarians; its vitality was not sapped by the devastation of World War I nor by the revolt of a socialist proletariat or a lower fascist middle class" (Kindle Edition, p. 257).

14 Hannah Arendt also underlines this point (H. Arendt (1951), *The Origins of Totalitarianism* (New York: Harcourt, Brace & Company):

The revolt of the masses against "realism," common sense, and all "the plausibilities of the world" (Burke) was the result of their atomization, of their loss of social status along with which they lost the whole sector of communal relationships in whose framework common sense makes sense. (Apple Books, p. 838).

15 K. Polanyi (1944), *The Great Transformation: The Political and Economic Origins of Our Time* (New York: Farrar & Rinehart): "The fascist solution to the impasse reached by liberal capitalism can be described as a reform of market economy achieved at the price of the extirpation of all democratic institutions" (Kindle Edition, p. 245).

Modern science & agriculture bubble

Focuses on extracting and controlling resources

Neoliberalism bubble

Prioritizes capital markets and individualism

Not compatible with:
- Finite resources
- Limits to access

Access to resources

Coordination tools

Not compatible with:
- Moral values
- Long-term issues
- Time sensitivity
- Cooperation
- Lack of signal
- Abrupt shifts
- Social bonds

Reinforces   Reinforces

Ways to represent the world

Not compatible with:
- Lack of signal
- Tipping points
- Entropy
- Living entities

Built on physics-based representations

World modelling bubble

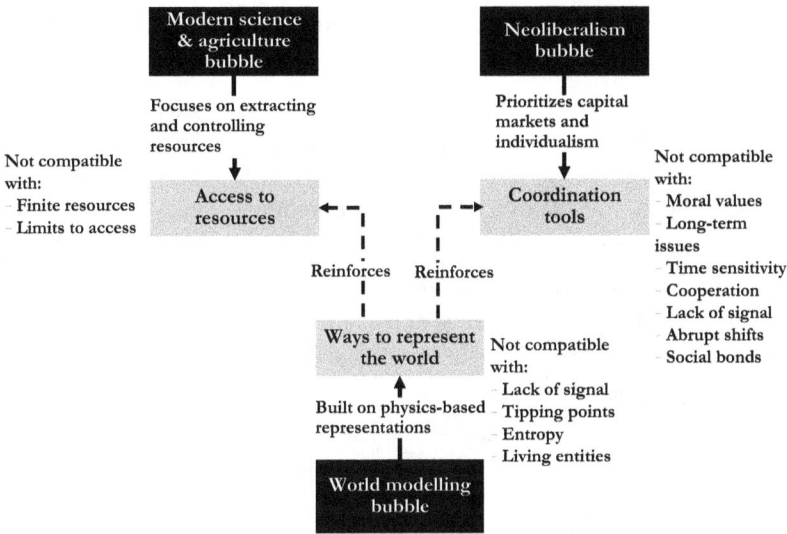

Figure 7.4 Graph of the mismatch between societal bubbles and climate specifics
Source: Author.
Note: All three bubbles formed during the natural selection of mechanisms by allowing us access to resources. Agriculture and modern science provided access to natural resources, neoliberalism provided access to human resources throughout the world, and world modeling provided access to all resources. However, the mechanisms they have created—in particular the logic of extraction in modern science and agriculture, the goal of resource allocation in financial markets, and the mechanistic view of the world in global modeling—clash head-on with the specific characteristics of climate change.

As a result, human beings find themselves in an impasse in terms of doing what is necessary: they can't do it (because they are bound by the logic of exploitation and the absence of signals); they don't know how to do it (in the absence of adequate instruments of societal coordination or ways of representing the world); and they don't want to do it (as it would impede their access to resources).

Developing a living organism

This investigation's central hypothesis is that societies function like living organisms, and that mechanisms enabling access to resources confer a competitive advantage. This led us to study in depth the mechanisms of representation of the world. One might wonder whether human structures share another trait of living organisms: evolving through the gradual formation of an organism. Without falling into finalism, we are seeking to test a hypothesis linked to a particularity of living beings, whereby organizational forms that allow access to more resources are selected.

Organ specialization

As we have seen, the analogy between corporations—structures of human cooperation—and living organisms seems apt. Employees (like cells), who start out as independent individuals like craftsmen or farmers, recognize each other, cooperate, and then specialize in specific functions. This specialization is accompanied by the creation of a "membrane" —the legal fiction that defines the corporation as an entity distinct from its members. It also develops a "brain function" in the form of general management, which coordinates activities and makes strategic decisions. Thanks to its organizational structure, the corporation is able to access resources that none of its cells (employees), taken individually, could obtain: social and intellectual capital, access to large-scale natural resources, and so on. This reflects an organic logic in which cooperation and specialization generate capacities superior to those of isolated individuals.

At the state level, a similar evolutionary process can be observed. Individuals gradually learn to recognize one another as members of the same community, eventually forming increasingly complex structures: villages, towns, and ultimately nation-states. These entities come to perform many of the essential functions of a "living organism." Borders act as membranes, defining the limits of the political entity and safeguarding its integrity. Citizens function as sensors, transmitting information about needs, expectations, and internal or external tensions. The army plays a defensive role, ensuring the security of both borders and society as a whole. Finally, the government fulfills a representative function: it synthesizes information, formulates action strategies, contributes to the establishment of collective values, and manages cooperation with other entities.

The same trend toward increasing coordination and specialization of "organs" could be observed. Individuals (like cells) learn to aggregate through the exchange of signals or the sharing of common value systems. Then, these communities structure themselves spatially by creating membranes such as cities and borders; they create specializations by assigning various roles and trades—such as crafts, commerce, management—to distinct groups, or "organs," and these, in turn, form larger interconnected "organs" that reinforce collective efficiency. The result is a single "living organism" that is interconnected at all levels, from local to global.

The emergence of a coordinating body

Today's societies may represent the third major stage in forming a "living organism" that is still under construction. After the emergence of the individual as a fundamental unit, followed by collective structures such as

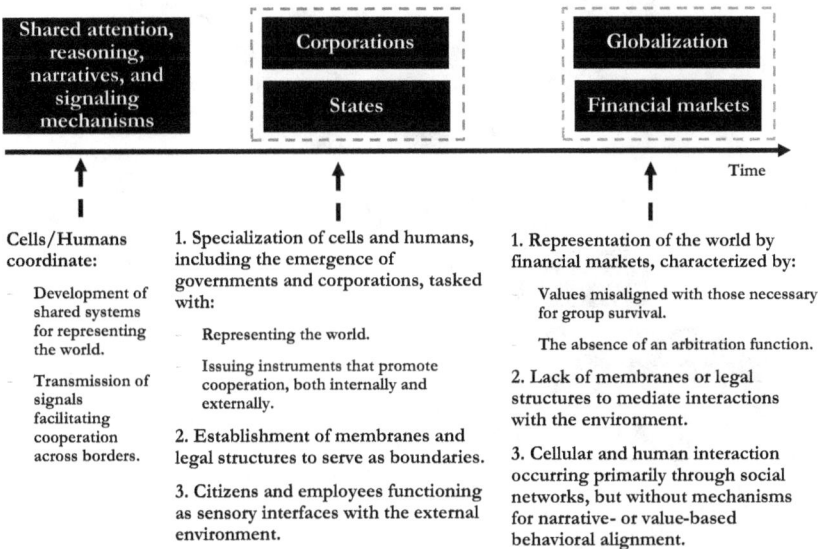

| Shared attention, reasoning, narratives, and signaling mechanisms | Corporations | Globalization |
| | States | Financial markets |

Cells/Humans coordinate:

- Development of shared systems for representing the world.

- Transmission of signals facilitating cooperation across borders.

1. Specialization of cells and humans, including the emergence of governments and corporations, tasked with:

- Representing the world.

- Issuing instruments that promote cooperation, both internally and externally.

2. Establishment of membranes and legal structures to serve as boundaries.

3. Citizens and employees functioning as sensory interfaces with the external environment.

1. Representation of the world by financial markets, characterized by:

- Values misaligned with those necessary for group survival.

- The absence of an arbitration function.

2. Lack of membranes or legal structures to mediate interactions with the environment.

3. Cellular and human interaction occurring primarily through social networks, but without mechanisms for narrative- or value-based behavioral alignment.

Figure 7.5 Graph of the progressive constitution of a societal "organism"

Source: Author.

Note: We can compare the evolution of societal coordination structures—such as cities, companies, states and, more recently, modern society—with the process of building sophisticated biological structures. Initially independent, cells develop shared systems of world representation and emit signals expressing the will to cooperate, enabling them to organize themselves into more complex organisms. This coordination increases their access to resources and thus their ability to survive. Then, with the emergence of cities, states, and corporations, these social cells specialize, creating protective membranes—such as city walls, state borders, or the legal existence of corporations—and coordinating structures—such as mayors, branches, or governments—enabling them to access resources on an even larger scale. In modern times, this dynamic has reached a new stage of development in financial markets, where minds seem to "merge," enabling collective coordination.

corporations and states, we are now at a stage where these elements are interconnected on a global scale, and are creating the outline of a unified, integrated cooperative system (see Figure 7.5).

The specialization of organs requires the gradual unification of different models of human representation, most recently seen in the emergence of a true "global brain": the financial markets (see Figure 7.6).

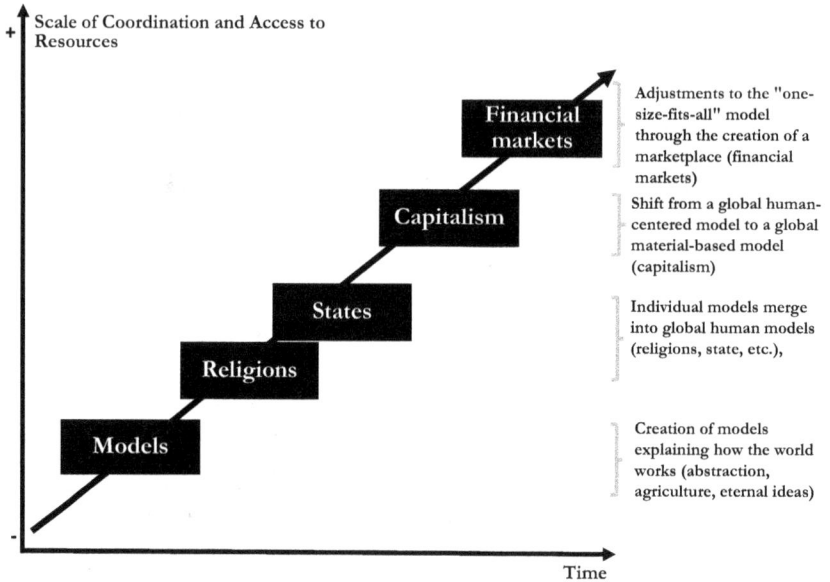

Figure 7.6 Graph showing the increasing integration of models representing the world

Source: Author.

Note: Human history, as observed through successive human structures as well as their domination of other organizational forms, traces a trajectory of increasing access to resources, whether human or natural. This progress is based, in particular, on the increasingly advanced integration of world models, enabling ever-greater coordination and resource exploitation.

Extended coordination

If we view it as an evolving organism, human history looks like a progressive homogenization of cooperation mechanisms that promote increasing individual integration. As we saw in Chapter 4, these mechanisms include the use of reason as a substitute for trust—the latter being costly in terms of energy because it is always difficult to infer the intentions of others, especially when hampered by constraints of distance and cultural diversity. Another mechanism is the emergence of capitalism, where social ties have been replaced by a form of cooperation mediated by objects such as money or goods. Cooperation expands at each of these stages, but does so at the cost of weakening the quality of our relationships (see Figure 7.7).

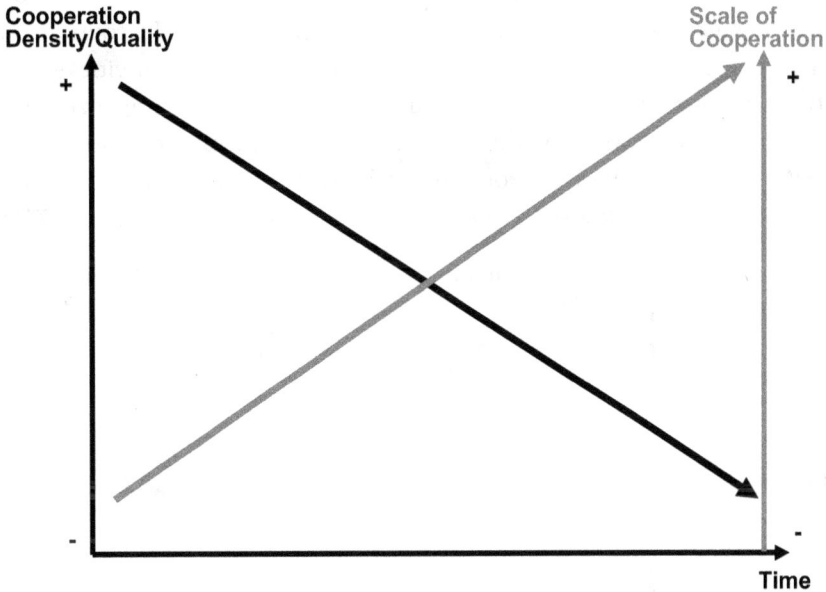

Figure 7.7 Graph of the evolution of cooperation: Quantity versus density/quality
Source: Author.
Note: Capitalism can be seen as an acceleration of a long-standing human process toward ever broader cooperation—fostering, among other things, human equality and democracy—but at the cost of reduced cooperation quality, moving from families to villages, to cities, and finally to social networks.

The "capitalism/modern science" moment is undoubtedly a point of acceleration or steepening of the curves, since, as we saw in Chapter 4, capitalism and Protestantism diminish the quality of attention given to others, while modern science erases the qualitative distinctiveness of nature. Both enable increased access to resources in terms of quantity.

Alternating symbols and structures

Looking back at human history, we can see that increasing coordination among people has activated different mechanisms, depending on the prevailing structure. In cases of significant human disparity (e.g., early com-munities) or extreme homogeneity (e.g., in the era of financial markets), symbols dominate. In contexts of disparity, such symbols bridge differ-ences in worldviews by externalizing the willingness—or unwillingness—to cooperate. At the other extreme, in situations of extreme homogeneity, symbols likewise sustain cooperation: the uniformity of representation models means a simple signal is enough to update them. In contrast, in intermediate situations—marked by moderate diversity, as in cities—it is structures that take over.[16] They coordinate actions through organized sys-tems, in particular through the specialization of roles and professions.

What's more, as human groups expand and diversify, cooperation tends to be based on the most universal objects possible, such as money. This

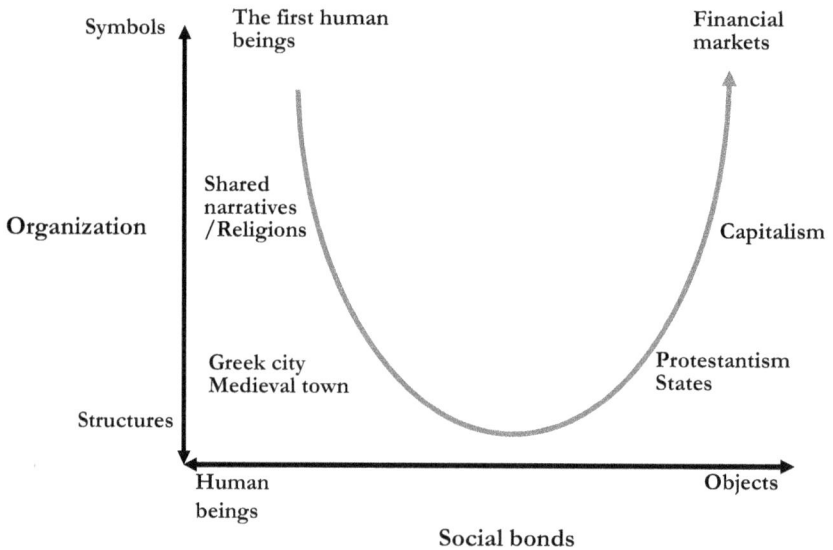

Figure 7.8 Graph of the evolution of structures in the West

Source: Author.

Note: Mechanisms of societal cooperation based on Bayesian cognitive inference evolve according to the specificities of human interactions in each period.

---

16 Greek culture and the rise of capitalism share a strong societal coordination structure: the city. This is paired with mechanisms of shared values, whether through a common perception of beauty in Greece or through religion, such as Protestantism. For cooperation to be satisfactory, another mechanism of solidarity is needed, whether it's the shared perception of beauty in Greece or the mecha-nisms of cooperation enabled by religions.

dynamic reflects the shift introduced by capitalism, which transformed relational cooperation into material-based mechanisms.

This reveals a dual evolution: a pendulum swing between structures and symbols, and a shift from social to material cooperation, where objects became the dominant means of cooperation (see Figure 7.8).

Correspondence through the ages

While there are myriad coordination mechanisms, some surprising similarities have emerged over time. Here is a selection drawn from what has been explored so far:

1. Between the small, colorful marine gastropods traded by *Homo sapiens* and a handshake or a smile:[17] a signal expressing a willingness to cooperate;
2. Between a nine-month-old baby and the ancient Greeks: shared attention as a basis for possible cooperation;
3. Between religious signs—e.g., a cross, a veil, or a yarmulke—and luxury items—e.g., a Vuitton bag: signals recognizable by all as adhesion to a particular worldview;
4. Between the Protestant Reformation, financial markets, and the consumer society: coordination via the object rather than the social link;[18]
5. From the emergence of reason to the rise of financial markets: a confrontation of rational perspectives, and thus the possibility of sidestepping the need for trust in others;
6. Between the emergence of agriculture and that of modern science: both brought about a transformation of relations between men and women, to the detriment of the latter;
7. Between the sea squirt and neoliberalism: both have eliminated their control organ—the brain and the state, respectively—in an environment perceived as stable.

---

17 S. Centorrino, E. Djemai, A. Hopfensitz, M. Milinski, and P. Seabright (2015), "A Model of Smiling as a Costly Signal of Cooperation," *Opportunities Adaptive Human Behavior and Physiology* 1 (3): 325–340.

18 Another way of putting it is that the emergence of capitalism in Western history represents a rupture, or a massive acceleration.

Ultimately, a "biological structure" of our human societies seems to be emerging. However, it seems to be incomplete, particularly in light of the specific nature of the climate challenge. First, as we have seen, the "global brain" formed by the financial markets does not have an arbitration function like that found in the human brain, and therefore cannot update its models when the time needed to refine its understanding of the situation would conflict with its desired objective. Second, it does not have values that prioritize the survival of the species over the allocation of resources. Furthermore, the organism does not have a mechanism for socializing with its environment. And finally, it lacks a membrane—a feature specific to living beings—that reduces the number of situations to be handled by different organs, as provided by the legal structure of corporations or the borders of states. In this case, human beings will be directly exposed to changes in their environment.

Comparison with other societal challenges

Now that we have a framework for understanding the reasons behind societies' failure to act in the face of climate change, we need to test it against other crises that human societies have successfully overcome.

We can analyze this using three main parameters. The first concerns whether or not there was a signal corresponding to the challenge in question. The second relates to whether the societal coordination tools at hand were suited to the nature of the challenge—that is, the mandate and structure of the institutions responsible for addressing the issue, the tools available for coordination, and the overall approach taken. The third involves whether the crisis threatened our access to natural or human resources.

Three factors to which we can also add the question, often raised, of whether the challenge will have an imminent impact on societies.

Let's look at a few concrete examples.

At the start of the First World War, the United States was not involved in the conflict, but the country eventually mobilized. There had been a signal—the war in Europe—but from the perspective of Americans in 1916, it didn't concern the United States, and so there was no sense of urgency to act. Woodrow Wilson, then President of the United States, was able to activate a powerful societal narrative, based on universal values— a certain idea of humanity—which convinced the American Congress to

enter the war in 1917 and rallied public opinion to support the mobilization. This combination of factors made it possible to send 2 million soldiers
to Europe, and helped bring the war to an end. Moreover, as in most wars,
there was no period of modeling before the intervention. Finally, involvement in this conflict did not impede access to essential natural or human
resources. Ultimately, the United States mobilized successfully.

In the aftermath of the Second World War, fears of nuclear conflict were
widespread. However, despite moments of acute tension—such as the
Cuban Missile Crisis—this scenario was ultimately avoided. Several factors contributed to averting disaster. First, the experience of Hiroshima
and Nagasaki acted as a powerful "signal"—although this is not the place
to debate its moral dimension. Second, the arms race, along with successive crises, created a sense of immediacy that heightened public awareness
and urgency. Third, the management of this threat remained in the hands
of nation-states, whose primary mission was to protect their citizens and
who had access to diplomatic mechanisms such as international treaties.
This problem could also be understood by means of a relatively "simple"
model inspired by game theory, which demonstrated the rational value of
cooperation. Finally, the prevention of nuclear escalation did not require
limiting access to essential natural or human resources. In the end, societies were able to mobilize effectively within this geopolitical framework.

As the Covid virus spread around the world, threatening human societies,
most of those societies were able to cope, despite some periods of chaos.
Several factors explain this relatively effective mobilization. First, there was
a clear "signal" with the outbreak of the epidemic, and the speed at which
the virus spread demonstrated the immediacy of the challenge. Second, governments (re)assumed a leadership role in managing the crisis, by imposing measures that were at times highly restrictive to limit the spread of the
virus, and by massively funding vaccine research. State control was based
on tried-and-tested mechanisms, such as quarantines, orders for drugs and
medical equipment, and financial support for research. In addition, there
was no prior modeling of the problem, but rather the most pragmatic
approach possible was taken. Finally, although management of the crisis
temporarily slowed economic growth, it did not impede access to essential
natural or human resources. Ultimately, societies mobilized successfully.

As many electronic systems recorded only the last two digits of years and
not the full century, in the runup to the year 2000 many feared multiple

catastrophes were about to occur—from pacemaker stoppages to plane crashes and operating room shutdowns. However, the world woke up on January 1, 2000, to find that none of these doomsday scenarios had come true. There were several reasons for this. First, although there had been no pre-crisis signal, the challenge was close at hand and governments took the lead by imposing precise rules on the various sectors concerned: flights were suspended on New Year's Eve, hospitals postponed operations that were not urgent, and so on. What's more, no prior modeling of the problem was undertaken; instead, a pragmatic approach was adopted, with all potential vulnerabilities identified. Second, the problem—a computer bug—was relatively easy to grasp, and governments could coordinate their responses around a narrative that everyone could understand. Finally, the challenge did not hinder access to essential natural or human resources. In the end, societies managed.

At a time when the ozone layer was threatening to disappear, putting human life at risk, society mobilized quickly and effectively, to such an extent that the situation is now almost back to normal. There are several reasons for this success. First, a clear signal was identified in 1985 with the scientific observation of a reduction in the ozone layer, corroborating a chemical analysis that had been conducted in the 1970s.[19] Even though the effects were distant, states reacted quickly by establishing international coordination tools: the adoption of the Montreal Protocol, which led to the ban on chlorofluorocarbons (CFCs) used in aerosol sprays and refrigeration systems. This negative externality was not corrected through market pricing, but by strict bans imposed by governments. Moreover, the problem was easy to model. Finally, the management of this crisis did not impede access to essential natural or human resources. Ultimately, societies mobilized successfully.

While the inhabitants of Easter Island had developed a sophisticated culture, they descended into cannibalism after exhausting their natural resources.[20] Several factors explain this collapse. Firstly, there was no warning signal before the crisis, making awareness of it difficult, and its impact remote. Secondly, the construction of the famous statues, which grew ever more imposing, seems to have been the result of exacerbated social

---

19 M. Molina and S. Rowland (1974), "Stratospheric Sink for Chlorofluoromethanes: Chlorine Atom-Catalysed Destruction of Ozone," *Nature* 249 (5460): 810–812.

20 As we saw in the introduction, this is Jared Diamond's thesis, although other explanatory frameworks also exist.

competition. Thirdly, the island's geographical isolation probably led to the formation of a "societal bubble" that lacked the institutional mechanisms that could have prevented disaster. Fourthly, there doesn't seem to have been any modeling of the problem. Finally, meeting this challenge would have meant preserving the island's trees, which meant restricting access to a resource essential to the islanders' way of life. Ultimately, this society failed to mobilize in time to prevent collapse (see Figure 7.9).

	WWI US Entry	Nuclear Threats	Ozone Layer	Y2K	Covid	Eastern Islands	Climate Change
Was there a signal?	No (Or not direct)	Yes (Hiroshima)	Yes (For scientists only)	Yes	Yes	No	No
Was the impact immediate?	No (Not directly involved)	Yes	No	Yes	Yes	No	No
Did the challenge align with:							
Societal organization	Yes (states)	Yes (States)	Yes (States)	Yes (States)	Yes (States)	No	No (Neoliberalism)
Coordination mechanisms	Yes (War declaration)	Yes (Treaties)	Yes (Global agreements)	Yes (Regulations)	Yes (State and corporations)	No (Social prestige)	No (Market-based coordination)
Existing frameworks	Yes (Moral framing)	Yes (Game theory)	Yes (Chemistry)	Yes (Industrial challenge)	Yes (Epidemiology)	No	No (physics and economics)
Were there constraints on access to resources?	No	Yes	Yes	Yes	Yes	Yes	Yes

Figure 7.9 Graph summarizing selected examples of societal challenges

Source: Author.

Note: The climate challenge is characterized by three specific features. First, one of the signals it is sending out is inappropriate: there is no perceptible direct climate alert, while indicators of economic progress and stability reinforce humanity's overconfidence in the dominant model, and the information society encourages short-term thinking. Second, this challenge does not fit the worldview of the societal structures in charge of managing it, e.g. dominant doctrines such as neoliberalism, instruments such as financial markets, and therefore our conceptualizations tend to have been limited to an economic approach, despite the biological and moral dimensions of the problem. Finally, it imposes a constraint on access to fossil fuels and natural resources, which have historically been central to the success of human societies.[21]

---

21 As far as the climate is concerned, the lack of immediate impact is often put forward as an explanation for the lack of mobilization. While short-termism does exist, as we saw in Chapter 6, as a result of overconfidence and the information

It's true that you can't build a reliable model from just a few isolated examples.[22] What's more, such an exercise could only be a decoy of Bayesian inference, as history is sometimes shaped by seemingly insignificant events. Just think of the three hundred or so votes in Florida that tipped the 2000 election in favor of George W. Bush, when Al Gore would very likely have placed the fight against climate change at the heart of American politics, thereby changing the course of history. It has to be said, however, that the climate challenge has some specific features rarely seen in past crises. The only case that comes close is Easter Island, where a societal organization focused on prestige, combined with extreme isolation, led to the creation of a "societal bubble" and a questioning of access to natural resources. As a result, humanity is now faced with a rare and unfavorable conjunction of critical factors.

*

So, we are gradually solving the mystery: human societies may legitimately be seen as functioning like living organisms. They are organized in a similar way—with membrane, cell coordination, organ specialization, etc.— and those societies with mechanisms of world representation are enabled to access greater resources, gaining a competitive advantage over others. With success comes overconfidence in these mechanisms, creating societal bubbles. There are three such bubbles: modern agriculture/science, neoliberalism, and world modeling.

But the problem is that these mechanisms, which have driven unprecedented improvements in our quality of life, directly conflict with our ability to deal with the unique characteristics of the climate challenge.

Of course, major perils such as the nuclear threat, Covid, or Y2K also had points of nonalignment with existing societal tools. But our societies were

---

society, other examples show that societies sometimes know how to get around this obstacle. For example, the entry of the United States into the First World War or the management of the disappearance of the ozone layer were not held back by the absence of immediate consequences, showing that this factor does not appear to be decisive in itself.

22 And there are certainly other factors in play. For example, states may be unwilling to implement climate strategies as governments lack a sense of responsibility (citing, for example, the fact that the results also depend on the actions of other states, or the need for global governance).

able to respond. What sets the climate challenge apart is that none of those earlier challenges asked us to question our access and use of resources. This distinction reinforces our core assumption that societies function like living organisms. What's more, it is central to explaining our collective inaction in the face of the climate challenge.

The roots of our inaction, as revealed through this archaeological deep dive, indeed lie deep within the workings of our brains and can be traced back to the origins of humanity.

Are we to conclude that we are doomed to remain its prisoners?

No. Now that the roots of our inaction have been brought to light, we can turn to the fundamental question of how to confront the challenge of global warming. But how?

That will be the subject of the next chapter.

8

TAKING ACTION IN THE HERE AND NOW

Three "bubbles" have been identified as the sources of our inaction in the face of the climate crisis. These are mechanisms that once granted humanity tremendous access to resources—but, having been selected precisely for that purpose, they are now proving inadequate when confronted with the specific challenges of climate disruption.

This situation presents us with two major imperatives. First, we must break free from the overconfidence embedded in these three societal bubbles. This means shifting from a logic of exploitation to one grounded in adaptation and exploration—drawing on human inventiveness to address today's challenges.[1] Breaking out of this logic requires not only new strate-

---

1 In both cases, this transition presents extreme challenges: the transition to adaptation can only take place in a context of increasing entropy. Exploration, on the other hand, requires the invention of new technologies and forms of cooperation, but time is running out.

DOI: 10.4324/9781003638384-8

gies, but a fundamentally different relationship to responsibility, action, and the living world. Second, we must stop emitting greenhouse gases.

To meet these challenges, I propose mobilizing the new interpretive framework that has emerged from our inquiry. Throughout this book, it has allowed us to revisit the past; now, it can guide us in formulating appropriate responses to the challenges of the present.

It can help us break out of our bubbles—while there is still time.

The imperative to act

Given the immensity of the task, discouragement may seem natural. Yet there is an imperative to act. Here and now.

We must move beyond our system of modeling. First, as discussed in Chapter 7, the act of modeling itself—anchored in a reductive engagement with a static, physical world—is misaligned with the unpredictable and emergent nature of ecological and climatic systems. Depending on the analytical perspective, this challenge involves tipping points, rising entropy, and heterogeneous states—such as life and death—that cannot be fully captured by physics-based mechanisms. The very inadequacy of modeling in the face of the specific challenges of climate change calls for a fundamental reorientation—one that privileges immediate, adaptive action over theoretical abstraction. As in times of war, the imperative is to identify and reinforce positive nodes while neutralizing dangerous ones—not to first model future outcomes and only then determine a course of action.

Second, the window of opportunity to avoid crossing critical thresholds is very narrow. Let's not forget that we only have a few years of carbon budget remaining. For a surgeon with a patient in the emergency room, once the diagnosis has been made, it is time to operate. The same applies here: too much time spent modeling or analyzing risks undermining the very goals we are seeking to achieve. If we wait too long, society's ability to adapt will be impeded by ever more physical constraints; so we need to act quickly.

Third, in the face of existential danger, action must take precedence. When someone collapses from cardiac arrest, calculating their chances of survival isn't the point—what matters is acting immediately. Because the climate challenge is fundamentally a moral issue—of responsibility toward the most disadvantaged and future generations—it's a matter of reactivating the primary human impulse, caring for the most vulnerable, rather than relying on conceptualizing the world. The moral imperative leaves no room for thought before action.[2] The law does not declare what is true—it defines what must be done. It's a question of prioritizing right action over right thinking; law over models; responsibility toward others over the pursuit of abstract truth.

In short, there are three converging imperatives for action: conceptual, operational, and moral.

The history of 20th-century Europe offers powerful examples of moments when this imperative to act became undeniable. Those who chose to mobilize against fascism sometimes set aside conceptual reflection in favor of necessary action—even risking their lives to do so. Among them were prominent figures such as Georges Canguilhem, François Jacob,[3] and Jean Cavaillès.[4] Though deeply immersed in abstract thought as a philosopher of mathematics, Cavaillès became a man of action when war broke out, co-founding a resistance movement and even planting explosives in a submarine base. In doing so, he became what Canguilhem would describe as the embodiment of "a philosopher of mathematics laden with explosives, clear-eyed and reckless, resolute yet without optimism";[5] someone who took "action without sparing the rear," with a total commitment to action. Furthermore, in early June 1941, it was impossible for those who mobilized against fascism to foresee the Normandy landings that would come three years later. At that time, neither the United States nor the USSR were involved in the conflict. This example shows that in moments of extreme uncertainty, when disorder dominates, only morally guided action can—and must—prevail.

Is that a solitary challenge? Starting from scratch? Certainly not; new positive dynamics have emerged. Indeed, while no significant progress had been made since the 1970s, the world has seen a major turning point in the last decade. In Paris in 2015, a previously unthinkable agreement between

---

2   Which is another great message in the work of Emmanuel Levinas. This perspective is in line with the position taken in Chapter 4, according to which these are initially two distinct channels of access to resources—one being cooperation, which in human beings evolved into a responsibility toward the most vulnerable.

3   F. Jacob (1988), *The Statue Within: An Autobiography*, translated by F. Jellinek (New York: Basic Books).

4   G. Ferrières (2000), *Jean Cavaillès: A Philosopher in Time of War 1903–1944*, translated by T. N. F. Murtagh (Lewiston, NY: The Edwin Mellen Press).

5   G. Canguilhem (2018), *Vie et Mort de Jean Cavaillès* (Paris: Allia), p. 35; my translation.

states was reached. The cost of renewable energies, once high, has fallen to the point of becoming competitive, particularly as compared with coal, the most polluting of the fossil fuels. What's more, climate change, once the preoccupation of governments and NGOs, has gained the attention of the financial sector, with the emergence of a profusion of coalitions[6] and financial innovations. What was once the domain of specialists is now central to public debate. China, once seen as an obstacle to the process, has become a driving force, particularly in the development of renewable energies. Lastly, government commitments to carbon neutrality, which only covered 10% of global emissions in 2018, had covered 70% by 2021.[7] In other words, while all the indicators were in the red just ten years ago, they have gradually shifted to yellow, or even green. This alignment of positive forces has created a dynamic in which each advance inspires the next.

These advances, while encouraging, will still not be enough for us to meet the 1.5°C temperature increase threshold set by the IPCC. However, they do mark a turning point: even if we are still a long way from the general mobilization required to fully meet this challenge, there are now soldiers on the battlefield where, not so long ago, there were none to be seen.

Paradigm shift: From exploitation to adaptation/ exploration

If action is necessary, we must still clarify its methods. The investigation carried out in the preceding chapters offers us some enlightening perspectives. If we consider society as a biological organism, it is imperative that it adapts and develops new mechanisms for harmonious co-evolution with its environment, thus avoiding the risk of collapse.

This approach builds on the framework of state, company, and society proposed by Samuel Bowles and Wendy Carlin,[8] while incorporating the key dysfunctions that have been identified throughout this work.

---

6 M. Andersson, P. Bolton, and F. Samama (2016), "Governance and Climate Change: A Success Story in Mobilizing Support for Corporate Responses to Climate Change," Journal of Applied Corporate Finance 28 (Spring): 1–13.

7 IEA (2021), Net Zero by 2050: A Roadmap for the Global Energy Sector, International Energy Agency.

8 B. Bowles and W. Carlin (2020), "Shrinking Capitalism," AEA Papers and Proceedings 110 (May): 272–276.

Rights enabling
socialization

Nature ← - - - - States

- -

Values and
action
(protection of
the weakest)

Coordination
(when
necessary)

- Shared observation
of the planet's
beauty
- Caring for the
weakest

New *Kharis*

Corporation

New
objectives:
exploration,
solutions

Corporation

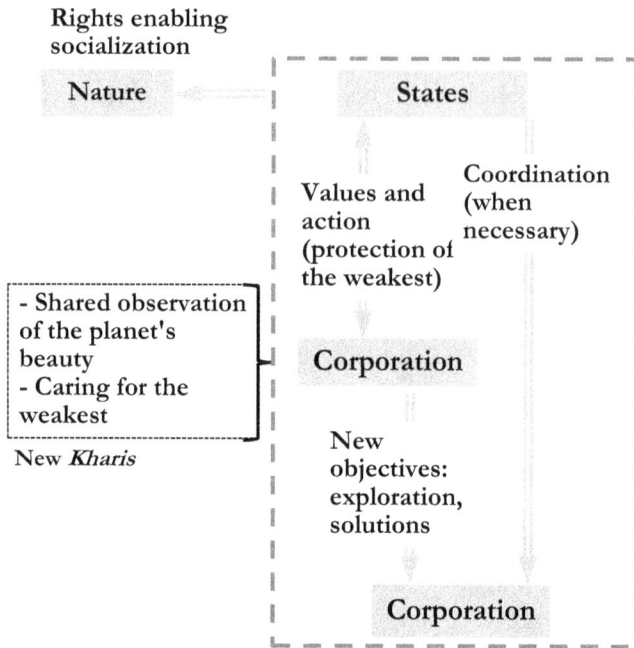

Figure 8.1 Graph summarizing the action that will be needed to meet the climate challenge

Source: Author.

Note: Society can be seen as a living organism with the "organs" necessary for its internal organization and co-development with its environment. This perspective highlights several dysfunctions or inadequacies of our current situation. First, we lack the arbitration function that is essential in times of crisis, which calls for a strengthened state that is also capable of reinforcing cooperation where it is needed. Second, the current economic logic, which is focused on maximizing profitability, does not guarantee that sufficient responsibility toward nature will be taken; it even tends to reduce it. It is therefore imperative to invent new mechanisms of respect and dialogue between society and its environment. What's more, the logic of maximizing profits for the benefit of shareholders pushes companies toward a logic of short-term optimization. A new balance is needed—one that favors exploration and solution-seeking in response to the climate challenge. Finally, society's growing fragility demands that we adopt new mechanisms to protect the most vulnerable. These are both internal challenges (reinforcing human solidarity, creating mobilizing narratives that encourage cooperation, redefining corporate objectives, "guided" corporate cooperation) and external ones, linked to our relationship with nature.

First, exploitation and overconfidence: we must move beyond the excessive logic of resource extraction and the blind faith we place in current economic mechanisms. Second, the hoarding of natural resources: sustainable management is now imperative. Third, the erosion of social ties: we must respond to the weakening of solidarity by reimagining the forms of cooperation we use and rebuilding social bonds (see Figure 8.1).

By drawing on this framework, it becomes possible to map out concrete avenues for collective action to meet the challenges posed by the ecological and societal crisis.

Rethinking the role of government

Neoliberalism reduced the role of the state, holding to the belief that it was no longer useful in a world it perceived as stable, as financial markets could ensure the optimal coordination of society. However, given the scale of today's challenges, cooperation is once again essential, and the state must return to playing a central role in organizing and structuring that society. It also has a fundamental responsibility to protect the most vulnerable, who will be hit first and hardest by the consequences of global warming.

That said, how can we mobilize people on a massive scale? As we have seen, since the appearance of *Homo sapiens*, the answer has been found in the ability to rebuild our shared values. But is it possible to rapidly transform a group's values? History provides us with a striking example: President Woodrow Wilson's shift in position when he decided to bring the United States into the First World War. This episode shows how, at times, the resolve of a single leader can alter the course of history.

In 1916, Wilson was re-elected, largely thanks to his support of US neutrality in the First World War; he even used the campaign slogan "He kept us out of war." In February 1917, the Quai d'Orsay sent Henri Bergson[9] to the White House to convince the American president that the war had deep moral implications.[10] Other events, such as attacks on defenseless American ships,

---

9   E. Kessler (2022), *Bergson, notre Contemporain* (Paris: Éditions de L'Observatoire/Humensis).

10   H. Bergson (1972), *Mélanges* (Paris: Presses universitaires de France, quoted by Emmanuel Kessler (E. Kessler (2022), *Bergson, notre Contemporain* (Paris: Éditions de L'Observatoire/Humensis)): "We had to show a naturally idealistic president the

confirmed this change in his position. In April 1917, Wilson committed the United States to war. Here is an extract from his speech to the US Congress:[11]

> I have called the Congress into extraordinary session because there are serious, very serious, choices of policy to be made, and made immediately [...]. It will involve the immediate addition to the armed forces of the United States already provided for by law in case of war at least 500,000 men [...].

He outlined his motivations and objectives:

> [...] let us be very clear, and make very clear to all the world, what our motives and our objects are [...] Our object now, as then, is to vindicate the principles of peace and justice in the life of the world as against selfish and autocratic power [...] The world must be made safe for democracy. Its peace must be planted upon the tested foundations of political liberty. We have no selfish ends to serve. We desire no conquest, no dominion.

He also set out what the American people should expect, or not expect, in return: "We seek no indemnities for ourselves, no material compensation for the sacrifices we shall freely make. We are but one of the champions of the rights of mankind."

A leader's role is, above all, to articulate a group's shared values—leading all its members to see what actions are necessary and generating new ways of cooperating.[12]

---

unique opportunity available to him to restore peace in the world [...] and to open a new era in the history of humanity." (Kindle Edition, p. 83; my translation).

11   W. Wilson, "Address to Congress Requesting a Declaration of War Against Germany," US Congress, April 2, 1917. Ultimately, 2 million Americans would be sent to Europe.

12   A French political "experiment" highlighted the recognition of this function: François Mitterrand, then a presidential candidate whose defeat was widely predicted, was questioned on television about the death penalty. He acknowledged that the majority of French people were in favor of the death penalty, but stated clearly and firmly that, if elected, he would abolish it. The next day, he was ahead of the incumbent President in the polls, and a few weeks later won the presidential election. Voters, though unfavorably disposed to the policy, recognized the leader's ability to set values for the group (https://www.ina.fr/ina-eclaire-actu/video/i00004518/francois-mitterrand-je-suis-contre-la-peine-de-mort).

In the field of climate change, a number of figures have played a decisive role in constructing mobilizing narratives. In 2006, Davis Guggenheim and Al Gore made their mark with their film *An Inconvenient Truth*, offering a clear, hard-hitting interpretation of the causes and impacts of global warming. Mark Carney, then Governor of the Bank of England, mobilized the financial community. On the political front, François Hollande asserted his determination to organize COP21, which, thanks to the expertise of Laurent Fabius, resulted in the first global agreement to limit global warming. This work has been continued by Emmanuel Macron through successive One Planet Summits.[13] Finally, Pope Francis brought a moral and spiritual dimension to the debate with his first encyclical dedicated to the subject, *Laudato Si'*.[14]

Political leaders have, therefore, launched initiatives around the world, but these remain scattered, are limited to certain territories, and are sometimes hampered by opposing forces. This highlights the need for more authoritative leadership—a role that is to some extent played by the IPCC, a remarkable collective experiment. With minimalist structure and a modest voluntary budget, this organization has succeeded in developing an authoritative narrative on global climate issues in a relatively short space of time. Yet its limited resources remain vastly disproportionate to the scale of the task, reducing its impact. Its statements, while important, struggle to capture the attention of the general public, and its highly technical reports are not aimed at a broad audience. It would be easy to imagine an enlarged,

---

13 Notably with the creation in Paris in December 2017 of the Network for Greening the Financial System, which brings together the central banks; this sends a strong message to the entire financial community of the issue's importance. See https://www.ngfs.net/en.

14 Pope Francis, *Laudato Si'*, Holy See, 2015, and in particular:

> These situations have caused sister earth, along with all the abandoned of our world, to cry out, pleading that we take another course. Never have we so hurt and mistreated our common home as we have in the last two hundred years. [...] The problem is that we still lack the culture needed to confront this crisis. We lack leadership capable of striking out on new paths and meeting the needs of the present with concern for all and without prejudice towards coming generations. The establishment of a legal framework which can set clear boundaries and ensure the protection of ecosystems has become indispensable; [...] men and women are still capable of intervening positively. For all our limitations, gestures of generosity, solidarity and care cannot but well up within us, since we were made for love.

better-funded structure that was capable of intervening more effectively in public debate and raising public awareness.

The emergence of authority in times of crisis is complex, yet some cultures have developed ways to construct it. As Pierre Clastres' analysis points out, Indigenous American societies had a nonhierarchical organizational system in times of peace:[15] "It is the lack of social stratification and the authority of power that should be stressed as the distinguishing features of the political organization of the majority of Indian societies."

This meant that the leader held no formal authority:[16]

> The chief is a "peacemaker"; he is the group's moderating agency, a fact borne out by the frequent division of power into civil and military. (2) He must be generous with his possessions, and cannot allow himself, without betraying his office, to reject the incessant demands of those under his "administration." (3) Only a good orator can become chief.

This situation changes in wartime:[17]

> It is truly remarkable that the features of the chieftainship stand in strong contrast to one another in time of war and in time of peace. Quite often the leadership of the group is assumed by two different individuals. [...] During military expeditions the war chief commands a substantial amount of power—at times absolute– over the group of warriors. But once peace is restored the war chief loses all his power.

The function of a leader in wartime[18] is to coordinate under existential constraints, to make the necessary trade-offs to ensure the survival of the

---

15 P. Clastres (1989), *Society Against the State: Essays in Political Anthropology*, translation by R. Hurley in collaboration with A. Stein (New York: Zone Books), Kindle Edition, Loc. 375.

16 P. Clastres (1989), *Society Against the State: Essays in Political Anthropology*, translation by R. Hurley in collaboration with A. Stein (New York: Zone Books), Kindle Edition, Loc. 398.

17 P. Clastres (1989), *Society Against the State: Essays in Political Anthropology*, translation by R. Hurley in collaboration with A. Stein (New York: Zone Books), Kindle Edition, Loc. 402.

18 This echoes Article 16 of the French Constitution of October 4, 1958. See https://www.conseil-constitutionnel.fr/la-constitution/quel-pouvoir- donne-l-article-16-de-la-constitution-au-president-de-la-republique.

collective and, if necessary, to orchestrate a rapid and profound change in the group's "values." When the United States entered the Second World War, this time constraint was particularly acute[19] and the scale of the adjustments to be made were immense. Christophe Prime illustrates this challenge by recalling that in 1940, the quantity of gunpowder available in the United States was sufficient for only one day's combat. In response to this emergency, the government set up a number of coordinating agencies[20] to mobilize production facilities and optimize resource allocation. At the beginning of 1942, carmakers abruptly ceased vehicle production to devote themselves to the war effort. The working week was extended from 38 to 48 hours, households were asked to save cooking fat for use in manufacturing explosives, and food rationing measures were introduced.[21] Mobilization was

---

Moreover, similarly to the Indigenous Americans' system, in Western societies, once peace has been achieved, the roles and authority of leaders can also be called into question. This is illustrated by the fate of Winston Churchill and Charles de Gaulle, who, although central figures during the Second World War, lost elections shortly after the end of the conflict. This transition reflects the need, in postcrisis contexts, to redefine collective priorities and forms of leadership suited to a new era.

19 F. D. Roosevelt (1942), "State of the Union Address," US Congress, January 6, 1942:

> Only this large-scale production will accelerate the final and total victory. It's speed that counts. Lost ground can always be regained, lost time never. Speed will save lives; speed will save this imperiled nation; speed will save our freedom and civilization.

20 C. Prime (2024), *America at War: 1933–1946* (Paris: Perrin):

> From now on, it is the federal government that will apply purchasing policy, set prices, and distribute contracts and raw materials: Big Government imposes its views on Big Business (employers) and Big Labor (unions), preferring cooperation to coercion. (Kindle Edition, p. 179; my translation)

21 C. Prime (2024), *America at War: 1933–1946* (Paris: Perrin):

> Reducing food waste is becoming a national goal. [...] Roosevelt asked his compatriots not to eat meat on Tuesdays [...] Candies, chocolate bars and fruit jellies became unobtainable, as these energy-giving treats were reserved for soldiers who consumed them in large quantities. The rationing system inevitably provoked discontent among American consumers unaccustomed to restrictions and this state takeover of their lives. (Kindle Edition, p. 230; my translation)

total, even creating migratory flows to the industrial towns,[22] which demonstrated a remarkable societal adaptability. In just two and a half years, the United States had transformed itself, recovering from the surprise attack on Pearl Harbor enough to organize the successful Normandy landings, illustrating a society's ability to reinvent itself under pressure.

Once reinstated in a coordinating role, the state can identify the forces at work, as well as the strategic points of bifurcation.[23] To do this, the state needs to map the forces present and consider possible actions on them. This approach reduces the field of possibilities and increases the likelihood of favorable situations arising. In August 1939, Franklin D. Roosevelt received a letter from Albert Einstein alerting him to the possibility that the Nazi regime might be developing a nuclear bomb. At the time, it was difficult for the American president to gauge the letter's importance. However, a new realm of possibilities had just emerged—one that Roosevelt chose to activate through the Manhattan Project. It is on these critical points that policymakers can focus their efforts, thereby steering their actions in a pragmatic manner based on the confirmation or refutation of the assumptions linked to these nodes. In the case of the climate, although many exploratory initiatives are underway, their slow pace remains a problem given the time constraints. This inertia can be explained by a pessimistic perception on the part of companies, who doubt they will be able to achieve the desired state, as shown by Philippe Aghion et al.[24] Furthermore, companies tend to

---

22 C. Prime (2024), *America at War: 1933–1946* (Paris: Perrin): "The country is traversed by large-scale migratory movements [...].Twenty-four million people are moving [...] In five years, six and a half million rural dwellers have left the countryside." (Kindle Edition, p. 220; my translation).

23 See M. Biesbroek, B. Glavovic, M. Haasnoot, J. Lawrence, R. Lempert, and V. Muccione (2020), "Defining the Solution Space to Accelerate Climate Change Adaptation," *Regional Environmental Change* 20 (37).

24 P. Aghion, C. Antonin, and S. Bunel (2020), *Le Pouvoir de la Destruction Créatrice* (Paris: Odile Jacob):

> The same applies to companies as to schoolchildren, and empirical studies corroborate this astonishing parallel: companies close to the technological frontier will innovate more to "escape competition"; conversely, other companies, far from the technological frontier, will be discouraged by competition. (Kindle Edition, p. 81; my translation)

In other words, in the logic of Bayesian cognitive inference, a company that is close to the technological frontier—i.e., using the most advanced technologies in its sector—believes that it alone can achieve the desired state—such as market

innovate in areas where they already have experience, thus limiting their field of exploration.[25]

Recent history offers a number of examples where European states have been able to organize international cooperation to overcome these limitations. The creation of Airbus, at a time when no individual player could offer a credible alternative to Boeing, is a real success story in this field. Similarly, initiatives such as the European Battery Industry[26] have brought together manufacturers and financiers to take steps that are essential to the energy transition. Last but not least, trust is a key success factor in the event of a crisis. According to the logic of Bayesian cognitive inference, trust removes noise about the values and desired states of others, and therefore promotes actions that will help achieve these states, notably through cooperation. And as shown by Yann Algan and Daniel Cohen[27] in the case of

---

domination—and implements an appropriate policy that involves competition with the other players. A company that is far from the probability of achieving this state does nothing.

25 As Philippe Aghion *et al.* have shown in the automotive sector (P. Aghion, A. Dechezleprêtre, D. Hemous, R. Martin, and J. Van Reenen (2016), "Carbon Taxes, Path Dependency and Directed Technical Change: Evidence from the Auto Industry," *Journal of Political Economy* 124 (1): 1–51).

26 https://www.eba250.com.

27 Y. Algan and D. Cohen (2021), "Les Français au Temps du Covid-19: Économie et Société face au Risque Sanitaire," *Les Notes du Conseil d'analyse économique*, no. 66, October:

> Two qualitative parameters play a crucial role: Interpersonal trust and trust in government. Measured before the onset of the crisis, they imposed themselves as a constraint on the government. [...] the higher the level of trust, the more limited the recession. [...] Countries that entered the crisis with higher levels of interpersonal trust thus resorted to less stringent containment policies in the first half of the year, relying more on trust between citizens. Moreover, it is possible that in a crisis situation, a low level of interpersonal trust makes it more difficult to coordinate actors to continue business [...]. Governments that entered the crisis with higher levels of trust were less systematic in enforcing such strict containment rules than others, and compliance with sanitary rules was also higher there. (My translation)

More generally, Karla Hoff, Allison Demeritt and Joseph Stiglitz show the impact of trust on the development of economies through the ages, with examples from Northern Italy, Africa, and areas close to gulags (K. Hoff, A. Demeritt, and J. Stiglitz (2024), "The Long Shadow of History," in *The Other Invisible Hand: The Power of Culture to Promote or Stymie Progress* (New York: Columbia University Press)).

Covid, trust must be considered as a public good to be preserved and reinforced, as it is essential to the smooth functioning of cooperative policies.

Similarly, there are also situations in which the state must assume an essential part of the exploration role.[28] History offers remarkable examples of this kind of leadership, such as that of NASA. Just eight years after President John F. Kennedy's address to Congress on May 25, 1961, the United States successfully carried out the first crewed lunar landing and return, exemplifying the effectiveness of coordinated state-led mobilization in achieving complex technological objectives.

In the case of climate, spending on green innovation remains largely insufficient, as the International Energy Agency (IEA) has pointed out.[29] It is imperative to accelerate the transition of technologies that are still at the prototype stage to large-scale deployment.[30] Some are calling

---

28 As was also the case with Covid, as Joseph Stiglitz reminds us (J. Stiglitz (2024), *The Road to Freedom: Economics and the Good Society* (W. W. Norton & Company)):

> Despite the mistaken general impression that the mRNA vaccine was the result of the skills and effort of private companies, the success was due to a partnership that worked. Pfizer's vaccine was actually codeveloped with BioNTech SE, a German biotechnology company that had received government subsidies. And every company's timely success was only possible because of previous government-funded and university-funded research on mRNA platforms. (Kindle Edition, p. 203)

29 IEA (2021), *Net Zero by 2050: A Roadmap for the Global Energy Sector* (International Energy Agency):

> Government R&D spending needs to be increased and reprioritized. Critical areas such as electrification, hydrogen, bioenergy and carbon capture, utilisation and storage (CCUS) today receive only around one-third of the level of public R&D funding of the more established low-carbon electricity generation and energy efficiency technologies. (p. 16)

30 IEA (2021), *Net Zero by 2050: A Roadmap for the Global Energy Sector* (International Energy Agency):

> Reaching net zero by 2050 requires further rapid deployment of available technologies as well as widespread use of technologies that are not on the market yet. [...] But in 2050, almost half the reductions come from technologies that are currently at the demonstration or prototype phase. (p. 15)

for a new Apollo[31] program for green innovation, or the creation of a "carbon NASA" to organize international development of concrete solutions—such as carbon-capture technologies deployed on a large scale and nuclear breakthroughs—within tight deadlines.[32]

The state can also support exploration by backing basic and applied research. The example of the fight against Covid-19 speaks for itself: when it launched Operation Warp Speed,[33] the US government injected $10 billion into promising vaccine technologies, enabling development and large-scale production in record time. Similarly, the German government's support for BioNTech contributed decisively to the rapid development of mRNA vaccines. As a result, countries like France had lifted most restrictions by March 2022, just two years after the WHO's designation of Covid-19 as a pandemic on March 11, 2020.

In the face of structural blockages linked to climate change, it would be naïve to think that companies will adjust to the scale of the challenge on their own. Carbon taxes, while useful, have been criticized for weakening the principle of responsibility by allowing polluters to pay financial compensation. A more radical alternative lies in prohibition rather than financial sanctions. The logic is simple: when a state wants to protect its citizens, it applies legal prohibitions rather than creating compensation

---

31 J. Browne, D. King, R. Layard, G. O'Donnell, M. Rees, N. Stern, and A. Turner (2015), *Global Apollo Programme to Combat Climate Change* (London: London School of Economics).

32 To buy some time, governments could also explore ways to reduce the amount of solar radiation reaching the Earth—though they would have to tackle significant governance challenges. See for example G. Davies and J. Vinders, (2025), "Geoengineering, the Precautionary Principle, and the Search For Climate Safety," *European Journal of Risk Regulation*.

33 M. Hepburn and M. Slaoui (2020), "Developing Safe and Effective Covid Vaccines-Operation Warp Speed's Strategy and Approach," *New England Journal of Medicine* 383 (18): 1701–1703:

> OWS's role is to enable, accelerate, harmonize, and advise the companies developing the selected vaccines. [...] OWS''s strategy relies on a few key principles. First, we sought to build a diverse project portfolio that includes two vaccine candidates based on each of the four platform technologies. [...] Second, we must accelerate vaccine program development without compromising safety, efficacy, or product quality. [...] Finally, OWS is supporting the companies financially and technically to commence process development and scale up manufacturing while their vaccines are in preclinical or very early clinical stages.

mechanisms. Fortunately, no one can go out simply pay a fine for having committed a murder; the law forbids it entirely. So, if global warming is rightly perceived as a threat to the group, the same protective mechanisms should apply to preserve that society and its environment.

It's not an illusory idea. In 2022, 65% of the cars produced in Europe were still powered by combustion engines, but the decision was made to ban these from sale from 2035 rather than simply imposing higher taxes on them. Similarly, the fight against the depletion of the ozone layer has been waged not by taxing chlorofluorocarbons, but by banning them altogether. As we shall see below, new laws are already being passed here and there to protect nature.

The state's financial institutions can play a crucial role in promoting public-goods innovation,[34] mobilizing public investors to fund prototype financial solutions that help to unblock critical problems. For example,[35] as highlighted by the IMF,[36] a World Bank subsidiary set up a public–private partnership to finance green infrastructure in emerging economies, mobilizing public resources to enable private capital to invest.[37] Similarly, the first financial innovation[38] to provide a large-scale solution[39] to address the Tragedy of the Horizon— a term coined by Mark Carney to describe the mismatch between the short time horizons of financial markets, businesses, and policymakers, and the much longer time horizon of climate change risks—[40] was backed by two public institutional investors.[41] These initiatives

34 P. Bolton, S. Levin, and F. Samama (2020), "Navigating the ESG World," in *Sustainable Investing: a Path to a New Horizon*, edited by H. Bril, G. Kell, and A. Rasche, pp. 131–150 (Princeton, NJ: Princeton University).

35 P. Bolton, X. Musca, and F. Samama (2020), "Global Public-Private Investment— Partnerships (GPPIPs): A Financial Innovation with a Positive Impact on Society," *Journal of Applied Corporate Finance* 32 (2) (Spring): 31–41.

36 IMF (2022), "Global Financial Stability Report: Navigating the High-Inflation Environment," *International Monetary Fund*.

37 P. Bolton, S. Peters, A. Rabah, F. Samama, and J. Stiglitz (2017), "From Global Savings Glut to Financing Infrastructures," *Economic Policy* 32 (90) (April): 221–261.

38 M. Andersson, P. Bolton, and F. Samama (2016), "Climate Change Hedging," *Financial Analysts Journal* 72 (3) (May-June): 13–32.

39 R. Eccles and S. Klimenko (2019), "The Investor Revolution," *Harvard Business Review*, May–June.

40 M. Carney (2015), "Breaking the Tragedy of the Horizon: Climate Change and Financial Stability." Speech presented at Lloyd's of London, London, September 29. *Bank of England*.

41 M. Andersson, P. Bolton, and F. Samama (2016), "Governance and Climate Change: a Success Story in Mobilizing Support for Corporate Responses to Climate Change," *Journal of Applied Corporate Finance* 28 (Spring): 1–13.

show how important it is for public authorities to have a detailed understanding of financial market mechanisms to mobilize them effectively.[42]

But steering requires steering tools. The state, as supervisor, must monitor the adjustment risks of entities that are important to the economy, i.e., banks. These supervision and monitoring tools can be deduced from the preceding analysis. If the objective is to maintain a trajectory compatible with a maximum temperature rise of 1.5°C, as discussed in Chapter 1, it is imperative to reduce the volume of CO_2 emitted each year by 24% between 2025 and 2050. By way of comparison, even in 2020, during the Covid-19 pandemic, emissions fell by just 7%. To achieve the necessary targets, a binding and robust framework is needed. In 2021, 113 countries— representing 70% of global emissions— committed to achieving carbon neutrality, and several of them, such as Canada, the UK, the EU, and Japan, incorporated these targets into their legislation. This empowers financial authorities in each country to question whether their banking systems align with climate commitments.[43] Given the time urgency, these authorities should ask all their banking institutions to provide an estimate of the future carbon footprint[44] of their balance sheets.[45] And, to support this process, public authorities should require companies to make public a future estimate of their carbon footprint (or *carbon guidance*[46]), modeled on "earnings guidance" they already provide.

---

42 J. Boissinot and F. Samama (2017), "Climate Change: A Policy Making Case Study of Capital Markets' Mobilization for Public Good," in *Coping with the Climate Crisis*, edited by R. Arezki, P. Bolton, K. El Aynaoui, and M. Obstfeld, pp. 179–200 (New York: Columbia University Press).

43 For a bank, not complying with these commitments would mean taking the material risk of depreciating its credits or assets linked to carbon-intensive sectors. For governments, such a situation would represent a major danger: A weakened banking system could lead to contagion effects, threatening the health of the entire economy.

44 P. Bolton, M. Kacperczyk, and F. Samama (2022), "Net-Zero Carbon Portfolio Alignment," *Financial Analysts Journal*, 78 (2): 19–33.

45 As well as a whole battery of "carbon greek letters," including the "carbon theta." The theta reflects the sensitivity of the option price to time, which, as we have seen, is essential in the case of climate change.

46 P. Bolton, M. Kacperczyk, and F. Samama (2022), "Net-Zero Carbon Portfolio Alignment," *Financial Analysts Journal*, 78 (2): 19–33. European regulations are already moving in this direction. Investors would be able to immediately identify companies that are already following a virtuous trajectory in terms of climate transition, thus facilitating the creation of portfolios based on these criteria. This transparency would also establish market discipline with regard to carbon

Rethinking the role of corporations

A corporation's economic weight carries with it a corresponding social responsibility. It must reinforce its role as a solution provider by developing technologies such as carbon capture, low-cost renewable energy production, and solutions to reduce energy consumption.

To encourage this mobilization, it is essential for civil society to engage in a profound reflection on the value of things and the objectives of corporations. Is this feasible? Yes, because the value of things, like the goals of corporations, are the result of a social consensus that has constantly evolved over time.[47] While the use of a pair of shoes, from Aristotle's sandal to a pair of NBA sneakers, has remained the same, its perceived value has changed considerably over the ages. Today, a new value has to impose itself: the living being, whose very existence is threatened by the climate crisis, must replace the consumer as the ultimate reference.

Likewise, we have also seen that the role of corporations has evolved considerably over the centuries. Initially, their role was to support governments in financing major industrial projects, before their benefits could be extended to the wider society. Today, their dominant objective is to maximize profits for shareholders, who are their legal owners, according to Milton Friedman's interpretation.[48] But this analysis is flawed for at least three reasons. First, it makes a logical "leap": equity investors, who often

---

neutrality commitments: companies that fail to meet their targets several times in a row would be penalized, as would those that fail to meet their earnings guidance forecasts. For the most part, this exercise would not be very complex, as companies already have good visibility of their business over the next three years.

47   See Mark Carney (M. Carney (2021), *Value(s): Building a Better World for All* (London: William Collins)), who also called for new values. Schematically, we first had Aristotle, who based the price of things on their utility and exchange value. Then, in the Middle Ages, and in particular with Saint Thomas Aquinas, came the notion of the "fair price," defined in terms of moral values such as avarice. This perception then evolved with the development of international trade, which emphasized the value of exchange, giving rise to mercantilism. Then value shifted to agricultural production, with the French physiocrats, and in particular François Quesnay's *Tableau économique*, showing the predominant role of farmers. Then, with the Industrial Revolution, value shifted to labor as the primary source of creation. Finally came the neoclassics, for whom a price depended on the subjective utility of the product, particularly from the consumer's point of view.

48   M. Friedman (1970), "The Social Responsibility of Business is to Increase Its Profits," *New York Times*, Sept. 13, 1970.

hold only a fraction of a corporation's capital, own neither that corporation nor its assets, but only shares—i.e., a financial security. Second, as briefly mentioned in Chapter 3, shareholders provide a specific financial resource: risk financing. This gives them certain rights, including the right to influence the corporation's development; but other stakeholders, such as bondholders, also contribute to this financing. Although the risk profile of bondholders is different—and generally lower than that of shareholders—they also play a key role, particularly in the event of major financial difficulties, when they can have a decisive influence on the corporation's fate. Finally, influence does not always mean ownership.[49] Consequently, the very idea of having to act exclusively in the interests of an "owner" dissolves by itself under closer examination.[50] This questioning opens the way to a redefinition of corporate objectives, and of whether these should also take society's interests into account, as without that society corporations would not exist.

In line with this trend, ESG—or Environmental, Social, and Governance—criteria have gained significant attention in recent years, prompting ongoing discussions about their role and effectiveness. This concept sits at the crossroads of several issues, including a broader reflection on the role of the company in society, but it can also be seen from two other perspectives.

---

49   If we consider another form of collective action, such as that taken by a country, the example of elections is illuminating. When an election is held, citizens participate in defining the country's "strategy" by choosing leaders who represent their will. However, this in no way means that they "own" the country: they can't sell it, let alone destroy it.

50   Or as Jean-Philippe Robé puts it (J.P. Robé (2012), "Being Done With Milton Friedman Accounting," *Accounting, Economics, and Law*, 2 (2), article 3):

> Milton Friedman made a "demonstration" that has the appearance of science but is totally fanciful. [...] The first is that since shareholders own the firm, says he, corporate executives must follow their masters' orders and maximize the owners' interest in the management of the firm [...] After the process of incorporation, shareholders have *no right of access* to the assets of the corporation; they *do not enter into any contract* in its name. No liability can arise for them from the corporate activity. They *do not run the corporation and do not own it*. [...] Referring to a property right that does not and cannot exist—and therefore to an agency relationship that does not and cannot exist—is a total incongruity, a fundamental flaw in Friedman's reasoning.

The first is the adaptation of the corporation to its environment.[51] The corporation of the 21st century is very different from that of the 1950s, particularly in the nature of its interaction with the outside world.[52] The number and sensitivity of the points at which the company interacts with its environment have greatly increased. These ESG criteria act as societal sensors—covering issues such as employee diversity, board diversity, gender parity policy, etc.—which enables companies to better perceive and respond to their stakeholders' expectations. This reinforces their legitimacy and their access to essential nonfinancial resources. Therefore, ESG criteria play a key role in filling the information gap for investors on a corporation's access to these essential resources. In this way, they enable us to better assess a corporation's ability to adapt and prosper in a complex and constantly evolving environment.[53]

The impact movement, which aims to limit the negative effects of corporations on their environment and society, is moving in a similar direction. However, it raises a major difficulty: how can we objectively measure the contribution of corporations to externalities, whether positive or negative? These are neither homogeneous across cultures, nor uniform throughout the world.[54] However, this problem is easier to address when it comes to the climate, for two main reasons. First, the climate challenge is a universal reality, which affects everyone on the planet. Second, climate risk is a top

---

51 P. Bolton, S. Levin, and F. Samama (2020), "Navigating the ESG World," in *Sustainable Investing: a Path to a New Horizon*, edited by H. Bril, G. Kell, and A. Rasche, pp. 131–150 (Abingdon: Routledge).

52 As we quickly saw in Chapter 6, if we take, for example, the IT leader of the time, IBM, it sold large computer systems in developed countries, to interlocutors similar to IBM's employees (white males), and for tasks limited to mass computing. Seventy years later, the new leader Apple operates worldwide, selling its products to billions of people who use them for sometimes private purposes (body data, etc.). These resources have also evolved over time. While financial capital was the most important resource when modern corporations were created, and again when accounting standards were codified in the wake of the 1929 crash, other types of capital have now become essential: human, societal, natural, and intellectual capital.

53 P. Bolton, S. Levin, and F. Samama (2020), "Navigating the ESG World," in *Sustainable Investing: a Path to a New Horizon*, edited by H. Bril, G. Kell, and A. Rasche, pp. 131–150 (Abingdon: Routledge).

54 A recent example illustrates this heterogeneity: after the San Bernardino terrorist attack in 2015, the FBI asked Apple to unlock the iPhone of one of the murderers. Apple refused, citing the protection of individual liberties. Conversely, Bill Gates took a different stance, arguing in favor of access to data, in the name of defending the collective interest.

priority for many corporations, whether in terms of disruptions to their supply chains, tighter environmental regulations, or changes in consumer expectations. This has made climate an indisputable priority in the integration of ESG criteria and the transformation of business models.[55]

Given the dominance of exploitative logic (as outlined in Chapter 6), it is essential that we encourage a culture of exploration. This could involve cultivating a kind of "societal dopamine" by fostering innovation and encouraging risk-taking. One solution would be to grant a special societal status to the explorer entrepreneur. This dynamic is already partially reflected in American capitalism, where iconic figures like Thomas Edison and Steve Jobs are celebrated as symbols of entrepreneurial exploration. This approach could be extended to other entrepreneurs, including those who have dared to explore without necessarily succeeding. This would mean recognizing that failure is an integral part of the exploration process, which in no way diminishes the value of such efforts for society. From this perspective, societal value is found not only in achieving final success, but also in the processes of exploring, testing, and innovating, as these help open up new avenues to meet contemporary challenges.

However, exploration means long-term. And corporations are facing a virtual absence of long-term investors. Indeed, whereas the average holding period for shares on the New York Stock Exchange was eight to nine years in the 1960s, it was reduced to 18 months in the early 1980s,[56] well before the advent of trading rooms and high-frequency trading. If its so-called "owners" are only around for a few months at most, a corporation will naturally tend to adopt a short-term strategy, focusing on immediate exploitation rather than exploration or transformation. Under these conditions, it is unrealistic to expect corporations to commit to medium- to long-term strategies, which take between five and seven years to bear fruit.

---

55 On the other hand, it's easy to see how this approach runs counter to the fundamental paradigm of capitalism, which is based on an amoral social organization. Today, however, the corporation finds itself at the heart of the societal challenge represented by climate change, due to its weight in society. It must therefore adapt to this new reality. This is all the more necessary if it is to continue to have access to the resources essential to its proper functioning, such as its human capital, which depends on its alignment with the environmental and social concerns of its time.

56 P. Bolton and F. Samama (2013), "Loyalty-Shares: Rewarding Long-Term Investors," *Journal of Applied Corporate Finance* 25 (3): 86–97.

This is where institutional investors, such as sovereign wealth funds or public pension funds, can play a decisive role. Players such as Norges Bank Investment Management in Norway or the Government Pension Investment Fund in Japan, with their size and long-term investment horizons, can positively influence companies, not only for the good of their own economies, but also for that of society as a whole.[57] Why not create a prestigious "steering committee" dedicated to the long-term, capable of attracting the best talent through a competitive remuneration policy? This structure would aim to align corporations with intergenerational objectives, providing them with the stability and support they need to focus on passing sustainable "wealth" to future generations. In short, such governance would give long-term aims the recognition and resources they deserve, and enable the corporation to establish itself as a pillar of the economy and society.

In the same vein, we could extend a mechanism that historically remunerates certain employees beyond their employment contracts—stock options—to all a corporation's loyal shareholders.[58] This would increase the weight of long-term investors among company shareholders, thus encouraging a strategy aligned with sustainable objectives.[59]

In line with this exploratory attitude, society also needs to make a clear distinction between optimization and resilience. Living beings do not seek the former, but the latter. Unlike optimization, which aims for maximum performance in a given context, resilience is about maximizing one's chances of survival in the face of uncertainty. It is based on the creation of systems capable of operating in various scenarios, while absorbing shocks that would jeopardize their survival, and then returning to a state that is as stable as possible. Where efficiency tends to eliminate redundancies in order to reduce costs, resilience retains certain redundancies that

---

57 As such, Hiro Mizuno, then Chief Investment Officer of Japan's Government Pension Investment Fund (GPIF), reflected on the role of his institution. Contributing to resilient financial markets was a benefit for Japanese pensioners. See R. Henderson, N. Jinjo, J. Lerner, and G. Serafeim (2019), "Should a Pension Fund Try to Change the World? Inside GPIF's Embrace of ESG," Harvard Business School, 9–319–067, March 1.

58 P. Bolton and F. Samama (2013), "Loyalty-Shares: Rewarding Long-Term Investors," *Journal of Applied Corporate Finance* 25 (3): 86–97.

59 J. Stiglitz (2015), *Rewriting the Rules of the American Economy: An Agenda for Growth and Shared Prosperity* (New York: Roosevelt Institute).

are essential in times of crisis. This distinction finds concrete application in the role played by the state in rescuing companies. The state sometimes intervenes to preserve critical sectors, such as banking or civil aviation. Yet its resources are limited, and should be devoted as a matter of priority to mechanisms that protect the group as a whole, rather than mobilized indefinitely in support of corporations that lack resilience. As a society, we therefore need to reflect on the mechanisms that will enable companies to absorb the increasing shocks associated with the entropy caused by climate disruption. The transition to a resilient society therefore also requires resilient capital structures,[60] as opposed to practices such as share buybacks, which are aimed solely at optimizing earnings per share.

While the recommendations made so far in this chapter have focused on strengthening adaptation and exploration to mitigate the risks associated with extreme entropy, another possible course of action is to reduce entropy itself. This is what governments are already doing when they make long-term commitments to reduce greenhouse gas emissions and implement binding or incentive measures to this end. Corporations, increasingly aware of the risks posed by high entropy, can help to reduce it by actively reshaping their environments.[61] They have an interest in cooperating with governments and sharing their industrial expertise to make public regulations as effective and relevant as possible. Obviously, this collaboration must not open the door to purely self-interested lobbying.[62] Greater transparency is essential to prevent abuses. Such precautions are gaining wide support as lobbying becomes increasingly risky in the age of social media and as intangible assets take on a growing role in companies. A transparent and constructive approach to interactions with governments is not only necessary for society, but also sensible for corporations.

---

60 P. Bolton and F. Samama (2012), "Capital Access Bonds: Contingent Capital with an Option to Convert," *Economic Policy* 27 (70): 275–317.

61 As in the case of COP 21, during which six oil groups asked negotiators for a price on carbon. Available at https://unfccc.int/ news/major-oil-companies-letter-to-un.

62 Especially to the so-called "connected" lobby, which is on the rise, as opposed to the so-called "technical" kind. See M. Bertrand, M. Bombardini, and F. Trebbi (2014), "Is it Whom You Know or What You Know? An Empirical Assessment of the Lobbying Process," *American Economic Review* 104 (12): 3885–3920.

Adjusting our representation of the world

The challenges we collectively face are clear: the first is to move away from a logic of exploitation, which is dangerous and ill-adapted to a world undergoing climate change. The second challenge is to reduce the consumption of fossil and natural resources, even though access to resources has historically been the driving force behind the cultures that have prevailed over the centuries. But how do we get out of our bubbles in a situation where rational discourse has failed? Where political leaders have failed to make climate change a civilizational struggle? Where solutions are known but not implemented? Where proposals are based on mechanisms selected over time to enable access to resources, while limiting that access is now the primary challenge? Where signals such as giant forest fires, endemic droughts, and recurring heatwaves are already front-page news? Where every human being on the planet has already had some experience of climate disruption?

One option is to generate a signal that will make us adjust our representation of the world right now—and not wait for a signal caused by climate disruption, which will come when it's too late. This signal would act as a shock that reactivates our values—and those values will, in turn, enable movement and collective action. To generate this driving signal, we can draw on one of the most powerful and recent images in human history: Earth, as seen from space (see Figure 8.2).

This image reveals three fundamental truths: the Earth is beautiful, fragile, and alive. This small, bright, and unique blue sphere contrasts with the icy black vastness of space, and this highlights its precious singularity.

Astronauts often report a profound shift in perspective after having seen the Earth from space, a phenomenon described by Frank White as the "Overview Effect." As he explains:[63]

> The Overview Effect is a shift in worldview reported by astronauts and cosmonauts during spaceflight, often while viewing the Earth from orbit, in transit between the Earth and the Moon, or from the lunar surface. It refers to the experience of seeing firsthand the reality that the Earth is in space, a tiny, fragile ball of life, "hanging in the void," shielded and nourished by a paper-thin atmosphere.

---

63   F. White (2023), *The Overview Effect: Space Exploration and the Human Evolution*, 4th edition, Multiverse Media Inc. (Oakland, CA: Multiverse); Kindle Edition, p. 28.

Figure 8.2 Photo of the Earth taken during the Apollo 17 mission

Source: NASA.[64]

Note: Although there have been other color photographs of the Earth, the first full imag—and perhaps the most iconic one—was taken by the Apollo 17 crew on December 7, 1972.

Although astronauts are typically selected for their ability to operate under extreme stress, many have described this experience as transformative:[65]

> The experience often transforms astronauts' perspective on the planet and humanity's place in the universe. Some common aspects of it are a feeling of awe, a profound understanding of the interconnection of all life, and a renewed sense of responsibility for taking care of the environment.

In witnessing Earth from this distant vantage point, astronauts come to fully perceive its fragility and the deep interdependence of all living beings. This reshaped perspective often leads to a sharpened awareness of humanity's collective responsibility toward the planet.

---

64 Available at: https://www.nasa.gov/image-article/blue-marble-image-of-earth-from-apollo-17/. The view of the Earth from space is already a theme of some environmental movements. See S. Jasanoff (2001), "Image and Imagination: The Formation of Global Environmental Consciousness," in *Changing the Atmosphere: Expert Knowledge and Environmental Governance*, edited by P. Edwards and C. Miller (Cambridge, MA: MIT Press).

65 F. White (2023), *The Overview Effect: Space Exploration and the Human Evolution*, 4th edition, Multiverse Media Inc. (Oakland, CA: Multiverse); Kindle Edition, p. 29.

Is it possible to experience a similar feeling without going into space? Yes, if we are to believe French President Georges Pompidou, whose February 28, 1970, speech in Chicago begins with this observation:[66]

> Human influence on nature has become such that it carries the risk of destroying nature itself. It is striking to note that at a time when so-called consumer goods are increasingly accumulating and spreading, it is the basic goods most necessary for life, such as air and water, that are beginning to be lacking. Nature appears to us less and less as the formidable power that man at the beginning of this century was still striving to master, but as a precious and fragile environment that must be protected so that the Earth remains habitable for man.

This calls for an environmental ethic: "We must create and spread a kind of 'environmental morality' requiring the state, local authorities and individuals to respect a few basic rules, without which the world would become unbreathable."

Then the French president shares his amazement:

> [...] the extraordinary epic of your astronauts setting out to conquer the Moon. Of all the images that television broadcast on that occasion, none struck me as much as that of the Earth, seen for the first time in interplanetary space. Enveloped in vapors, adorned with impressionist colors, the Earth appeared to us as an island lost in the middle of immensity, but one that we know is endowed with the fragile and perhaps unique privilege of life.
>
> What better vision than this, strange and yet familiar, could make us aware of the precariousness of our earthly universe and the duties of solidarity involved in safeguarding the human home?

Finally, let's hear from William Shatner, the iconic actor from *Star Trek*. Passionate about space exploration, in 2021 he had the opportunity to see the Earth from space himself, as those first astronauts had done:[67]

---

66   G. Pompidou (2016), *Discours de Chicago: La Crise des Civilisations*, Selected Texts No. 2 (Paris: Institut Georges Pompidou), available at https://www.georges-pompidou. org/publications/discours-chicago. My translation, here and below.

67   W. Shatner (with J. Brandon) (2022), *Boldly Go: Reflections on a Life of Awe and Wonder* (New York: Simon & Schuster), Kindle Edition, p. 89.

That beauty, that magnificence of the evolutionary process, struck me so hard in that moment because when I looked in the opposite direction, into space, there was no mystery, no majestic awe to behold... all I saw was death. I saw a cold, dark, black emptiness. [...] I turned back toward the light of home. I could see the curvature of Earth, the beige of the desert, the white of the clouds and the blue of the sky. It was life. Nurturing, sustaining, life. Mother Earth. Gaia.

This caused him to question his beliefs profoundly:[68]

Everything I had thought was wrong. [...] I had thought that going into space would be the ultimate catharsis of that connection I had been looking for between all living things—that being up there would be the next beautiful step to understanding the harmony of the universe [...] I had a different experience, because I discovered that the beauty isn't out there, it's down here, with all of us. Leaving that behind made my connection to our tiny planet even more profound.

Where Shatner had expected a symbiosis between Earth and space, he instead felt a profound shock at the difference he perceived between the Earth—alive—and the rest of space— empty, dead: "It was the opposite of life."

Beauty, fragility, and uniqueness of life. Rather than waiting for the harmful effects of global warming to update our representations of the world, it is possible—and it is certainly necessary—to transform our perceptions now. With this in mind, the image of the Earth as a symbol of the beauty, of its vulnerability,[69] and of the uniqueness of life could become a valuable tool in awakening a collective and universal consciousness.

How can we make this message resonate in people's minds? Why not start each morning at school with a moment of reflection, showing an image of the Earth from space, reminding students of their connection to

---

68 W. Shatner (with J. Brandon) (2022), *Boldly Go: Reflections on a Life of Awe and Wonder* (New York: Simon & Schuster), Kindle Edition, p. 89.

69 This fragility is also highlighted in all the reports on biodiversity. See P. Dasgupta (2021), *The Economics of Biodiversity: The Dasgupta Review* (London: HM Treasury). Moreover, according to Johan Rockström (C. Chapin et al. (2009), "A Safe Operating Space for Humanity," *Nature* 461 (September 24): 472–475), only the stabilization of climatic conditions on Earth has enabled the development of agriculture, and hence of human beings. It is this very stability that we are calling into question through climate disruption.

this unique planet? This could be extended with lessons on the social life of animals or the communication mechanisms of plants. Or, on a larger scale, why not organize a global broadcast of a view of the Earth from space, on a public holiday? Or at a global event, like the opening ceremony of the Olympic Games? Or even more ambitiously, why not set up a planetary event in which every country, time zone by time zone, takes part in a temporary blackout for a defined period, creating a kind of global wave,[70] joyful,[71] united, and visible from space?

Such collective experiences in which we share our awareness of Earth's beauty, the uniqueness of living beings, and the fragility of the planet are within our grasp. Modern communication and global synchronization technologies make them possible. This experience could activate fundamental human mechanisms for living together.

The first mechanism lies in a shared aesthetic experience. According to Immanuel Kant, beauty arouses disinterested and universalizable pleasure, which accustoms us to judge that which is beyond ourselves, as we do in the moral realm. Indeed, beyond the fact that beauty, like morality, does not operate through concepts,[72] it represents a transcendence of interest.[73]

> 1) The beautiful pleases **immediately** (but only in reflecting intuition, not, like morality, in the concept). 2) It pleases **without any interest** (the morally good is of course necessarily connected with an interest, but not with one that precedes the judgment on the satisfaction, but rather with one that is thereby first produced)[.]

---

70 Just like *Earth Hour.* See https://www.lemonde.fr/planete/article/2021/03/28/earth-hour-cities-around-the-world-turn-off-their-lights-for-the-planet_6074738_3244.html.

71 As seen above, happiness reinforces trust and therefore cooperation; see J. Dunn and M. Schweitzer (2005), "Feeling and Believing: The Influence of Emotion on Trust," *Journal of Personality and Social Psychology* 88(5): 736–748.

72 On the point of the absence of conceptualization, we can make the hypothesis that if the Bayesian movement is a search for laws from observations, there is an initial moment of exploration of the mind, which when it is not looking for laws, can become autonomous; this is creation, which moreover benefits from a moment of satisfaction in a harmony found, and that aesthetics is the manifestation of this phenomenon, which is also autonomous of the search for invariants.

73 I. Kant (2000), *Critique of the Power of Judgment* (The Cambridge Edition of the Works of Immanuel Kant), translation by P. Guyer and E. Matthews (Cambridge: Cambridge University Press, Kindle Edition, p. 227.

And, also like morality, beauty tends toward the universal:[74]

> 4) The subjective principle for judging of the beautiful is represented as **universal**, i.e., valid for everyone, but not as knowable by any universal concept (the objective principle of morality is also declared to be universal, i.e., knowable for all subjects, and at the same time also for all actions of one and the same subject, yet by means of a universal concept).

Therefore, contemplating nature activates a mechanism similar to that of morality:[75]

> We call buildings or trees majestic and magnificent, or fields smiling and joyful; even colors are called innocent, modest or tender, because they arouse sensations that contain something analogical to the consciousness of a mental state produced by moral judgments.

And thus it gently prepares human beings for morality:[76]

> Taste as it were makes possible the transition from sensible charm to the habitual moral interest without too violent a leap by representing the imagination even in its freedom as purposively determinable for the understanding and teaching us to find a free satisfaction in the objects of the senses even without any sensible charm.

Furthermore, as we saw in Chapter 4, faced with the challenge of living together in the Greek city, our predecessors invented new societal tools, including a shared perception of beauty. This was manifested in particular through the contemplation of public buildings, visible to all within the city. The ancient Greeks thus appear to have identified a fundamental human

---

74 I. Kant (2000), *Critique of the Power of Judgment* (The Cambridge Edition of the Works of Immanuel Kant), translation by P. Guyer and E. Matthews (Cambridge: Cambridge University Press), Kindle Edition, p. 227.

75 I. Kant (2000), *Critique of the Power of Judgment* (The Cambridge Edition of the Works of Immanuel Kant), translation by P. Guyer and E. Matthews (Cambridge: Cambridge University Press), Kindle Edition, p. 228.

76 I. Kant (2000), *Critique of the Power of Judgment* (The Cambridge Edition of the Works of Immanuel Kant), translation by P. Guyer and E. Matthews (Cambridge: Cambridge University Press), Kindle Edition, p. 228.

mechanism, as we saw with Michael Tomasello: the creation of shared values through collective observation. These shared values, in turn, fostered cooperation. Transposed to the current challenge of preserving nature, this shared perception of beauty now extends to the entire planet, paving the way for the establishment of a new social bond.

The second mechanism is responsibility. As we saw with Charles Darwin, morality, with care for the weakest at its core, drove the rise of the human species.[77] The fragility of the planet echoes the fragility of the human being, as seen by the philosopher Emmanuel Levinas, whose thinking follows in the footsteps of Edmund Husserl.[78] At the beginning of the 20th century, Husserl developed a philosophical theory known as phenomenology, which rethinks access to things: they are never given in their immediacy, for there is always a consciousness or an intentional act that perceives them. Only through a succession of perspectives is their essence disclosed.[79] Emmanuel Levinas, a student of Edmund Husserl and the one who introduced his work to the French public, takes up this reflection, but applies it to human beings.[80] He makes a fundamental distinction: things that can be grasped, possessed and known lend themselves to unlimited appropriation, whereas the human face resists this grasp and imposes a different relationship, marked by ethics:[81]

> The face is an irreducible mode in which being can present itself in
> its identity. A thing can never be presented personally and ultimately

---

77 Today, some business leaders such as Hubert Joly also rely on the mechanism of expressing vulnerability to encourage managerial mutual aid (H. Joly (2021), *The Heart of Business: Leadership Principles for the Next Era of Capitalism* (Boston: Harvard Business Review Press)).

78 E. Husserl (1960), *Cartesian Meditations: An Introduction to Phenomenology*, translated by D. Cairns (The Hague: Martinus Nijhoff).

79 By circling a chair, an exercise Edmund Husserl calls "eidetic variations," we perceive its specificities, revealing its essence. Transposed to Bayesian cognitive inference, this approach shows that different perspectives enable us to establish a categorization of the object, as illustrated with the Tufas in Chapter 2.

80 Not unimportantly, Emmanuel Levinas followed in the footsteps of Franz Rozenzweig (F. Rozenzweig (2005), *The Star of Redemption* (Modern Jewish Philosophy and Religion: Translations and Critical Studies), translated by B. Galli (Madison: The University of Wisconsin Press)). The two professional philosophers, confronted with two world wars, questioned Western philosophy at its Platonic roots—i.e., where absolute truths exist.

81 E. Levinas (1990), *Difficult Freedom: Essays on Judaism*, translated by S. Hand (Baltimore: Johns Hopkins University Press), p. 8.

has no identity. Violence is applied to the thing, it seizes and disposes of the thing. Things *give*,—they do not offer a face. They are beings without a face.

And possession can lead to violence, because it is absolute and implies the possibility of destroying the object. The face, on the other hand, escapes all forms of possession.[82]

The face [...] is inviolable; those eyes, which are absolutely without protection, the most naked part of the human body, none the less offer an absolute resistance to possession [...] To see a face is already to hear "You shall not kill" [...].

Distinct from things, the face invites a relationship based on responsibility:[83]

The first obvious thing in the other's face is the directness of exposure and that defenselessness. The human being in his face is the most naked; nakedness itself [...] The face looks at me, calls out to me. It claims me. What does it ask for? Not to leave it alone [...] My presence, of no avail perhaps, but a gratuitous movement of presence and responsibility for the other.

This impossibility of abandoning others leads to a true "love of neighbor":[84]

If we want to define what that famous love of ones neighbour—a shop-worn saying—is, [...] we have to return to that relation to the face qua mortality of ones neighbour and the impossibility of leaving him to his isolation.

This duty or free responsibility is independent of my actions:[85] "A gratuitous responsibility: independent of what I may or may not have committed.

---

82 E. Levinas (1990), *Difficult Freedom: Essays on Judaism*, translated by S. Hand (Baltimore: Johns Hopkins University Press), p. 8.

83 E. Levinas (1999), *Alterity and Transcendence*, translated by M. Smith (New York: Columbia University Press), p. 163.

84 E. Levinas (1999), *Alterity and Transcendence*, translated by M. Smith (New York: Columbia University Press, pp. 163–164.

85 E. Levinas (1999), *Alterity and Transcendence*, translated by M. Smith (New York: Columbia University Press), p. 129.

The non-transferrable responsibility of my logically indiscernible unique-ness. Responsibility which is also the stern name of love without lust."

This responsibility calls for no reciprocity, as Emmanuel Levinas points out:[86] "A responsibility without concern for reciprocity: I have to respond for another without attending to an other's responsibility in regard to me." This responsibility opens the way to sociability: "Love without concupis-cence; it is sociability itself."[87] Finally, this sociability transcends the natu-ral struggle for survival:[88]

> The fundamental trait of being is the preoccupation that every par-ticular being has with its very being. Plants, animals and all living things cling to their very existence. For everyone, it's the struggle for life. [...] And here in the human being is the possible appearance of an ontological absurdity: concern for others prevails over concern for oneself. (My translation)

In other words, the thing leads to possession, which can engender vio-lence, and to solitude.[89] With the face, on the other hand, a human being first appears to another as someone who cannot be possessed, thus curbing potential violence. Then, its fragility elicits a call to care for it, whatever its actions, without expecting reciprocity and without being able to avoid it. Finally, from this recognition emerges a sociability so profound that con-cern for the other can override the instinct for self-preservation. This is the first step toward ethics.

According to Emmanuel Levinas, a temptation to totality is thus (re)closed, opening the way to the infinite.[90] The totality of philosophical systems—and therefore of models—where truths are imposed on all and potentially

---

86 E. Levinas (1998), *Of God Who Comes to Mind*, translated by B. Bergo (Stanford, CA: Stanford University Press), Foreword, p. xv.

87 E. Levinas (1999), *Alterity and Transcendence*, translated by M. Smith (New York: Columbia University Press), p. 164.

88 E. Levinas (1994), *Les Imprévus de l'Histoire* (Paris: Fata Morgana), p. 201.

89 E. Levinas (1990), *Difficult Freedom: Essays on Judaism*, translated by S. Hand (Baltimore: Johns Hopkins University Press): "The violent man does not move out of himself. He takes, he possesses. Possession denies independent existence. To have is to refuse to be. Violence is a sovereignty, but also a solitude." (p. 9)

90 To use Emmanuel Levinas' title and thesis in *Totality and Infinity* (E. Levinas (1969), *Totality and Infinity: An Essay on Exteriority*, translated by A. Lingis (Pittsburgh: Duquesne University Press)).

generate violence, is opposed by the infinity of our responsibility toward others. This is because others, elusive in their singularity and fragility, cannot be reduced to a totality. This fragility calls for infinite responsibility (see Figure 8.3).[91]

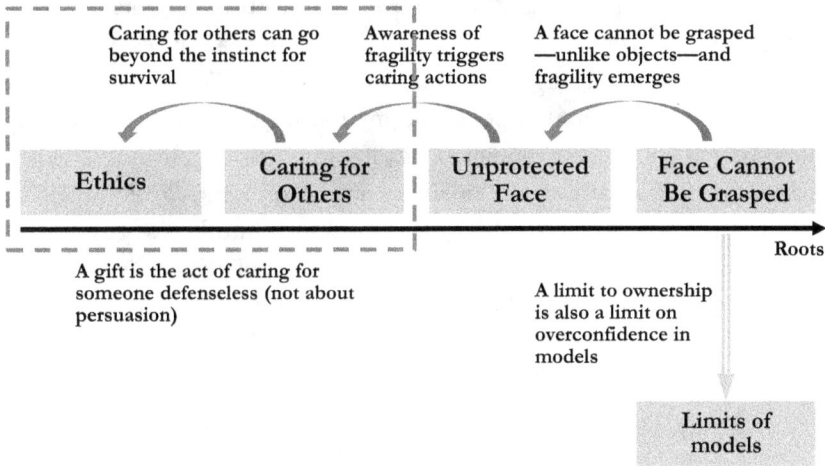

Figure 8.3 Synthetic diagram of Emmanuel Levinas' responsibility toward others
Source: Author.
Note: Unlike things, faces cannot be "grasped." This impossibility has two consequences. First, it curbs the belief that everything can be modeled. Second, it reveals the fragility of the face, which, being defenseless, calls for care. This concern for the other creates a movement away from the self, thus founding ethics, or responsibility toward others, beyond the instinct for self-preservation.

This "ethical" moment can also take place in the legal sphere, by granting rights to nature. New Zealand, for example, has already adopted this approach, granting legal personality (and the rights that go with it) to Te Urewera National Park and the Whanganui River. Representatives are appointed to defend these rights, in the same way as children's advocates are appointed ex officio before the courts.[92] Similarly, in 2008, nature's legal

---

91 Then comes the codification of this movement, in other words, its inscription as an explicit rule of group functioning, notably through the law; this is the case for the prohibition of murder or non-assistance to a person in danger.

92 As Michel Serres pointed out (M. Serres (2000), *Retour au Contrat Naturel*, Paris: Éditions de la Bibliothèque nationale de France), the history of law is marked by a progressive extension of the beneficiaries of legal protection:

personality was enshrined in Ecuador's Constitution, granting it various rights[93] and paving the way for a renewed relationship with it: "The people have decided to build a new form of civic life, in diversity and in harmony with nature to achieve the good life, sumak kaxsay" (my translation).

As François Ost points out,[94] this movement to attribute rights to nature is spreading, and is not limited to so-called emerging countries. For example, in a debate on fracking, the Pennsylvania Supreme Court ruled in favor of "preserving the natural values of the environment."[95] What's particularly interesting about this movement is that it was about establishing a global relationship with nature, as evidenced by the recognition of the rights given to the Ganges referred to by François Ost.[96] In other words, giving rights to nature is not just a way of protecting it, but above all a recognition of the relationship that human beings have with it. It comes down to accepting a sociability with nature.

[...] the whole history of law shows the progressive universalization of the right to become a subject of law: slaves once became so, children later, and women much more recently, a decision whose recent date is a disgrace to humanity. (Kindle Edition p. 26; my translation)

93   F. Ost, in P. Descola (ed.), (2018), *Les Natures en Question* (Paris: Odile Jacob), Kindle Edition, p. 214; my translation.
94   F. Ost, in P. Descola (ed.), (2018), *Les Natures en Question* (Paris: Odile Jacob):

Bolivia followed Ecuador's lead in 2010, passing the Mother Earth Rights Act; this law guarantees the rights to life, biodiversity, water, clean air, balance, restoration and non-pollution. It calls on the state and citizens to respect nature's rights, and provides an ombudsman for nature to protect its interests. (Kindle Edition, p. 215; my translation)

95   F. Ost, in P. Descola(ed.), (2018), *Les Natures en Question* (Paris: Odile Jacob), Kindle Edition p. 216; my translation.
96   F. Ost, in P. Descola (ed.), (2018), *Les Natures en Question* (Paris: Odile Jacob):

The granting of legal personality to a river the size of the Ganges by the Supreme Court of a common law state is unquestionably a legal event. [...] It is not ecological considerations based on the intrinsic value of the river that motivate this option, but rather the cultural rights of the Hindus, while the emphasis is placed, at the operational level, on very precise methods of managing this common asset. [...] the Ganges and the Yamuna are sacred to the Hindus, who have a deep spiritual relationship with them - a relationship of adoration and respect. (Kindle Edition, p. 217; my translation)

Mechanisms of this kind already exist in certain societies, as shown by Philippe Descola using the example of the Achuar of Amazonia. In contrast to the practices of European social structures,[97] these people dialogue with nature[98] and animals[99] through incantations[100] and dreams, forming relationships with them similar to those between human beings:[101]

> The Achuar were not [...] a society parachuted into an environment to which it had to adapt. Rather, they were a collective of humans interacting with nonhuman collectives perceived as being of the same nature as themselves. [...] Nonhuman people were hunted (animals) or eaten (plants), but they were seen as ontologically similar to humans. (My translation)

Socialization in the Amazon was shaped by a worldview profoundly different from that in Europe:[102]

---

97 P. Descola (2019), *Une Écologie des Relations* (Paris: CNRS Éditions, De Vive Voix): "The Indigenous Americans of this great rainforest [...] did not live in states or kingdoms, they had no established religion or clergy, they had no temples." Kindle Edition, p. 11; my translation.

98 P. Descola (2019), *Une Écologie des Relations* (Paris: CNRS Éditions, De Vive Voix): "These plants and animals appeared to the dreamers in human form and delivered a message to them. [...] the Achuar saw the plants and animals as social partners, as interlocutors, as people." Kindle Edition, p. 19; my translation.

99 P. Descola (2019), *Une Écologie des Relations* (Paris: CNRS Éditions, De Vive Voix).

100 P. Descola (2019), *Une Écologie des Relations* (Paris: CNRS Éditions, De Vive Voix):

> The Achuar spent a large part of their time singing magical incantations to communicate with beings who were either very far away or present but did not speak their language. [...] these are speeches from the heart, speeches from the soul [...] They are injunctions addressed to distant relatives or spouses [...] or songs of appeasement used in relation to plants and animals. (Kindle Edition, p. 18; my translation)

101 P. Descola (2019), *Une Écologie des Relations* (Paris: CNRS Éditions, De Vive Voix), Kindle Edition, p. 20.

102 P. Descola (2019), *Une Écologie des Relations* (Paris: CNRS Éditions, De Vive Voix). This approach echoes that of Marcel Hénaff (M. Hénaff (2002), "De la Philosophie à l'Anthropologie: Comment Interpréter le Don? Interview with Marcel Hénaff," *Esprit* (February) (1): 135–158), who traces the distinction between hunter-gatherers and pastoralist-farmers:

> These hunter-gatherer societies do not practice sacrifice; [...] their relationship with the animal world is one of constant, egalitarian exchange, [...] this

> In Europe, we think that humans are a species (Homo sapiens sapiens) completely apart because they have an interiority. [...] In animist societies [...] the opposite was true. Most nonhumans (not all) also had a soul, a kind of internal disposition, an interiority similar to that of humans. On the other hand, physical dispositions varied according to species, each occupying a particular kind of ecological niche. (My translation)

Is this mode of sociability with nature accessible to Western city-dwellers? To answer this question, allow me to share some of my experiences with large animals.

I witnessed a buffalo being attacked by lionesses. The next day, satiated, they were dozing, their bellies full, while a cub, its snout plunged into the carcass, continued to feed. Suddenly, all the lionesses turned their heads in the direction of a lion that had just appeared at the top of an embankment. It roared, then galloped toward the carcass. Immediately, the lionesses formed a circle around the remains of the buffalo, the lion cub still absorbed in his feast. The lion approached the carcass and began to eat, but soon let out a growl in the direction of the cub, who ignored it. Suddenly, with a flick of his paw, he threw the young animal into the air. Falling back onto its paws, the animal ran to take refuge with what seemed to be its mother, uttering little cries. The scene was disturbingly reminiscent of certain episodes in human life.

Later, at the edge of a clearing, I observed impalas rubbing shoulders with monkeys. The former could sense the presence of lions thanks to their sense of smell, while the latter could spot them from the treetops. Two species had pooled their natural aptitudes to better protect each other.

Finally, during a walk on the savanna, as soon as we stepped out of the vehicle, an old cerebral mechanism, inherited from our distant ancestors, kicked in. Still human, but suddenly perceived—wrongly—as potential hunters, and above all as game, our senses sharpened. We were no longer mere observers, at a distance from the animals, but animals among animals.

These moments—the family life of animals, the cooperation between species, and the felt sense of our own animal nature—profoundly reshaped

---

animal world is also a world of spirits, [...] the fundamental link between humans and nonhumans is a relationship of alliance; [...] this world of alliance [...] is the opposite of the world of filiation that dominates among pastoralists-farmers. (My translation)

our representation of the world. Without sending contingents of children to the savanna, it is essential to teach them about the rich social life of animals from an early age. Similarly, learning about plant life in the field could help awaken a new sensitivity toward living things and nature.[103] Children would be astonished to discover, for example, that acacia trees, when attacked by kudu, make their leaves astringent and therefore inedible, thus scaring the animals away. Even more fascinating, these trees transmit a defense signal to those around them by releasing a gas.[104] Certain other plants emit another gas capable of triggering rain.[105] In children, this sense of wonder would trigger the release of dopamine—the molecule which, as we saw in Chapter 2, rewards exploration and produces a deep feeling of satisfaction. Beyond its benefits for the human body—lower blood pressure, etc.—[106] immersion in nature can be a source of wellbeing and happiness.[107]

The third mechanism is the recognition of the specificity and uniqueness of living things. As we saw in Chapter 6, the emergence of agriculture coincides with the moment when human beings invent an explanatory framework governing the workings of nature. They then establish a dialogue with the gods, so as to receive, in a give-and-take exchange, the natural elements necessary for their survival, such as water, fodder for theirs livestock, and so on. The mechanism is effective because trust in this new representation of the world, in addition to allaying fears of loss, also strengthens faith in the agricultural system itself. This in turn encourages

---

103 A relationship with nature that has faded with the spread of cities, but also through the representation of the world that is offered to children, as Susan Clayton et al. have shown by studying the presence of nature in Walt Disney films (S. Clayton, A.-C. Julliard, and R. Julliard (2014), "Historical Evidence for Nature Disconnection in a 70-year Time Series of Disney Animated Films," *Public Understanding of Science* 24 (6): 672–680).

104 F. Hallé (2022), *In Praise of Plants*, translated by D. Lee (Portland, OR: Timber Press), referring to Wouter van Hoven (W. Van Hoven (1991), "Mortalities in Kudu (*Tragelaphus Strepsiceros*) Populations Related to Chemical Defence in Trees," *Journal of African Zoology* 105 (2): 141–145).

105 D. Bourg and S. Swaton (2021), *Primauté du Vivant: Essai sur le Pensable* (Paris: Presses Universitaires de France/Humensis).

106 M. Le Van Quyen (2022), *Cerveau et Nature: Pourquoi nous Avons Besoin de la Beauté du Monde* (Paris: Flammarion).

107 This is tantamount to returning the human being to their position as an animal among their fellow creatures, a position abandoned with the advent of agriculture, as we saw in Chapter 6. It is therefore a reversal of perspectives that have been anchored for over 10,000 years.

a greater allocation of resources, consolidating that system's success. As a corollary effect, human beings are extracted from nature and rise above it, as evidenced by their portrayal in rock paintings.

Then comes the shock of life's uniqueness, stirred by the sight of Earth from space.

First of all, this experience of the uniqueness of life naturalizes the very process of thought and situates it within its broader evolution: a basic brain mechanism (Bayesian cognitive inference), a development to gain access to resources (persistence hunting), an adoption as a cooperation mechanism (reasoning), the creation of an entirely new mechanism replicating it (financial markets), growth in its societal use (from marginal to dominant), and finally, overconfidence as a result of its success. In other words, where thought has been overhanging nature since agriculture, its naturalization reintegrates it into the life's great adventure.

Second, this living world, in contrast to the world of planets and the immutable laws of physics, highlights the distinction made by Henri Bergson which we saw in Chapter 7. Science, born of the mechanisms of cognitive Bayesian inference, looks for invariants in order to establish laws. But in the living world, in life, a permanent process of creation is taking place. The living world therefore limits our overconfidence in understanding the world by means of the thinking mechanisms that stem from our desire to act. This sense of humility echoes the thinking of Emmanuel Levinas: the encounter with another's face is an acute expression of the singularity of the living, an irreducible otherness that escapes all modeling— and, consequently, all forms of overconfidence.

What's more, this view from space puts us back in the midst of the living world of which we are a part, even if we thought we had extracted ourselves from it with the advent of agriculture. Is there a thought experiment in European culture that places the human being back in nature? Yes, that of Baruch Spinoza. After pointing out that the two basic mechanisms of understanding are the passions and reason, the Dutch philosopher proposes a third path, that of intuitive science, which enables us to perceive the unity of nature: "*Deus, sive Natura*" or "God, or Nature."[108] This is Baruch

---

108 B. Spinoza (1985), *The Collected Works of Spinoza, Volumes I and II*, edited and trans- lated by Edwin Curley (Princeton, NJ: Princeton University Press, "On Human Bondage, or the Powers of the Affects," Apple Books, p. 1363.

Spinoza's great message: a monism that extracts human beings from all transcendence, as Robert Misrahi points out:[109]

> This is because the rational system of infinite Nature, both Spirit and Matter, knowable by reason, frees the human spirit from all dependence on a personal God or Nature Providence. Because this system is a monism, it frees man from all transcendence. (My translation)

This leads to a reversal of the "agricultural moment"—i.e., of the desire for control:[110] "Wisdom will not be a mastery of mind over matter, or a victory of freedom over determinism: it will be another way of existing."

This other way of existing leads to wisdom:[111] "The unity of the whole of Nature and its absolute autonomy, by making immanence the place where humanity lives, makes possible the task of wisdom, which is to build the best of all possible lives."

And this wisdom is that of living, according to Baruch Spinoza:[112] "No one can desire to be blessed, to act well and to live well, unless at the same time he desires to be, to act, and to live, i.e., to actually exist."

It's also a joyful wisdom:[113] "To anthropomorphic and affective monotheism Spinoza thus substitutes a wisdom of perfect Joy through understood immanence."

This has its corollary, gratitude, the result of thankfulness for that which has made this happiness possible, according to Baruch Spinoza:[114] "Love is joy accompanied by the idea of an external cause."

---

109 R. Misrahi (2005–2013), *Spinoza—Une Philosophie de la Joie* (Paris: Éditions Médicis-Entrelacs), Kindle Edition, p. 51; my translation.

110 R. Misrahi (2005–2013), *Spinoza—Une Philosophie de la Joie* (Paris: Éditions Médicis-Entrelacs), Kindle Edition, p. 49; my translation.

111 R. Misrahi (2005–2013), *Spinoza—Une Philosophie de la Joie* (Paris: Éditions Médicis-Entrelacs), Kindle Edition, p. 51; my translation.

112 B. Spinoza (1985), *The Collected Works of Spinoza, Volumes I and II*, edited and translated by Edwin Curley (Princeton, NJ: Princeton University Press), "Part IV, Proposition 21," Apple Books, p. 1393.

113 R. Misrahi (2005–2013), *Spinoza—Une Philosophie de la Joie* (Paris: Éditions Médicis-Entrelacs), Kindle Edition, p. 117; my translation.

114 B. Spinoza (1985), *The Collected Works of Spinoza*, Volumes I and II, Part III, edited and translated by Edwin Curley (Princeton, NJ: Princeton University Press), "Definitions of the Affects, Definition VI," Apple Books, p. 1337.

Love is therefore not completeness, as in Plato, but gratitude for the external presence that makes happiness possible.

The consequences of this are manifold. First of all, as Baruch Spinoza says, totality, in its infinity, has no exterior, or cause other:[115] "By substance I understand that which is in itself and is conceived through itself—that is, that whose concept does not require the concept of another thing, from which it must be formed."

De facto, the absence of any other cause halts the process of Bayesian cognitive inference. In other words, since substance is infinite and therefore by definition without exteriority, it does not lend itself to the process of "escalation" inherent in explanatory inference, in the sense of an ever more abstract search for an explanatory framework, and thus halts its deployment. The shock of perceiving the living as unified and absolute then becomes a practical opportunity to close the parenthesis of the runaway process of Bayesian cognitive inference, born of agriculture. This was a tremendous moment for human development, but it also generated a split with the living world, which would abruptly be revealed by the climate challenge.

Furthermore, explanatory abstraction has always come up against the challenge of finding an observable element to validate the model, with multiple responses depending on the culture. By placing the human in nature, immanence resolves an intrinsic and unsurpassable incompleteness. Life is there, before our very eyes, and is self-sufficient. From now on, by setting a limit to the process of explanatory "escalation," a harmony is established, the source of the happiness spoken of by Baruch Spinoza.

Moreover, as human beings are reintegrated into nature through their physicality, they rediscover that air, water, etc. are essential to their survival. And just like any element that enables the body to function, attention must be paid to these resources, which calls for a form of sociability. Just like food or relationships with loved ones, we do not allow them to deteriorate.

---

115 B. Spinoza (1985), *The Collected Works of Spinoza, Volumes I and II*, edited and translated by Edwin Curley (Princeton, NJ: Princeton University Press,), "Part I, Definitions, III," Apple Books, p. 1073.

Furthermore, the recognition that nature enables us to live leads to gratitude toward it. Gratitude is a source of happiness, as the cognitive sciences have also shown,[116] and reinforces our renewed social ties with nature.

Moreover, the uniqueness of this living being makes up for the lack of a "membrane," as identified in the constitution of the living human organism in Chapter 7. But a membrane already exists: the one that separates us from the rest of the universe.[117] Nature, then, becomes part of our global organism, which is indeed the case, since without oxygen or water, the cells that we human beings are cease to function. This extra body must be given the care it deserves. And this, too, reinforces our sociable relationship with nature.

Finally, this shock to the living reminds us that the purpose of human beings is not to know, but to live. Admittedly, knowing how the world works has enabled us and continues to enable us to live better. But this form of knowledge, first, clashes with the climate challenge in its own way and contributes to our vulnerability; second, knowledge was never an end in itself, but a means—selected over time—to improve our chances of survival. The climate challenge forces us to reconsider our priorities.

In short, the shared perception of the Earth's beauty—when joined with an awareness of its fragility and the irreducible uniqueness of living beings—acts as a new cognitive signal. It reshapes our representation of the world by activating deep-seated moral mechanisms within us. Beauty becomes a vector for collective morality. Fragility stirs our instinctive movement toward protection and care for what is defenseless. And life itself—resisting abstraction and resisting reduction—invites us to reinhabit our place within the living world, not above it. In this way, the gaze from space may not only update our vision of the world—it may recalibrate our moral compass (see Figure 8.4).

---

116 As seen previously with Antonio Damasio et al. (A. Damasio, H., Damasio, G. Fox, and J. Kaplan (2015), "Neural Correlates of Gratitude," *Frontiers in Psychology* 6: 1491).

117 A lesser version of this perspective is to lower the membrane threshold to greenhouse gas limitation agreements, applying the Paris climate agreement. In so doing, a "membrane" is created, as human beings are placed inside it (like employees in a corporation) and it reduces the need for adjustments, which is its primary utility function.

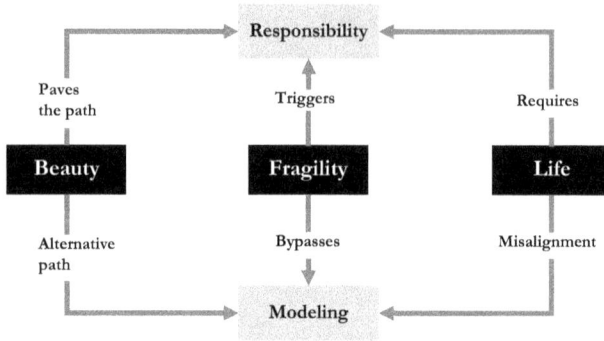

Figure 8.4 Graph illustrating how signals of beauty, fragility, and life both shrink the world-modeling bubble and trigger a sense of responsibility

Source: Author.

Note: The three pillars of shared perception—beauty, the recognition of fragility, and reintegration into the living world—each act as a brake on world modeling: by activating alternative circuits (beauty), by short-circuiting them (responsibility), and by revealing a fundamental mismatch (the living world). At the same time, they lead to the activation of mechanisms that lead to responsibility. The shared perception of beauty reinforces a common value that leads to morality and, as a result, activates cooperation, which leads to morality. Next, the recognition of fragility leads us to care for others beyond our instinct for self-preservation. Finally, the reintegration of life into the human sphere also leads to a sense of responsibility toward that which enables us to live.

All of which opens up possible ways to rise to the major challenges of overconfidence and the decline of living conditions on Earth.

The first response is the observation that living things, whether they take the form of faces or other aspects of nature, resist control. The thoughts of a cheetah or a tortoise remain a mystery to human beings. What's more, the abundance and quality of living things cannot be reduced to physicist's models, built for action in a world of solids. This puts the brakes on overconfidence in our very modeling of the world, and thus provides an answer to challenge No. 1, that of overconfidence, the driving force behind "societal bubbles."

Second, the recognition of fragility, in this case that of the planet, activates the primary human mechanism of responsibility, creating a social bond with the Earth. As a result, mankind rediscovers its own fragility, as a result of climate disruption, which reactivates this same sense of responsibility. From then on, this recognition enables the emergence of a broader social bond, based on a shared perception of beauty and a relationship with others founded on responsibility. This concordance paves the way for the foundations of a new social bond—opportunity no. 1.[118]

The new social bonds between human beings can harmonize with the need to take care of our planet, which is both vulnerable and necessary for our survival, as our own physicality reminds us. This harmony, by inspiring widespread action, offers a possible response to challenge no. 2: climate change and limiting greenhouse gas emissions.

Moreover, our departure from the logic of exploitation is strengthened by a sense of wonder at the richness and complexity of nature, as well as by our feeling of belonging to the world. This recognition triggers a sense of gratitude toward nature, further strengthening our social bond with it. The harmony generated by the uniqueness of living things and gratitude are sources of happiness, constituting opportunity no. 2.

Finally, the perception of nature's fragility reminds us of the fragility of the human body, reinforced by that of the uniqueness of living beings. This reminds us of our status as biological beings, and of our purpose, which is to live and not to possess or to know, something that has been all too often forgotten since the rise of agriculture, and which constitutes opportunity no. 3.

Complementary mechanisms will reinforce this process, notably through such methods as the granting of rights to nature or the emission of signals testifying to the acceptance of these new values (see Figure 8.5).

*

In conclusion, it would be naïve to believe in a miracle solution. But—standing on the shoulders of the giants who came before us—we can adopt their approach: as we saw with Albert Hirschman, three centuries ago when Europe was faced with perpetual wars, many thinkers were reflecting on how to live together well. This contributed to capitalism, and all

---

118 In the modern era, we'll certainly have to invent digital mechanisms to issue signs indicating adherence to this representation of the world.

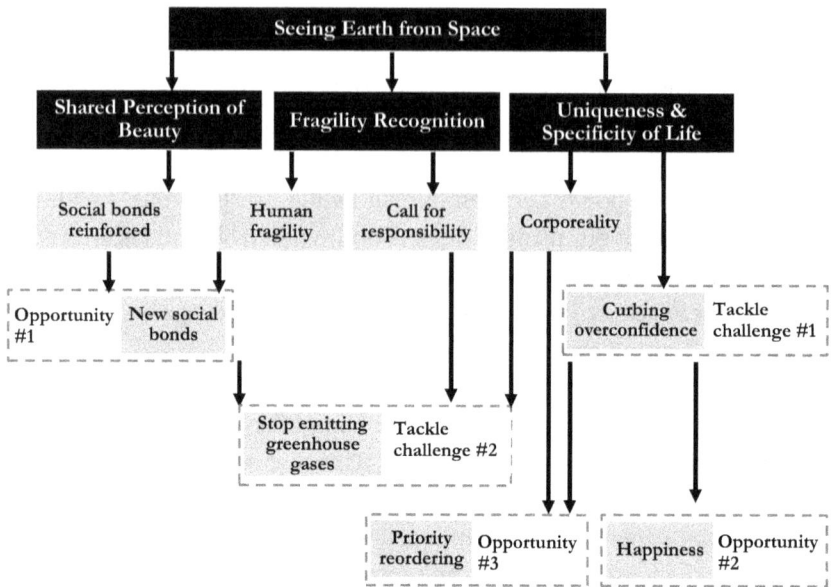

Figure 8.5 Graph of the articulation of new links with the planet and between human beings

Source: Author.

Note: Recognition of the unique nature of living things puts a brake on our over-confidence, providing an answer to challenge no. 1. A shared perception of beauty activates a powerful social bonding mechanism. At the same time, recognition of fragility fosters a sense of responsibility toward the planet, and by extension, an awareness of the fragility of human beings themselves, as living beings. This dual feeling is the basis of a responsibility which, reinforced by the inspiration of shared beauty, can restore a social bond, offering opportunity no. 1. This strengthened social bond, combined with an awareness of the fragility of the planet and the need to protect it in order to ensure our continued bodily functioning, creates the conditions for mobilization and therefore a response to challenge no. 2, that of climate change, and in addition, a break from the dopamine-inducing logic of exploitation, reinforced by the discovery of the stress-reducing uniqueness of nature. All of these factors contribute to wellbeing and happiness, thus activating opportunity no. 2. Finally, the perception of the planet's fragility, which recalls the fragility of our bodies, coupled with the uniqueness of living beings, reminds us of our status as living beings, and repositions our order of priorities, making knowledge as a means to a better life rather than an end in itself, which is opportunity No. 3.

It is not this simple chain of forces themselves but their mutual reinforcement that can contribute to a real change of perspective for humanity.

the success we associate it with today. Three centuries later, it is certainly time to revisit this approach and make the necessary changes. And—as in wartime—heterodox approaches should not be ruled out, especially when they hold considerable potential. As in war, collective action on this must be based on shared values. And when the politician's speech is delayed, a signal may activate this collective mechanism. As we have seen, societies have historically thrived when they secure access to resources. This trajectory of success has led to the emergence of agriculture and modern science, neoliberalism, and our approach to world modeling. Yet their very success has led to our becoming trapped in societal bubbles that create systemic fragility and hinder society's ability to chart new paths—although this is all the more necessary in a context growing entropy. Those bubbles now appear to be misaligned with the specific demands of the climate crisis. Finally, the essential driver of societal success—access to resources—is now facing severe constraints.

Then, perhaps, comes the view of Earth from space—a moment that stirs a threefold awareness: its beauty, its fragility, and the uniqueness of life itself.

It is a signal that could help us update our models of the world, prompting the reemergence of moral values. These values could play a role in four ways. First, they might offer us an opportunity to question the overconfidence we have placed in the mechanisms developed to access resources. Beauty awakens a moral impulse, curbing the logic of exploitation that began with agriculture and was amplified by modern science. Fragility reactivates the social bonds that neoliberalism has frayed. And life itself—irreducible to any model—reminds us that the living world cannot be confined within systems of abstraction. Second, the very same values provide the foundations for climate mobilization: a revived moral compass, a renewed sense of care for others, and a reintegration into the web of life. With a renewed DNA, society can mobilize the full extent of its capacities for innovation and solidarity—just as it has done before in times of war. Third, it tempers the cascade of abstract reasoning, opening a path toward a more grounded sense of happiness. Fourth, it brings human beings back to eye level with the living world. It recenters our attention—not on means of survival such as resources, which have become the focus of a losing battle in a world of limited resources—but on life itself as the ultimate purpose (see Figure 8.6).

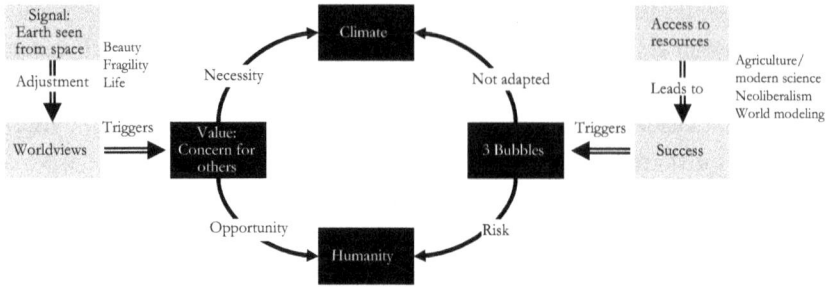

Figure 8.6 Graph showing how a representational shock activates new values, creating an opportunity for humanity and for addressing climate change

Source: Author.

Note: Three major modes of access to resources—world modeling, modern agriculture and science, and neoliberalism—have been remarkably successful. Yet their very success has given rise to three "bubbles" that now contribute to societal fragility and which are poorly suited to help us meet the unique challenges posed by the climate crisis. Access to resources has long driven the success of human societies, but now it is reaching its limits. In combination, the bubbles are putting us at more risk.

Then comes the iconic image of Earth from space—a powerful symbol of shared beauty, fragility, and life. This view invites us to update our representation of the world. Shared beauty calls for moral responsibility; fragility calls us to care for one another; and life calls for humans to be re-embedded within nature, closing the parenthesis of ecological surplomb—the detached, elevated stance that began with agriculture. These are three paths toward reinventing our social bonds.

This shift in values is both a necessity and an opportunity. First, it provides a response to the societal bubbles that have become sources of fragility. Second, it opens a path for societies to more effectively confront and respond to the climate crisis. Third, it restores a sense of happiness. And fourth, it recenters life itself as the ultimate priority—reminding us that access to resources is only a means, not an end.

Social ties, happiness, life.

All the cards we need are already on the table. All that remains is for us to pick them up.

CONCLUSION

The origins of this book lie in a fundamental question: why has climate change—recognized for decades as an existential risk caused by our own actions—failed to inspire widespread mobilization? To shed new light on this paradox, we conducted a Bayesian cognitive inference exercise: when observations contradict our existing explanatory frameworks—when our suicidal inaction clashes with the commonly accepted idea that humans are rational beings—we must seek a new model. Staying within a Darwinian framework, we expanded the idea of world representations as tools shaped by selection to access resources, giving societies that develop them a competitive edge over others.

We have identified two "societal bubbles," each arising from pivotal shifts in access to natural resources—first with the birth of agriculture, then with the rise of modern science—and to human resources, shaped by neoliberalism. Alongside these, a "modeling bubble" emerged, in which conceptualization of the world gradually supplanted human connection as the primary means of accessing resources.

These bubbles have introduced systemic fragility and led to the adoption of societal coordination mechanisms that are poorly suited to the unique challenges posed by the climate crisis. Moreover, climate change is undermining access to resources, even though such access has historically been the engine of success for societies capable of securing them.

DOI: 10.4324/9781003638384-9

Three imperatives for action have therefore emerged: the urgency of the problem, its complexity, and the ethical questions it raises. These demand that states reclaim their role in coordination and in protecting the most vulnerable. They also urge businesses to reengage as solution creators by reconnecting with their exploratory mission. As for society, it must fundamentally rethink its functioning—especially its overreliance on the notion that the world can be fully modeled.

To counter this overconfidence and activate new values, a signal—reminding us of the planet's beauty, its fragility, and the uniqueness of life—could trigger a readjustment in our models of the world. This shift would allow deep mechanisms of social connection, collective responsibility, and a rediscovery of our priorities as living beings to reemerge. Driven by these renewed values, society—much like in times of war—could then mobilize at scale. This shift would open the door to Homo sapiens naturans: a wise human who acts within nature, not above it. A human reanchored in the living world, capable of socializing with nature. This would not be a return to the past, but an evolution of consciousness—a necessary adaptation for survival.

It seems an overwhelming story as it is—but is there even more to it? Perhaps we need to broaden our perspective even further: we are witnessing a deeper immersion into a new form of globalization. For the first time in history, 8 billion people are connected within a single shared space. Have we ever before experienced a moment of such global reach combined with such profound social disconnection? The technical advances and massive migrations of the 19th century created a similar dislocation—whether across continents or from rural villages to sprawling cities.[1] What followed is well known:[2] the reaction was an intensified call for social cohesion, even in its worst forms, with nationalism, fascism, and ultimately two

---

1 See Daniel Cohen (D. Cohen (2006), *Globalization and Its Enemies*, translated by J. Baker (Cambridge, MA: Massachusetts Institute of Technology Press)):

> [...] the telegraph, the railroad, and the telephone disrupted distances much more radically than the Internet does today. [...] Starting in 1865, London and Bombay were connected by cables laid underwater and across land. [...] If the era of the Spanish Conquistadors marked the first act in modern globalization, then the second one took place in the nineteenth century at the English merchant houses. (Kindle Edition, p. 254)

2 As we saw in Chapter 7, with Claude Lévi-Strauss, Karl Polanyi, and Hannah Arendt.

world wars. Isn't that the central issue? How can we forge a sense of collective belonging in a world dominated by individualism? How can we prepare to welcome climate migrants without rethinking our relationship with others? And in a historical moment that echoes past challenges, how can we avoid repeating the tragic mistakes of earlier generations? How can we resist the lure of rigid, dangerous structures that offer the illusion of belonging at the cost of our humanity?

Last but not least, climate change represents the first truly universal value: a value rooted in shared responsibility. Religions have long aimed to build cohesion, but their competing frameworks often fell short of universality. Capitalism, in contrast, achieved a kind of universality—but at the price of promoting an individualistic doctrine that weakened bonds both between people and between humanity and nature. Now nature offers us the first truly universal value: a responsibility shared by all humanity. And the good news is that this responsibility also contains within it a deep source of happiness.

The question before us is both simple and profound: we are standing at the crossroads of an existential challenge and a historic opportunity. Will we rise to meet this moment?

It is up to each and every one of us to transform that moment into a movement of collective mobilization.

Beyond its conceptual exploration, the sole purpose of this book is to contribute to that difficult action.

BIBLIOGRAPHY

Adamo, S., V. Clement, A. de Sherbinin, B. Jones, K. K. Rigaud, N. Sadiq, J. Schewe, and E. Shabahat. 2021. *Groundswell Part 2: Acting on Internal Climate Migration*. Washington, DC: World Bank. https://openknowledge.worldbank.org/handle/10986/36248.

Aghion, P., C. Antonin, and S. Bunel 2020. *Le Pouvoir de la Destruction Créatrice*. Paris: Odile Jacob.

Aghion, P., A. Dechezleprêtre, D. Hemous, R. Martin, and J. Van Reenen. 2016. "Carbon Taxes, Path Dependency and Directed Technical Change: Evidence from the Auto Industry." *Journal of Political Economy* 124 (1): 1–51. https://doi.org/10.1086/684581.

Algan, Y., and D. Cohen. 2021. "Les Français au Temps du Covid-19: Économie et Société Face au Risque Sanitaire." *Les Notes du Conseil d'Analyse Économique*, no. 66. https://www.cae-eco.fr/les-francais-au-temps-du-covid-19-economie-et-societe-face-au-risque-sanitaire.

Anderson, P. W. 1972. "More Is Different." *Science* 177 (4047): 393–396. https://doi.org/10.1126/science.177.4047.393.

Andersson, M., P. Bolton, and F. Samama. 2016. "Climate Change Hedging." *Financial Analysts Journal* 72 (3): 13–32. https://doi.org/10.2469/faj.v72.n3.4.

Andersson, M., P. Bolton, and F. Samama. 2016. "Governance and Climate Change: A Success Story in Mobilizing Support for Corporate Responses to Climate Change." *Journal of Applied Corporate Finance* 28 (Spring): 1–13. https://doi.org/10.1111/jacf.12171.

Arendt, H. 1951. *The Origins of Totalitarianism*. New York: Harcourt, Brace & Company.

Arrhenius, S. A. 1896. "On the Influence of Carbonic Acid in the Air upon the Temperature of the Ground." *Philosophical Magazine and Journal of Science* 41 (fifth series, no. 251): 237–276. https://doi.org/10.1080/14786449608620846.

Bachelier, L. 1900. "Théorie de la Spéculation." *Annales Scientifiques de l'École Normale Supérieure*, 3rd ser., 17: 21–86.

Barthalon, É. 2014. *Uncertainty, Expectations and Financial Instability: Reviving Allais's Lost Theory of Psychological Time*. New York: Columbia University Press.

Baumard, N. 2019. "Psychological Origins of the Industrial Revolution." *Behavioral and Brain Sciences* 42: 1–58. https://doi.org/10.1017/S0140525X1800211X.

Bayes, T. 1763. "An Essay Towards Solving a Problem in the Doctrine of Chances." *Philosophical Transactions of the Royal Society of London* 53: 370–418. https://royalsocietypublishing.org/doi/pdf/10.1098/rstl.1763.0053.

Bayliss, A. P., P. Cannon, M. Paul, and S. P. Tipper. 2006. "Gaze Cuing and Affective Judgments of Objects: I Like What You Look at." *Psychonomic Bulletin & Review* 13 (6): 1061–1066. https://doi.org/10.3758/BF03213926.

Bergson, H. 1972. *Mélanges*. Paris: Presses Universitaires de France.

Bergson, H. 2007. *The Creative Mind: An Introduction to Metaphysics*. Translated by M. Andison. Mineola, NY: Dover Publications.

Bergson, H. 2023. *Creative Evolution*. Translated by D. Landes. London: Routledge.

Berlin, I. 1996. *Karl Marx: His Life and Environment*. 4th ed. Oxford: Oxford University Press.

Bernanke, B. 2004. "The Great Moderation." Meetings of the Eastern Economic Association, Washington, DC, February 20. https://www.federalreserve.gov/boarddocs/speeches/2004/20040220/default.htm.

Bertrand, M., M. Bombardini, and F. Trebbi. 2014. "Is It Whom You Know or What You Know? An Empirical Assessment of the Lobbying Process." *American Economic Review* 104 (12): 3885–3920. https://doi.org/10.1257/aer.104.12.3885.

Berthoz, A. 2000. *The Brain's Sense of Movement*. Translated by G. Weiss. Cambridge, MA: Harvard University Press.

Black, F., and M. Scholes. 1973. "The Pricing of Options and Corporate Liabilities." *Journal of Political Economy* 81 (3): 637–654. https://doi.org/10.1086/260062.

Bloomberg. 2020. "Exxon Faces Historic Write-Down After Energy Markets Implode." November 30.

Boissinot, J., and F. Samama. 2017. "Climate Change: A Policy Making Case Study of Capital Markets' Mobilization for Public Good." In *Coping with the Climate Crisis*, edited by R. Arezki, P. Bolton, K. El Aynaoui, and M. Obstfeld, 179–200. New York: Columbia University Press.

Bolton, P., and F. Samama. 2012. "Capital Access Bonds: Contingent Capital with an Option to Convert." *Economic Policy* 27 (70): 275–317. https://doi.org/10.1111/j.1468-0327.2012.00284.x.

Bolton, P., and F. Samama. 2013. "Loyalty-Shares: Rewarding Long-Term Investors." *Journal of Applied Corporate Finance* 25 (3): 86–97. https://doi.org/10.1111/jacf.12033.

Bolton, P., M. Després, L. Pereira da Silva, F. Samama, and R. Svartzman. 2020. *The Green Swan: Central Banking and Financial Stability in the Age of Climate Change*. Basel: Bank for International Settlements. https://www.bis.org/publ/othp31.pdf.

Bolton, P., M. Després, L. Pereira da Silva, F. Samama, and R. Svartzman. 2020. "Penser la Stabilité Financière à l'Ère des Risques Écologiques Globaux: Vers de Nouveaux Arbitrages entre Efficience et Résilience des Systèmes Complexes." *Revue d'Économie Financière* 138: 41–58. https://doi.org/10.3917/ecofi.138.0041.

Bolton, P., M. Kacperczyk, and F. Samama. 2022. "Net-Zero Carbon Portfolio Alignment." *Financial Analysts Journal* 78 (2): 19–33. https://doi.org/10.1080/0015198X.2022.2033105.

Bolton, P., S. Levin, and F. Samama. 2020. "Navigating the ESG World." In *Sustainable Investing: A Path to a New Horizon*, edited by H. Bril, G. Kell, and A. Rasche, 131–150. London: Routledge.

Bolton, P., X. Musca, and F. Samama. 2020. "Global Public-Private Investment-Partnerships (GPPIPs): A Financial Innovation with a Positive Impact on Society." *Journal of Applied Corporate Finance* 32 (2): 31–41. https://doi.org/10.1111/jacf.12403.

Bolton, P., S. Peters, A. Rabah, F. Samama, and J. E. Stiglitz. 2017. "From Global Savings Glut to Financing Infrastructure." *Economic Policy* 32 (90): 221–261. https://doi.org/10.1093/epolic/eix005.

Boole, G. 1854. *An Investigation into the Laws of Thought, on Which Are Founded the Mathematical Theories of Logic and Probabilities*. London: Macmillan & Co.

Bourg, D., and S. Swaton. 2021. *Primauté du Vivant: Essai sur le Pensable*. Paris: Presses Universitaires de France/Humensis.

Bowles, B., and W. Carlin. 2020. "Shrinking Capitalism." *AEA Papers and Proceedings* 110 (May): 272–276. https://doi.org/10.1257/pandp.20201001.

Braudel, F. 1985. *La Dynamique du Capitalisme*. Paris: Arthaud.

Braudel, F. 2025. *L'Aube, la Terre, la Mer: La Méditerranée, une Histoire. Extrait de La Méditerranée: L'Espace et l'Histoire*. Paris: Éditions Flammarion.

Brunnermeier, M. 2021. *The Resilient Company*. New York: Endeavor Literary Press.

Business Roundtable. 2019. "Business Roundtable Redefines the Purpose of a Corporation to Promote 'An Economy That Serves All Americans.'" https://www.businessroundtable.org/business-roundtable-redefines-the-purpose-of-a-corporation-to-promote-an-economy-that-serves-all-americans.

Canguilhem, G. 2018. *Vie et Mort de Jean Cavaillès*. Paris: Allia.

Carney, M. 2015. "Breaking the Tragedy of the Horizon: Climate Change and Financial Stability." Speech presented at Lloyd's of London, London, September 29. *Bank of England*. https://www.bankofengland.co.uk/speech/2015/breaking-the-tragedy-of-the-horizon-climate-change-and-financial-stability.

Carney, M. 2021. *Value(s): Building a Better World for All*. London: William Collins.

Case, A., and A. Deaton. 2015. "Rising Morbidity and Mortality in Midlife among White Non-Hispanic Americans in the 21st Century." *Proceedings of the National Academy of Sciences of the United States of America* 112 (49): 15078–15083. https://doi.org/10.1073/pnas.1518393112.

Case, A., and A. Deaton. 2020. *Deaths of Despair and the Future of Capitalism*. Princeton, NJ: Princeton University Press.

Cavaillès, J. 1940. "Du Collectif au Pari: À Propos de Quelques Théories Récentes sur les Probabilités." *Revue de Métaphysique et de Morale* 47 (2): 139–163. https://doi.org/10.2307/2268177.

Centorrino, S., E. Djemai, A. Hopfensitz, M. Milinski, and P. Seabright. 2015. "A Model of Smiling as a Costly Signal of Cooperation Opportunities." *Adaptive Human Behavior and Physiology* 1 (3): 325–340. https://doi.org/10.1007/s40750-015-0026-4.

Clastres, P. 1989. *Society Against the State: Essays in Political Anthropology*. Translated by R. Hurley in collaboration with A. Stein. New York: Zone Books.

Clavero, B. 1996. *La Grâce du Don: Anthropologie Catholique de l'Économie Moderne*. Paris: Fayard.

Cohen, D. 2006. *Globalization and Its Enemies*. Translated by J. Baker. Cambridge, MA: MIT Press.

Coll, S. 2013. *Private Empire: ExxonMobil and American Power*. New York: The Penguin Press.

Craig, K. 1943. *The Nature of Explanation*. Cambridge: Cambridge University Press.

Dams, L. 1984. *Les Peintures Rupestres du Levant Espagnol*. Paris: Picard.

Darwin, C. 1871. *The Descent of Man, and Selection in Relation to Sex*. London: John Murray.

Dasgupta, P. 2021. *The Economics of Biodiversity: The Dasgupta Review*. London: HM Treasury.

Davies, G., and J. Vinders. 2025. "Geoengineering, the Precautionary Principle, and the Search for Climate Safety." *European Journal of Risk Regulation*. Advance online publication. https://doi.org/10.1017/err.2025.14.

Day, R., K. Laland, and J. Odling-Smee. 2003. "Rethinking Adaptation: The Niche-Construction Perspective." *Perspectives in Biology and Medicine* 46 (1): 80–95. https://doi.org/10.1353/pbm.2003.0003.

Deane, H. 1963. *The Political and Social Ideas of St. Augustine*. New York: Columbia University Press.

Deimler, M., and M. Reeves. 2011. "Adaptability: The New Competitive Advantage." *Harvard Business Review* 89 (7–8): 7.

Descartes, R. 2006. *A Discourse on the Method*. Translated with an Introduction and Notes by I. MacLean. Oxford: Oxford University Press.

Descola, P. 2013. *Beyond Nature and Culture*. Translated by J. Lloyd. Chicago: University of Chicago Press.

Descola, P. ed. 2018. *Les Natures en Question*. Paris: Odile Jacob.

Descola, P. 2019. *Une Écologie des Relations*. Paris: CNRS Éditions, De Vive Voix.

Descola, P. 2024. *Avec les Chasseurs-cueilleurs*. Paris: Bayard.

Diamond, J. 1997. *Guns, Germs, and Steel: The Fates of Human Societies*. New York: W. W. Norton & Company.

Diamond, J. 2021. *The Last Tree on Easter Island*. London: Penguin.

Donatti, C., G. Fedele, D. Delforge, R. Below, J. Blatter, P. Moraga, K. Nicholas, N. Speybroeck, and A. Zvoleff. 2024. "Global Hotspots of Climate-Related Disasters." *International Journal of Disaster Risk Reduction* 108: Article 104488. https://doi.org/10.1016/j.ijdrr.2024.104488.

Dunbar, R. 2016. "The Social Brain Hypothesis and Human Evolution." *Oxford Research Encyclopedia of Psychology*. https://doi.org/10.1093/acrefore/9780190236557.013.44.

Dunn, J. R., and M. E. Schweitzer. 2005. "Feeling and Believing: The Influence of Emotion on Trust." *Journal of Personality and Social Psychology* 88 (5): 736–748. https://doi.org/10.1037/0022-3514.88.5.736.

Eccles, R., and S. Klimenko. 2019. "The Investor Revolution." *Harvard Business Review*, May–June.

Falk, A., and N. Szech. 2013. "Morals and Markets." *Science* 340 (6133): 707–711. https://doi.org/10.1126/science.1231566.

Fama, E., L. Fisher, M. Jensen, and R. Roll. 1969. "The Adjustment of Stock Prices to New Information." *International Economic Review* 10 (1): 1–21. https://doi.org/10.2307/2525569.

Ferrières, G. 2000. *Jean Cavaillès: A Philosopher in Time of War 1903–1944*. Translated by T. N. F. Murtagh. Lewiston, NY: The Edwin Mellen Press.

Fiske, S. T., A. J. C. Cuddy, P. Glick, and J. Xu. 2002. "A Model of (Often Mixed) Stereotype Content: Competence and Warmth Respectively Follow from Perceived Status and Competition." *Journal of Personality and Social Psychology* 82 (6): 878–902. https://doi.org/10.1037/0022-3514.82.6.878.

Fox, G. R. 2017. "What Can the Brain Reveal about Gratitude?" *Greater Good Magazine.* August 4. https://greatergood.berkeley.edu/article/item/what_can_the_brain_reveal_about_gratitude.

Fox, G. R., J. Kaplan, H. Damasio, and A. Damasio. 2015. "Neural Correlates of Gratitude." *Frontiers in Psychology* 6: 1491. https://doi.org/10.3389/fpsyg.2015.01491.

Friedman, M. 1973. "The Social Responsibility of Business Is to Increase Its Profits." *New York Times*, September 19.

Friston, K. J., M. Lin, C. D. Frith, G. Pezzulo, J. A. Hobson, and S. Ondobaka. 2017. "Active Inference, Curiosity and Insight." *Neural Computation* 29 (10): 2633–2683. https://doi.org/10.1162/neco_a_00999.

Friston, K. J., P. Schwartenbeck, T. FitzGerald, M. Moutoussis, T. Behrens, and R. J. Dolan. 2014. "The Anatomy of Choice: Dopamine and Decision Making." *Philosophical Transactions of the Royal Society B: Biological Sciences* 369 (1655): Article 20130481. https://doi.org/10.1098/rstb.2013.0481.

Friston, K. J., T. Shiner, T. FitzGerald, J. M. Galea, R. Adams, H. Brown, R. J. Dolan, R. Moran, K. E. Stephan, and S. Bestmann. 2012. "Dopamine, Affordance and Active Inference." *PLOS Computational Biology* 8 (1): e1002327. https://doi.org/10.1371/journal.pcbi.1002327.

Fukuyama, F. 1992. *The End of History and the Last Man.* New York: Free Press.

Galbraith, J. K. 1979. *The Great Crash 1929.* 50th Anniversary Edition. Boston: Houghton Mifflin Company.

Galbraith, J. K. 1990. *A Short History of Financial Euphoria: Financial Genius Is Before the Fall.* New York: Whittle Books.

Galilei, G. 1623. *Il Saggiatore.* Rome.

Gershman, S. J., E. J. Horvitz, and J. B. Tenenbaum. 2015. "Computational Rationality: A Converging Paradigm for Intelligence in Brains, Minds, and Machines." *Science* 349 (6245): 273–278. https://doi.org/10.1126/science.aac6076.

Gilson, R. J., and R. Kraakman. 1984. "The Mechanisms of Market Efficiency." *Virginia Law Review* 70: 549–644. https://doi.org/10.2307/1073080.

Gneezy, U., and A. Rustichini. 2000. "A Fine Is a Price." *Journal of Legal Studies* 29 (1): 1–17. https://doi.org/10.1086/468061.

Gneezy, U., and A. Rustichini. 2000. "Pay Enough or Don't Pay at All." *The Quarterly Journal of Economics* 115 (3): 791–810. https://doi.org/10.1162/003355300554917.

Goode, M., N. Mead, and K. Vohs. 2006. "The Psychological Consequences of Money." *Science* 314 (5802): 1154–1156. https://doi.org/10.1126/science.1132491.

Goodman, N. D., T. D. Ullman, and J. B. Tenenbaum. 2011. "Learning a Theory of Causality." *Psychological Review* 118 (1): 110–119. https://doi.org/10.1037/a0021336.

Greif, A. 1994. "Cultural Beliefs and the Organization of Society: A Historical and Theoretical Reflection on Collectivist and Individualist Societies." *The Journal of Political Economy* 102 (5): 912–950. https://doi.org/10.1086/261959.

Griffiths, T. L., C. Kemp, and J. B. Tenenbaum. 2018. "Bayesian Models of Cognition." In *The Cambridge Handbook of Computational Cognitive Modeling*, edited by R. Sun, 59–100. Cambridge: Cambridge University Press. https://doi.org/10.1017/CBO9780511816772.006.

Grosos, P. 2023. *La Philosophie au Risque de la Préhistoire.* Paris: Les Éditions du Cerf.

Haasnoot, M., J. Lawrence, R. Lempert, V. Muccione, R. Biesbroek, and B. Glavovic. 2020. "Defining the Solution Space to Accelerate Climate Change Adaptation." *Regional Environmental Change* 20 (37). https://doi.org/10.1007/s10113-020-01623-8.

Haddad, G. 2021. *À l'Origine de la Violence: D'Oedipe à Caïn, une Erreur de Freud?* Paris: Éditions Salvador.

Hallé, F. 2002. *In Praise of Plants*. Translated by D. Lee. Portland, OR: Timber Press.

Hamayon, R. 1990. *La Chasse à l'Âme: Esquisse d'une Théorie du Chamanisme Sibérien*. Nanterre: Société d'Ethnologie.

Hansmann, H., and R. Kraakman. 2001. "The End of History for Corporate Law." *Georgetown Law Journal* 89 (2): 439–68. https://openyls.law.yale.edu/entities/publicatio n/47662087-2b0c-4947-8034-e54982ee6590.

Harari, Y. N. 2015. *Sapiens: A Brief History of Humankind*. New York: Harper.

Hayek, F. A. von. 1945. "The Use of Knowledge in Society." *American Economic Review* 35 (4): 519–530.

Hénaff, M. 2000. "L'Éthique Catholique et l'Esprit du Non-capitalisme." *Revue du MAUSS* 15: 35–67.

Hénaff, M. 2002. "De la Philosophie à l'Anthropologie. Comment Interpréter le Don ? Entretien avec Marcel Hénaff." *Esprit*, February 2002 (no. 1): 135–158.

Hénaff, M. 2003. "Religious Ethics, Gift Exchange and Capitalism." *European Journal of Sociology* 44 (3): 293–324. https://doi.org/10.1017/S0003975603001309.

Hénaff, M. 2008. "Rethinking Sacrifice. Nouvelles Approches Anthropologiques." *Archivio di Filosofia* 76 (1–2): 171–192.

Hénaff, M. 2009. "Repenser la Réciprocité et la Reconnaissance : Relecture de l'Essai sur le Don de Marcel Mauss." *Revista Portuguesa de Filosofia* 65: 5–26.

Hénaff, M. 2010. *The Price of Truth: Gift, Money, and Philosophy*. Translated by J.-L. Morhange. Stanford, CA: Stanford University Press.

Hénaff, M. 2010. "La Valeur du Temps: Remarques sur le Destin Économique des Sociétés Modernes." *Esprit*, no. 1 (January): 164–184. https://doi.org/10.3917/ espri.1001.0164.

Hénaff, M. 2017. "L'Europe, une Genèse Paradoxale." *Esprit*, no. 440 (December).

Henderson, R., G. Serafeim, J. Lerner, and N. Jinjo. 2019. "Should a Pension Fund Try to Change the World? Inside GPIF's Embrace of ESG." *Harvard Business School Case* 9–319–067 (January 2019; revised February 2020).

Henrich, J. 2020. *The Weirdest People in the World: How the West Became Psychologically Peculiar and Particularly Prosperous*. New York: Farrar, Straus and Giroux.

Hepburn, M., and M. Slaoui. 2020. "Developing Safe and Effective Covid Vaccines— Operation Warp Speed's Strategy and Approach." *New England Journal of Medicine* 383 (18): 1701–1703. https://doi.org/10.1056/NEJMp2027405.

Hesp, C., R. Smith, T. Parr, M. Allen, K. J. Friston, and M. J. D. Ramstead. 2021. "Deeply Felt Affect: The Emergence of Valence in Deep Active Inference." *Neural Computation* 33 (2): 398–446. https://doi.org/10.1162/neco_a_01341.

Hirschman, A. O. 1977. *The Passions and the Interests: Political Arguments for Capitalism Before Its Triumph*. Princeton, NJ: Princeton University Press.

Hoff, K., and J. E. Stiglitz. 2010. "Equilibrium Fictions: A Cognitive Approach to Societal Rigidity." *Policy Research Working Paper* 5219, World Bank.

Hoff, K., A. Demeritt, and J. Stiglitz. 2022. "The Long Shadow of History." Excerpted from *The Other Invisible Hand: The Power of Culture to Promote or Stymie Progress*. New York: Columbia University Press.

Hohwy, J., A. Roepstorff, and K. J. Friston. 2008. "Predictive Coding Explains Binocular Rivalry: An Epistemological Review." *Cognition* 108 (3): 687–701. https://doi.org/10.1016/j.cognition.2008.05.010.

Hong, H., and J. C. Stein. 2007. "Disagreement and the Stock Market." *Journal of Economic Perspectives* 21 (2): 109–128. https://doi.org/10.1257/jep.21.2.109.

Hublin, J.-J. 2022. *Homo Sapiens, une Espèce Invasive*. Paris: Librairie Arthème Fayard and Collège de France.

Hublin, J.-J. 2024. *La Tyrannie du Cerveau*. Paris: Robert Laffont.

Hull, J. 2018. *Options, Futures, and Other Derivatives*. 10th ed. Boston: Pearson.

Husserl, E. 1960. *Cartesian Meditations: An Introduction to Phenomenology*. Translated by D. Cairns. The Hague: Martinus Nijhoff.

Iacoboni, M. 2009. "Neurobiology of Imitation." *Current Opinion in Neurobiology* 19: 661–65. https://doi.org/10.1016/j.conb.2009.09.008.

IEA (International Energy Agency). 2021. *Net Zero by 2050: A Roadmap for the Global Energy Sector*. https://www.iea.org/reports/net-zero-by-2050.

IMF (International Monetary Fund). 2022. *Global Financial Stability Report: Navigating the High-Inflation Environment*. October. https://www.imf.org/en/Publications/GFSR/Issues/2022/10/11/global-financial-stability-report-october-2022.

Innosight. 2018. *2018 Corporate Longevity Forecast: Creative Destruction Is Accelerating*. https://www.innosight.com/wp-content/uploads/2017/11/Innosight-Corporate-Longevity-2018.pdf.

IPBES (Intergovernmental Science-Policy Platform on Biodiversity and Ecosystem Services). 2019. *Global Assessment Report on Biodiversity and Ecosystem Services: Summary for Policymakers*. https://files.ipbes.net/ipbes-web-prod-public-files/2020-02/ipbes_global_assessment_report_summary_for_policymakers_en.pdf.

IPCC (Intergovernmental Panel on Climate Change). 2021. *Contribution of Working Group I to the Sixth Assessment Report of the Intergovernmental Panel on Climate Change*. https://www.ipcc.ch/report/ar6/wg1/downloads/report/IPCC_AR6_WGI_SPM.pdf.

Isler, K., and C. Van Schaik. 2014. "How Humans Evolved Large Brains: Comparative Evidence." *Evolutionary Anthropology* 23: 65–75. https://doi.org/10.1002/evan.21403.

Jacob, F. 1988. *The Statue Within: An Autobiography*. Translated by F. Jellinek. New York: Basic Books.

Jasanoff, S. 2001. "Image and Imagination: The Formation of Global Environmental Consciousness." In *Changing the Atmosphere: Expert Knowledge and Environmental Governance*, edited by P. Edwards and C. Miller, 309–337. Cambridge, MA: MIT Press.

Jeffreys, H. 1939. *The Theory of Probability*. Oxford: Oxford University Press.

Joly, H. 2021. *The Heart of Business: Leadership Principles for the Next Era of Capitalism*. Boston: Harvard Business Review Press.

Julien, F. 2022. *Moïse ou la Chine: Quand ne se Déploie pas l'Idée de Dieu*. Paris: Éditions de l'Observatoire/Humensis.

Kahneman, D., and A. Tversky. 1979. "Prospect Theory: An Analysis of Decision under Risk." *Econometrica* 47 (2): 263–291. https://doi.org/10.2307/1914185.

Kant, I. 2000. *Critique of the Power of Judgment*. Edited by P. Guyer. Translated by P. Guyer and E. Matthews. Cambridge: Cambridge University Press.

Kaufmann, R., P. Gupta, and J. Taylor. 2021. "An Active Inference Model of Collective Intelligence." *Entropy* 23 (7): 830. https://doi.org/10.3390/e23070830.

Kessler, E. 2022. *Bergson, notre Contemporain*. Paris: Éditions de l'Observatoire/Humensis.

King, D., R. Layard, G. O'Donnell, M. Rees, N. Stern, A. Turner, and J. Browne. 2015. *Global Apollo Programme to Combat Climate Change*. London: London School of Economics.

https://cep.lse.ac.uk/pubs/download/special/Global_Apollo_Programme_Report.pdf.

Klein, E. "How Thought Experiments Advanced Science." Available at https://www.youtube.com/watch?v=V5oV3SVkbJE (in French). Accessed July 30, 2025.

Koyré, A. 1985. Études d'Histoire de la Pensée Scientifique. Paris: Gallimard, Tel.

Kruglanski, A. W., K. Jasko, and K. J. Friston. 2020. "All Thinking Is 'Wishful' Thinking." Trends in Cognitive Sciences 24 (6): 413–424. https://doi.org/10.1016/j.tics.2020.03.004.

Le Van Quyen, M. 2022. Cerveau et Nature: Pourquoi nous Avons Besoin de la Beauté du Monde. Paris: Flammarion.

Lebreton, M., S. Kawa, B. Forgeot d'Arc, J. Daunizeau, and M. Pessiglione. 2012. "Your Goal Is Mine: Unraveling Mimetic Desires in the Human Brain." Journal of Neuroscience 32 (21): 7146–7157. https://doi.org/10.1523/JNEUROSCI.4821-11.2012.

Levinas, E. 1969. Totality and Infinity: An Essay on Exteriority. Translated by A. Lingis. Pittsburgh: Duquesne University Press.

Levinas, E. 1990. Difficult Freedom: Essays on Judaism. Translated by S. Hand. Baltimore: Johns Hopkins University Press.

Levinas, E. 1994. Les Imprévus de l'Histoire. Paris: Fata Morgana.

Levinas, E. 1998. Of God Who Comes to Mind. Translated by B. Bergo. Stanford, CA: Stanford University Press.

Levinas, E. 1999. Alterity and Transcendence. Translated by M. B. Smith. New York: Columbia University Press.

Levinson, M. 2016. The Box: How the Shipping Container Made the World Smaller and the World Economy Bigger. 2nd ed. Princeton, NJ: Princeton University Press.

Lévi-Strauss, C. and D. Eribon. 1991. Conversations with Claude Lévi-Strauss. Translated by Paula Wissing, Chicago: The University of Chicago Press.

Liebenberg, L. 2014. The Origin of Science: On the Evolutionary Roots of Science and Its Implications for Self-Education and Citizen Science. Cape Town: CyberTracker.

McAnany, P., and N. Yoffee, eds. 2010. Questioning Collapse: Human Resilience, Ecological Vulnerability, and the Aftermath of Empire. Cambridge: Cambridge University Press.

Maddison, A. 2003. The World Economy: Historical Statistics. Paris: OECD.

Malinowski, B. 1972. Les Argonautes du Pacifique Occidental. Paris: Gallimard.

Mauss, M. 1954. The Gift: Forms and Functions of Exchange in Archaic Societies. Translated by I. Cunnison. London: Cohen & West.

Mayer, C. 2018. Prosperity: Better Business Makes the Greater Good. Oxford: Oxford University Press.

Mercier, H., and D. Sperber. 2017. The Enigma of Reason: A New Theory of Human Understanding. Cambridge, MA: Harvard University Press.

Milo, D. 2019. Good Enough: The Tolerance for Mediocrity in Nature and Society. Cambridge, MA: Harvard University Press.

Milward, A. 1977. War, Economy, and Society, 1939–1945. Berkeley: University of California Press.

Misrahi, R. 2005–2013. Spinoza—Une Philosophie de la Joie. Paris: Éditions Médicis-Entrelacs.

Molina, M., and S. Rowland. 1974. "Stratospheric Sink for Chlorofluoromethanes: Chlorine Atom-Catalysed Destruction of Ozone." Nature 249 (5460): 810–812. https://doi.org/10.1038/249810a0.

Montesquieu. 1989. The Spirit of the Laws. Translated by T. Nugent. Edited by A. Cohler, B. Miller, and H. Stone. Cambridge: Cambridge University Press.

Mora, C., F. Powell, A. Shea, C. Trauernicht, H. Tseng, C. Bielecki, I. Caldwell, C. Counsell, B. Dietrich, B. Dousset, E. Johnston, R. Geronimo, T. Giambelluca, E. Hawkings, L. Leon, L. Louis, M. Lucas, and M. McKenzie. 2017. "Global Risk of Deadly Heat." *Nature Climate Change* 7: 501–506. https://doi.org/10.1038/nclimate3322.

Park, H.-J., and K. J. Friston. 2013. "Structural and Functional Brain Networks: From Connections to Cognition." *Science* 342 (6158): 1238411. https://doi.org/10.1126/science.1238411.

Patault, M.-A. 1989. *Introduction Historique au Droit des Biens*. Paris: Presses Universitaires de France.

Pearl, J., and D. Mackenzie. 2018. *The Book of Why: The New Science of Cause and Effect*. New York: Basic Books.

Peters, A., B. S. McEwen, and K. J. Friston. 2017. "Uncertainty and Stress: Why It Causes Diseases and How It Is Mastered by the Brain." *Progress in Neurobiology* 156: 164–188. https://doi.org/10.1016/j.pneurobio.2017.05.004.

Poincaré, H. 1952. *Science and Hypothesis*. Translated by W. J. Greenstreet. New York: Dover.

Polanyi, K. 1944. *The Great Transformation: The Political and Economic Origins of Our Time*. New York: Farrar & Rinehart.

Pomeranz, K. 2000. *The Great Divergence: China, Europe, and the Making of the Modern World Economy*. Princeton, NJ: Princeton University Press.

Pompidou, G. 2016. *Discours de Chicago : La Crise des Civilisations*. Selected Texts No. 2. Paris: Institut Georges Pompidou.

Pope Francis. 2015. *Laudato Si'*. Vatican City: Holy See.

Popper, K. 1945. *The Open Society and Its Enemies*. London: Routledge.

Pörtner, H. O., R. J. Scholes, A. Arneth, D. K. A. Barnes, M. T. Burrows, S. E. Diamond, C. M. Duarte, W. Kiessling, P. Leadley, S. Managi, P. McElwee, G. Midgley, H. T. Ngo, D. Obura, U. Pascual, M. Sankaran, Y. J. Shin, and A. L. Val. 2023. "Overcoming the Coupled Climate and Biodiversity Crises and Their Societal Impacts." *Science* 380 (6642): eabl4881. https://doi.org/10.1126/science.abl4881.

Prévot-Julliard, A.-C., R. Julliard, and S. Clayton. 2015. "Historical Evidence for Nature Disconnection in a 70-Year Time Series of Disney Animated Films." *Public Understanding of Science* 24 (6): 672–680. https://doi.org/10.1177/0963662513519042.

Prime, C. 2024. *America at War: 1933–1946*. Paris: Perrin.

Rand, A. 1943. *The Fountainhead*. Indianapolis: Bobbs-Merrill.

Rauch, E. 2017. "Climate Stress Seen Through Munich Re's Risk and Opportunity Lens." Munich RE.

Reagan, R. 1981. "Inaugural Address, January 20, 1981." *The American Presidency Project*. https://www.presidency.ucsb.edu/documents/inaugural-address-10.

Reagan, R. 2003. *A Life in Letters*. New York: Free Press.

Reeves, M., and F. Candelon, eds. 2021. *The Resilient Enterprise: Thriving amid Uncertainty*. Berlin/Boston: De Gruyter. https://doi.org/10.1515/9783110745511.

Robé, J.-P. 2012. "Being Done with Milton Friedman." *Accounting, Economics, and Law: A Convivium* 2 (2): Article 3. https://doi.org/10.1515/2152-2820.1047.

Rockström, J., W. Steffen, K. Noone, Å. Persson, F. S. Chapin III, E. Lambin, T. M. Lenton, M. Scheffer, C. Folke, H. Schellnhuber, B. Nykvist, C. A. de Wit, T. Hughes, S. van der Leeuw, H. Rodhe, S. Sörlin, P. K. Snyder, R. Costanza, U. Svedin, M. Falkenmark, L. Karlberg, R. W. Corell, V. J. Fabry, J. Hansen, B. Walker, D.

Liverman, K. Richardson, P. Crutzen, and J. Foley. 2009. "A Safe Operating Space for Humanity." *Nature* 461 (September 24): 472–475. https://doi.org/10.1038/461472a.

Roosevelt, F. D. 1942. "State of the Union Address." Speech, US Congress, January 6, 1942. *Franklin D. Roosevelt Presidential Library and Museum.* https://www.fdrlibrary.org.

Rosenzweig, F. 2005. *The Star of Redemption* (Modern Jewish Philosophy and Religion: Translations and Critical Studies). Translated by B. Galli. Madison: University of Wisconsin Press.

Rosling, H., A. Rosling Rönnlund, and O. Rosling. 2018. *Factfulness: Ten Reasons We're Wrong About the World—and Why Things Are Better Than You Think.* Translated by A. Rosling Rönnlund and O. Rosling. New York: Flatiron Books.

Samuelson, P. A. 1965. "Proof That Properly Anticipated Prices Fluctuate Randomly." *Industrial Management Review* 6 (2): 41–49.

Sandel, M. 2020. *The Tyranny of Merit: What's Become of the Common Good?* New York: Farrar, Straus and Giroux.

Schultz, W. 2016. "Dopamine Reward Prediction Error Coding." *Dialogues in Clinical Neuroscience* 18 (1): 23–32. https://doi.org/10.31887/DCNS.2016.18.1/wschultz.

Schwartenbeck, P., T. H. B. FitzGerald, R. J. Dolan, and K. J. Friston. 2013. "Exploration, Novelty, Surprise, and Free Energy Minimization." *Frontiers in Psychology* 4: Article 710. https://doi.org/10.3389/fpsyg.2013.00710.

Schwartenbeck, P., J. Passecker, T. U. Hauser, T. H. B. FitzGerald, M. Kronbichler, and K. J. Friston. 2019. "Computational Mechanisms of Curiosity and Goal-Directed Exploration." *eLife* 8: e41703. https://doi.org/10.7554/eLife.41703.

Serres, M. 1995. *The Natural Contract.* Translated by E. MacArthur and W. Paulson. Ann Arbor: University of Michigan Press.

Serres, M. 2000. *Retour au Contrat Naturel.* Paris: Éditions de la Bibliothèque nationale de France.

Shatner, W., with J. Brandon. 2022. *Boldly Go: Reflections on a Life of Awe and Wonder.* New York: Simon & Schuster.

Shepard, R. N. 1987. "Toward a Universal Law of Generalization for Psychological Science." *Science* 237 (4820): 1317–1323. https://doi.org/10.1126/science.3629243.

Shepard, R. N. 1994. "Perceptual-Cognitive Universals as Reflections of the World." *Psychonomic Bulletin & Review* 1 (1): 2–28. https://doi.org/10.3758/BF03200759.

Simon, H. A. 1956. "Rational Choice and the Structure of the Environment." *Psychological Review* 63 (2): 129–138. https://doi.org/10.1037/h0042769.

Simon, H. A. 1962. "The Architecture of Complexity." *Proceedings of the American Philosophical Society* 106 (6): 467–82. https://www.jstor.org/stable/985254.

Sims, C. A. 2003. "Implications of Rational Inattention." *Journal of Monetary Economics* 50 (3): 665–690. https://doi.org/10.1016/S0304-3932(03)00029-1.

Slaoui, M., and M. Hepburn. 2020. "Developing Safe and Effective Covid-19 Vaccines— Operation Warp Speed's Strategy and Approach." *New England Journal of Medicine* 383 (18): 1701–1703. https://doi.org/10.1056/NEJMp2027405.

Smith, A. 1776. *An Inquiry into the Nature and Causes of the Wealth of Nations.* London: Strahan and Cadell.

Sornette, D., P. Cauwels, and G. Smilyanov. 2017. "Can We Use Volatility to Diagnose Financial Bubbles? Lessons from 40 Historical Bubbles." *Swiss Finance Institute Research Paper Series* 17–27. https://doi.org/10.3934/QFE.2018.1.1.

Spinoza, B. 1985. *The Collected Works of Spinoza*. Edited and translated by E. Curley. Princeton, NJ: Princeton University Press.

Steffen, W., J. Rockström, K. Richardson, T. M. Lenton, C. Folke, D. Liverman, C. P. Summerhayes, A. D. Barnosky, S. E. Cornell, M. Crucifix, J. F. Donges, I. Fetzer, S. J. Lade, M. Scheffer, R. Winkelmann, and H. J. Schellnhuber. 2018. "Trajectories of the Earth System in the Anthropocene." *Proceedings of the National Academy of Sciences of the United States of America* 115 (33): 8252–8259. https://doi.org/10.1073/pnas.1810141115.

Stendhal. 1925. *The Charterhouse of Parma*. Translated by C. K. Scott Moncrieff. New York: Boni and Liveright.

Stevens, J. R., T. Pachur, and L. J. Schooler. 2013. "Rational Analysis of the Adaptive and Predictive Nature of Memory." *Journal of Applied Research in Memory and Cognition* 2 (4): 251–53. https://doi.org/10.1016/j.jarmac.2013.10.006.

Stiglitz, J. E. 2015. *Rewriting the Rules of the American Economy: An Agenda for Growth and Shared Prosperity*. New York: Roosevelt Institute.

Stiglitz, J. E. 2024. *The Road to Freedom: Economics and the Good Society*. New York: W. W. Norton & Company.

Stout, L. 2012. *The Shareholder Value Myth: How Putting Shareholders First Harms Investors, Corporations, and the Public*. San Francisco: Berrett-Koehler Publishers.

Strathern, A. 1971. *The Rope of Moka: Big-Men and Ceremonial Exchange in Mount Hagen New Guinea*. Cambridge: Cambridge University Press.

Talhelm, T. 2022. "The Rice Theory of Culture." *Online Readings in Psychology and Culture* 4 (1): 1–18. https://doi.org/10.9707/2307-0919.1172.

Tenenbaum, J. B., C. Kemp, T. L. Griffiths, and N. D. Goodman. 2011. "How to Grow a Mind: Statistics, Structure, and Abstraction." *Science* 331 (6022): 1279–85. https://doi.org/10.1126/science.1192788.

Thallinger, G. 2025. "Climate, Risk, Insurance: The Future of Capitalism." *LinkedIn*, 2025. https://www.linkedin.com/pulse/climate-risk-insurance-future-capitalism-günther-thallinger-smw5f/.

Tomasello, M. 2019. *Becoming Human: A Theory of Ontogeny*. Cambridge, MA: Harvard University Press.

Tort, P. 2008. *L'Effet Darwin: Sélection Naturelle et Naissance de la Civilisation*. Paris: Éditions du Seuil.

Van Hoven, W. 1991. "Mortalities in Kudu (*Tragelaphus strepsiceros*) Populations Related to Chemical Defence in Trees." *Journal of African Zoology* 105 (2): 141–145.

Vernant, J.-P. 1996. *Entre Mythe et Politique*. Paris: La Librairie du XXe Siècle, Seuil.

Vohs, K. D., N. L. Mead, and M. R. Goode. 2006. "The Psychological Consequences of Money." *Science* 314 (5802): 1154–1156. https://doi.org/10.1126/science.1132491.

Von Neumann, J., and O. Morgenstern. 1944. *Theory of Games and Economic Behavior*. Princeton, NJ: Princeton University Press.

Wack, P. 1985. "Scenario: Shooting the Rapids." *Harvard Business Review* 63 (6): 139–150. https://hbr.org/1985/11/scenarios-shooting-the-rapids.

Weinstein, N. D. 1980. "Unrealistic Optimism about Future Life Events." *Journal of Personality and Social Psychology* 39 (5): 806–20. https://doi.org/10.1037/0022-3514.39.5.806.

White, F. 2023. *The Overview Effect: Space Exploration and the Human Evolution*. 4th ed. Oakland, CA: Multiverse Media Inc.

Williamson, O. 1985. *The Economic Institutions of Capitalism*. New York: Free Press.

Wilson, W. 1917. "Address to Congress Requesting a Declaration of War Against Germany," April 2, 1917. Speech delivered to US Congress. National Archives. https://www.archives.gov/milestone-documents/address-to-congress-declaration-of-war-against-germany.

Wong, B. "Top Social Media Statistics and Trends." https://www.forbes.com/advisor/business/social-media-statistics/.

World Bank Group. "Urban Development." https://www.worldbank.org/en/topic/urbandevelopment/overview#1.

Xu, F., and V. Garcia. 2008. "Intuitive Statistics by 8-Month-Old Infants." *Proceedings of the National Academy of Sciences of the United States of America* 105 (13): 5012–5015. https://doi.org/10.1073/pnas.0704450105.

Young, M. 1958. *The Rise of the Meritocracy.* London: Thames and Hudson.

NAME INDEX

SUBJECT INDEX

Note: *Italic* page numbers refer to figures.

For Product Safety Concerns and Information please contact our EU
representative GPSR@taylorandfrancis.com
Taylor & Francis Verlag GmbH, Kaufingerstraße 24, 80331 München, Germany

www.ingramcontent.com/pod-product-compliance
Lightning Source LLC
Chambersburg PA
CBHW050643280326
41932CB00015B/2762